TIME WILL TELL

Memoirs

◆

Yvonne Kapp

Edited by Charmian Brinson and Betty Lewis
and with a preface by Alison Light

VERSO

London · New York

Frontispiece: Yvonne in the grounds of the hotel in Pardigon, February 1926.
Drawing by Edward Wolfe

Every effort has been made to obtain permission to use copyright material reproduced in this book.
Should there be any omissions in this respect we apologise and will be pleased to make the appropriate
acknowledgements in any future edition of the work. All illustrations are reproduced courtesy of
Betty Lewis unless otherwise indicated.

First published by Verso 2003
© Betty Lewis 2003
Preface © Alison Light 2003
Afterword © Charmian Brinson 2003
All rights reserved

Verso
UK: 6 Meard Street, London W1F 0EG
USA: 180 Varick Street, New York NY 10014-4606
www.versobooks.com

Verso is the imprint of New Left Books

ISBN 1–85984–510–X

British Library Cataloguing in Publication Data
A catalogue record for this book is available from the British Library

Library of Congress Cataloging-in-Publication Data
A catalog record for this book is available from the Library of Congress

Typeset in Monotype Fournier by The Running Head Limited, Cambridge, UK
www.therunninghead.com
Printed and bound in the USA by R. R. Donnelley & Sons

Contents

Preface

Alison Light

Memoirs are a form of licensed indiscretion. Suspense and curiosity keep the reader reading. Memoirs, in other words, are often as compelling for what they don't say (and for the ways in which they don't say it), as for what they do. Their air of informality reminds us that their origins lie in the art of conversation, which eighteenth-century authors took as their literary model: actresses relaying the tittle-tattle of the day, courtesans appealing for public sympathy or felons who wrote to set the record straight. More lofty personages also appeared off-duty or off-guard in their memoirs – aristocrats, statesmen, military men (and their wives), unbuttoning themselves on matters of controversy or flirting with society scandal. Often little more than table-talk, a string of anecdotes or impressions, memoirs seem closer to memories and as unreliable. Choosing at random from an inexhaustible fund, telescoping some events and expanding others, the memoirist would rather take a stroll down memory lane than attempt the autobiographer's more strenuous task of charting a life's progress step by step.

Yvonne Kapp begins her memoirs in the spirit of freedom. In one's eighties, she suggests, there is little to lose and little to prove; no need to

curry favour and, best of all, no one to contradict. Her disclaimers, though
– 'my memoirs lack gravitas', she writes – are also a form of permission.
Despite the fact that we live in a publicity-culture (or maybe because of the
emphasis upon 'celebrity'), many people find it hard to write about themselves. There is the fear of wounding others, certainly, but also of seeming
arrogant or vain, exhibitionist. To write about yourself is to assume that
others will want to read about you; it takes nerve but it is also an act of faith,
an assertion of the value of your life. Autobiographers often feel they must
justify their writing (the defensiveness of 'an apology' for one's life), and
life-stories frequently take the shape of moral lessons. Memoirs may seem
less egocentric, less soul-searching or confessional, but they too must go
against authority and inhibition, all those forbidding presences in the world
and in oneself who sternly pose the question: who do you think you are?

The satisfaction of defying authority is the opening theme of these
memoirs. Yvonne Kapp was born Yvonne Mayer in 1903, the second child
and only daughter of a German-Jewish family in London. She remembers
herself as a mutinous child ('Shan't, so there!' is her favourite phrase),
smarting under the wounds of childhood, especially those to self-esteem,
and chafing against the restrictions placed on her as a little girl. Not nostal-
gic for her younger self whom she finds 'tiresome', she remembers childhood as a hurtful place, full of illness and anxiety and resentment (insisting
on fasting like her brother and then being sick in the ladies' gallery of the
Great Portland Street synagogue was perhaps an early version of protest).
Adolescence figures as a political experience in which she discovers a 'suffocating sense of injustice' and the gulf between herself and her parents. In
fact much pleasure is derived from the memoirist toppling the tyrants of
her childhood, especially her mother who 'showed all the makings of a
colonial governor' (her father, by contrast, is merely 'a mild, good tem-
pered man of limited outlook'). Moments of physical release like roller-
skating and cycling (till her mother banishes her machine) and playing
truant are joyfully remembered. Her happiest snapshot of herself matches

freedom with responsibility: being allowed by her Bavarian relatives to 'man' the level-crossing in the village.

Yvonne Kapp belongs to that generation of girls growing up in the early twentieth century who became modern women by leaving home. Rebellion turned into the search for independence. It meant earning one's own living, so she takes a course in the new subject called 'journalism' at London University and determines to write. It meant sexual emancipation. Rejecting the 'mawkish' Edwardian sentimentalism of her parents, she falls in love with members of both sexes, runs off at eighteen and eventually marries a penniless artist, already her lover and twelve years her senior. She bobs her hair, picks up a rucksack and embarks on a 'walking honeymoon' in the Riviera. She tries to be breezily promiscuous and unpossessive, though she is frequently burdened with the shopping, cooking, and in due course a baby, while her husband has time to paint and 'fornicate' (her word). The experiments in freedom don't all work – they depend, for instance, on a devoted nanny – but there is plenty of excitement: she learns to balance on a surf-board lashed to a speed-boat, adores driving, and tries to get her pilot's licence, flying an Avro Cadet. And she begins to publish occasional pieces under the name of Yvonne Cloud.

Yvonne Cloud, as Yvonne Kapp fashions her, is a bit of a snob, elevating herself through the artistic and literary life (she had long ago scorned her parents' philistine tastes). With her 'Piccadilly baby' and her tiny studio flat in Orange Street, off Leicester Square, she finds herself among the bohemians in cosmopolitan Soho on the fringes of theatreland and the Bloomsbury Group (whose paintings and writings she apparently despised).* By 1930, however, things begin to fall apart and the free life starts to turn sour. She endures a painful divorce (allowing her husband temporary custody of

---

* Quentin Bell, *Elders and Betters*, London: John Murray, 1995, p. 11. See also the memoirs of Kathleen Hale, a close friend of Kapp's, *A Slender Reputation*, London: Frederick Warne, 1994.

her daughter) and hits an all-time low. Living alone, a year or so of strict Freudian analysis with Adrian Stephen, Virginia Woolf's brother, structures her life for a while. (Melanie Klein subsequently refuses to treat Yvonne's daughter on learning that Kapp has affairs with women.) Floating adrift in the nebulous literary underworld, on the edge of breakdown, she seeks distraction; the short story 'A Day in a Night-Club' (republished here, p. 152) bitterly evokes that season in hell. Friendships save her, as does the unexpected success of her first novel. A more resolute character was soon to emerge.

In 1935 Yvonne Kapp joined the Communist Party and remained a member until her death in 1999. From being merely disaffected or rebellious, she found serious work and purpose, a sense of belonging and an authority, we might say, she could at last respect. The Party introduced her to the terrible poverty in which a great many Londoners lived and she got to know men and women in the working classes (as the middle-class daughter of a businessman, she'd had no organic connection to socialism and is as mocking of the bearded, sandal-wearing simple-lifers as George Orwell famously was). She was 'magnificently active', the opposite of a 'parlour communist',* always campaigning and involved. Her political life was a creative response rather than an automatic one; urgent, energetic, it made life difficult, even dangerous at times. Her work in the 1940s as a Research Officer for the Amalgamated Engineering Union extended her political education. She learnt about the British labour movement, its culture and traditions, and the radical past of the country in which she had grown up. (The warm and humorous story she tells of saving the library of John Burns shows how at home she became in this world.)

As Charmian Brinson suggests in her afterword, Yvonne Kapp's memoirs are a political autobiography; as much in the contours they give to her life's experience, however, as in their content. *Time Will Tell* has much in

---

* Bell, *Elders and Betters*, p. 156.

common with the life-stories of earlier socialists who drew their inspiration from those 'conversion' narratives or spiritual autobiographies (beginning with St Paul), where a passage from darkness to light leads to the moral transformation of a life. The reprobate becomes a believer and spreads the good word. Kapp's road to Damascus began as literary editor of Paris *Vogue*, feeling she was a 'parasite' and that her concerns 'lacked dignity and moral justification'. The turning point comes in a meeting with Harry Pollitt, Chairman of the British Communist Party. Nevertheless political discussion is kept to a minimum. Her memoirs give us an intensely peopled world, but what it meant to remain loyal to the Party for the rest of her life is left largely unexplored.

Yvonne Kapp ends her account with the writing of *Eleanor Marx*, her marvellous biography of Marx's youngest daughter. The two volumes, which took her ten years and brought her much acclaim, were published in the 1970s.* Completed when she was seventy-three, the biography drew on all her strengths and skills: the capacity for tireless research (martialling a vast array of sources and statistics for her picture of Victorian London); her knowledge of early socialism and communism (including her own translations of Engels's correspondence and the mass of international writings); her understanding of the Marxes' cosmopolitan milieu. A novelist as well as a historian, she could shape her unwieldy material, animating a huge gallery of characters and their inter-relations, whilst keeping her heroine firmly to the fore. An affectionate description of the Micawber-like struggles of the Marx family, living on potatoes and keeping up appearances amidst the ferment of immigrant Soho, might be effortlessly followed by a brisk summary of Marxian theory; she breathes life into those stern, bearded patriarchs and stiffly-bonnetted ladies whilst offering sober accounts of the many events

---

* Originally published by Lawrence & Wishart, and subsequently by Virago, they are being reprinted in a one-volume edition to accompany these memoirs: Yvonne Kapp, *Eleanor Marx*, London and New York: Verso, 2003.

and causes, from the Paris Commune of 1871 to the London strikes of the 1880s, which inspired and galvanized Eleanor Marx.

Every biographer, or so they say, is an autobiographer in disguise. Yvonne Kapp says little about why she wrote the book (though she is entertaining on the 'grandeur and the miseries of research') but it is hard not to see Eleanor Marx as an alter ego: her gaiety and vitality, her love of the arts, her 'clear logical brain' and her desire 'to try something' and to live a life 'in the service of her fellowmen' (not to mention her revolt against housekeeping) all recommend her. (Kapp is especially caustic about Edward Aveling, the married man and comrade who treated Eleanor so badly, because he is rebellious rather than truly socialist: 'a gasbag, whom time has rudely deflated'.) Writing in the mid-1970s, Yvonne Kapp could rely on her British readership being familiar with trade unionism (their leaders were still household names) and its history – 'the Dock Strike', she felt, needed no chroniclers, 'its immortalization rests too secure'. Yet her scathing comments about university Marxists (she must be thinking of the New Left) and socialism being 'misappropriated to make capitalism more viable' suggest her own sense of an ending, and how hard it was to keep the faith. Eleanor Marx's socialism combined an 'understanding of theory with deep human feeling, uncommon in the world of politics'. The biography returned its author to the original moral optimism and heartfelt sympathy for the poor which had fuelled that earlier generation, to a more humane and utopian, less doctrinaire Marxism. Perhaps writing biography also opened up the path to thinking about herself.

Members or former members of the Communist Party might not necessarily seem best suited to writing autobiography. Since 'the Party's work came before everything that was personal',* communists were expected to subordinate their own needs and accept group discipline; to see oneself

---

* See Eric Hobsbawm, 'Being Communist', in his *Interesting Times: A Twentieth-Century Life*, London: Allen Lane, 2002, p. 135.

as exceptional smacked of 'bourgeois individualism' (Kapp, for instance, has some difficulty with singling out Eleanor Marx for study as opposed to other workers). The language of communist politics – anonymous, abstract, collectivist – was the opposite of a personal 'style' and being a writer was dubious unless it served the Party. For activists believing in 'faith, hope and struggle',* introspection could easily seem defeatist and might lead to despair, the ultimate taboo. (Yvonne Kapp sees no aggression in Eleanor Marx's suicide, only a desperate response to feeling 'ineffectual'.) Given the emphasis upon self-forgetfulness and self-sacrifice, the self-centredness of writing memoirs seems a bold stroke in itself.

Yvonne Kapp is certainly not of the generation who enjoyed 'navelgazing' or 'letting it all hang out', and whether by dint of training or temperament, her instincts as a writer are to exercise restraint. Yet there are times when the memoirs are remarkably uninhibited. She can be frank and remain impersonal. She is candid about her marriage and her sex life, but untormented. Her no-nonsense approach to love affairs reminds us how much this generation of emancipated women disliked the hothouse emotionalism of their childhood, finding emotional 'displays' and any form of demonstrativeness distasteful. (When Eleanor Marx gives way to self-pity, her biographer sees it as 'incontinent' and 'neurotic'.) Kapp dismisses psychoanalysis mischievously, all that talking about childhood – which could as easily be applied to autobiography – is 'pure swank'. When she describes herself weeping 'amniotic tears' at her mother's death, the rare confession is all the more powerful. It feels like reconciliation if not forgiveness.

The legacy from her mother made it possible for her to become a fulltime writer again; ironically it also separated her once and for all from her

---

* For another autobiographical account of being communist, see Raphael Samuel's two articles on 'The Lost World of British Communism', *New Left Review*, 154, Nov./Dec. 1985; 156, Mar./April 1986.

brother. Yvonne Kapp's hates remain as fierce as her loves. Such ambivalence prevents sentimentality – there is no feel-good factor here for the reader, no romance of kindly old age. Rather it suggests something steely in this story of becoming the author of one's own life. Such self-determination is not possible, perhaps, without some iron in the soul.

Time Will Tell confirms that Yvonne Kapp, in her own words, had 'always been a writer'.* In a crowded life, the place of writing was often precarious and relegated (a thirty-five-year gap at one point). She may have suffered from her own modesty, her uncompromising literary standards and devotion to the great writers, disparaging her novels and her translations (including distinguished work on the letters of Engels). Typically her Author's Note to *Eleanor Marx* instructs the reader to ignore the 'elaborate furniture' of references, 'smacking as it does of social climbing for this class of work'. Only a writer, however, could produce her elegant prose, at once precise and vigorous, and often witty, drawing on a rich vocabulary and able to conjure the beautiful description or vivid phrase, like the memory of 'the heady, pungent scent' of the blue plums in the vats at her uncle's factory or of the local boys 'with shaven heads like dirty eggs'.

The curiosity value of memoirs should not be underestimated, though. As Yvonne Kapp's title suggests, what posterity will make of a life is unpredictable. Much that strikes the writer now as important will fade; historians and specialists will raid the life ruthlessly for their own specialist purposes, and new chapters of the past will be prompted (I'd like to know more, for instance, about the Jewish Cambridge of her husband, Edmond Kapp). For the general reader, however, the pleasure of life-writing lies not only in

---

* '"I Have Always Been a Writer" – Yvonne Kapp, Writer and Socialist', interviewed by Sally Alexander in 1987, in Alexander, *Becoming a Woman, and Other Essays on 19th and 20th Century Feminist History*, London: Virago, 1995. The interview is fascinating, amongst other things, for their different perspectives on feminism: 'Why do all you girls hate men?' Kapp asks provocatively.

seeing history – national crises, political movements – from the inside,*
but in glimpses of another kind of history altogether, of emotional and
psychological life, a history *of* inside, of what makes people tick.

In memoirs and autobiographies the incidental is as historically suggestive as the major event – like the game of Dr Crippen and Miss Le Neve
('thrillingly dressed as a boy') which Yvonne and her brother play in childhood, his jokes, which she realizes no contemporary child would understand, or the sailor suits and caps they wore. (And why does she remember
scoffing twelve bars of Fry's chocolate cream at the outbreak of war in
1914?) Life-stories, however formal or informal, remind us that history is
also about the making of ourselves, through our fears and fantasies, and
that the world inside and the world outside are lived in tandem, like the
present and the past: the woman in her eighties remembers the little girl of
six who is in turn imagining herself a despatch-rider on a confidential
mission, 'whizzing' about the lawn on her new cycle and 'leaving a pattern
of crushed silver snakes on the sparkling grass'.

Alison Light

January 2003

---

* Hobsbawm, 'Being Communist', p. xiv.

TIME WILL TELL

FOR BETTY LEWIS

Souvenez-vous qu'à mon âge
Vous ne vaudrez guère mieux.
(Bear in mind that at my age
You won't be doing much better.)
Corneille, from 'Stances' (1658)

Autobiography can't be written until one is old,
can't hurt anyone's feelings, can't be sued for libel
or, worse, contradicted.
Nadine Gordimer, from 'A Bolter and
the Invincible Summer' (1963)

Foreword and Acknowledgement

In the eighty-seventh year of my age, having worked diligently for the greater part of my lifetime, while awaiting the uncertain but inevitable hour, I have decided to write my memoirs.

My reminiscences lack gravity. I have never kept a journal and, even had I, should not consult it now, in the same way that I have forborne – save in two instances – to quote from such old letters as I have kept, partly out of sheer laziness – the old do only what comes easily – electing to rely upon my fallible, fitful and selective memory, fully aware of the pitfalls that presents. But what good would it do, when all is said and done, to interlard what I can recollect with matters that, no doubt for excellent reasons, I have conveniently forgotten? Thus, here are no well-researched and authenticated facts: merely the anecdotes that have remained vivid to me.

It is probable that what I have set down will not be read until I am beyond the reach of ridicule and criticism; therefore I am not deterred by apprehension nor inhibited by false shame.

My thanks to Elisabeth Russell Taylor for reading this work in its early stages and making many valuable comments.

Y. K.

Highgate 1989

Part One

Beginnings

I

My mother was born in Bradford in 1878, the daughter of a wool-merchant of German-Swedish origin. His forebears had been called Homel, a name derived, I am convinced, from that of the Byelorussian town of Gomel where a large Jewish population is known to have dwelt since the twelfth century.

The first Homel – and, as it turned out, the last but one – who can be traced was Josef, born in 1690 in Bielefeld, the centre of the linen trade in the Westphalian Duchy of Brandenburg. At some stage in his life he moved to Deutz, a suburb of Cologne on the east bank of the Rhine. His son, Löb Joseph, born there in 1717, adopted the name of his father's birth-place. Thereafter the family was called Bielefeld.

For another couple of generations they remained in Deutz: then Löw Bielefeld – great-grandson of Josef Homel – went to live in Karlsruhe where his five children, four sons and a daughter, were born between 1806 and 1817. Two of those sons, Josef and Adolph, married sisters, Henrietta and Johanna Massenbach of Bühl, a small town in Baden near the Alsatian border, to which the elder couple moved, while Adolph stayed in Karlsruhe where he set up as a bookseller, publisher and printer. I have a pretty little engraving that he made of the marketplace with its incongruous pyramid at its centre (like the thing outside the Louvre in Paris), which was the tomb of Karl, Margrave of Baden who, in 1715, founded the town that bears his name, and there in the foreground stands the substantial corner house with the name A. Bielefeld over its doors.

Meanwhile Josef, settled in his wife's home town, fathered two sons of whom the younger, Emil, born in 1839, became my grandfather, the Bradford wool-merchant. He was to die in my parents' south London house in 1904. I dimly remember crawling about his bed, but I cannot be said to have known him for I was scarcely a year old. My brother, nearly three years senior, spoke of him as Poppapa.

In April 1870, at the age of thirty-two, Emil Bielefeld had married a Hamburg girl, Johanna Daus, then eighteen; but when and why they emigrated to England – the only Bielefelds of a dozen or more collaterals to leave their native land – putting down roots among many other German Jews in the textile town of Bradford, I do not know. They had certainly done so when their first child, a son, Charles Hermann, was born. My mother, Clarisse Fanny, followed to grow up in a large solid, grey stone house in what was then Walmer Place, now Villas, off Manningham Lane.

To run that establishment must have needed a pack of servants and, indeed, cooks and housemaids, nannies and bootboys figured extensively in my mother's reminiscences of childhood. The large domestic staff will have denoted, for that time and place, no more than moderate middle-class prosperity which, however, did not last. The business failed and the Bielefelds moved to London when my mother was eighteen. Her brother, something of a scapegrace, had left home for America by then. My grandfather was, in the parlance of the day, 'ruined', and his daughter went out to earn her living as a governess on a daily basis. What she can have taught is something of a mystery, as also, for that matter, is her choice of a profession for she did not much like children, save as decoration. In later life she confided in me that when she met my father she had been deeply in love with somebody else: a married man. I wondered whether, in keeping with romantic fiction, this might have been the father of her pupils; but this and all other matters concerning her personal life remained a closed book.

Indeed, of the intimate life of my entirely obscure parents I know nothing, nor have I any means of finding out. I was once scornful of my mother's limited range of reading but, as if to demonstrate the unreliability of hindsight and old people's memories, I overlooked the evidence of the bookshelves in my parents' house – with their collected editions of George Eliot, Thackeray, Byron, Tennyson and the single volumes of works by Turgenev, Wilde, Elizabeth Barrett Browning and Matthew Arnold – and now, quite recently, I unearthed from an old trunk in the attic a little sheaf of manuscript torn from a commonplace book kept by my mother in the first decade of this century.

It is a meagre enough inheritance that had lain there, disregarded, since, following my mother's death in 1961, I had gathered it up, together with ancient family photographs: my parents feeding pigeons in St Mark's Square; my mother, circa 1909, wearing an enormous hat and a flirtatious smile and carrying a bunch of flowers as she steps out in some foreign spa, escorted by a posse of laughing gentlemen sporting straw boaters. But there are some rather odd things about it. In the first place, it bore her maiden name – Clarisse Bielefeld – above the address where she had been living for five years after her marriage. Again, why, when no other documents or letters of hers had survived the long years, should she have preserved with care – for the pages were barely yellowed – this testimony to her tastes and opinions of so long ago? On good, thick paper, in her bold hand, she had inscribed passages from the works of Ruskin and Darwin, Dickens, Thackeray and Ibsen, as well as such popular novelists of the day as E. F. Benson, Marion Crawford, 'Elizabeth', Bulwer-Lytton, Dumas and Edna Lyall.

The recurrent theme of these chosen passages is epitomized in an extract from *Vanity Fair*: 'Never tell all you feel or (a better way still) feel very little.' And, from Bulwer-Lytton's *Godolphin*: 'The best way to preserve the happy equilibrium of the heart is to blunt its susceptibilities.'

My parents' first meeting in 1898 – contrived by a little old couple of German-Jewish amateur matchmakers called Loewe whose gloomy great house in Porchester Square I remember visiting as a small child – took place at the Royal Academy's Summer Exhibition. The little old people had been on the look-out to find a suitable bride for the promising young businessman recently arrived from America to take over his family's firm.

There are no records of my father's antecedents and, although my paternal grandmother's first name – Hélène, spelt in the French style – is incorporated in my own, I am not even sure of her maiden name, which is the kind of information the Italian police wish to know if you are robbed in the street. My father always claimed that he came from a long line of horse-thieves, but it is just possible that this was his way of deflating my mother's foolish pretensions; for she was fond of relating, without a shred of evidence, how an ancestress of hers had been an ornament of the Imperial Court, complimented by no less a person that the Empress upon the grace and beauty of her dancing. This charmer had in addition an elevated character, being exceptionally kind to her noble but decrepit parents. I fancy my mother believed several valuable lessons – in deportment no less than moral fibre – were to be drawn from these fables.

My father was born in Worms on 13 January 1871, in the year, the very month and fifteen days before Paris capitulated to the victorious Prussian troops of the newly-proclaimed first Emperor of Germany. Worms, on the west bank of the Rhine in Hesse-Darmstadt, one of the oldest cities in Germany, is associated for most people with the name of Luther, to whom a monument was unveiled in 1868; for here, in 1521, was held the Diet where he refused to recant and made his famous affirmation, 'Here I take my stand . . .' But it also had a Jewish community so ancient that it was said to have existed continuously since before the Christian era. There was even a local tradition that the Jews of Worms had voted against the crucifixion but that their messenger had arrived in Judaea too late. However that may be, the Romans occupied the city whose records go back to the sixth century AD. During the Thirty Years War the French laid waste to it and, just over a century later, in 1801 by the Peace of Lunéville, all that region – Liebfraumilch country – was annexed to France.

Thus it came about that many of my father's kin exercised their right to French citizenship and departed for Paris. My grandfather, however, chose England, for some obscure reason, to found a business. Since it is an attested fact that my father's sister, Florentine, and his brother, Henry, both older than he by more than a decade, were born in England, whereas he was born in Germany, I surmise that my grandmother left her husband and, with her two children, returned to her native Worms to give birth to this third child – my father, Max Alfred – quite soon after which she died. The children were left in the care of aunts who proved to be both niggardly and cold-hearted. I never heard any mention of uncles and must suppose that these women, whose names were never pronounced, were unmarried and perhaps not well-off. It may be that although my grandfather had made provision for his children, their guardians were too mean to spend the money on them.

There was a touch of sly irony in my father's description of his own father as a gentleman of landed property. It appears that Hermann Mayer, though established as a vanilla merchant of Crutched Friars in the City of London, had bought a small vineyard on the outskirts of Worms and when, after his wife's death, he visited his orphaned children growing up in the town he would step out on a Sunday morning, wearing a brown bowler hat and brown morning coat to inspect his vines. He died before I was born; but that picture of him – the little Jewish businessman, unsuitably clad for a country walk, strutting proudly about his tiny plot of land on summer Sundays – is more vivid to me than many a remembrance of things seen.

I have an old photograph of the family house in Worms that had belonged to my great-grandfather which was where my father grew up. It was a simple, low, white-washed building of some charm with a short flight of shallow, railed steps running along the side of the house up to the front door. It looks more like a farmhouse than any type of urban dwelling, which may well be because the chief resource of Worms was viticulture and its working population mostly wine growers.

My father did not often speak of his childhood and never with self-pity, yet when he did he evoked a singularly sad young life. One of his recollections was of skating on a frozen pond one bitter winter when he was about seven years old and a stranger suddenly thrusting a hot spiced bun into his chilly small hands. This was a most treasured memory, as though in adult life he could still savour the delicious taste no less than the warmth and rare kindness it represented. Equally touching I found his account of visiting some bedridden old neighbour who, upon catching sight of the little boy, gave him enormous pleasure by exclaiming: 'Aha, you have a fine new green cap.' These tiny incidents, so long stored up in my father's mind, made it clear that the child never had enough good things to eat or to wear. He must always have been cold and hungry. Losing his mother at the earliest age, the coldness and hunger he experienced will have been something more than purely physical.

Once, when I was grown up and my father and I had become companionable after years of estrangement, he told me that he had always believed, owing to his own deprivation, that the loving care of the young was, as he put it, 'the mother's business'. Disabused on this point – too late – he sorely regretted not having played a greater part in his own children's upbringing. It was on this same occasion that he advised me to ignore my mother's stormy moods and let her 'stew in her juice'. Those were his words, which struck me as emotionally coarse, wrung out from bitterness; but the advice was certainly sound and he himself lived by it in his middle years.

He took up all manner of pursuits outside the home: he played the violin in the Civil Service orchestra; was a chess player of tournament standard; won innumerable hideous trophies at golf and for fencing, all of which meant that he was out many evenings and always at the weekend. In old age he confessed to me that he had for many years entertained a longing to retreat to one of the vanilla-growing islands in the Indian Ocean. (Vanilla, it should be said, was not only his merchandise but among his greatest interests: he knew of every region ringing the globe, all equidistant from the equator, where it grew and could talk about its provenance, cultivation and habits by the hour, from which I learnt that the sex-life of the vanilla pod – whose name derives from 'little vagina' – is decidedly rum.)

A mild, good-tempered man of limited outlook, he could and, as it turned out, did learn from experience. With advancing years his sympathies broadened and his tolerance increased, while at all times he had the saving grace of a crisp and pawky sense of humour, sometimes expressed in short letters to *The Times* newspaper on such subjects as the Roman occupation of the Rhineland and the changing flavour of tomatoes. (That letter ended with the words: 'Now, though it will be of no moment to the readers of *The Times*, I like them.') He had a fund of good stories, though was perhaps over-fond of repeating them. One which I heard rather often was of a political candidate he claimed to have heard in America who ended his address with the words: 'Them's my sentiments, and if you don't like 'em, I'll change 'em.'

As a young man, after doing his compulsory military service, my father had fled Germany to join his brother Henry – now known as Hy – who had become a successful illustrator and cartoonist in New York. My father – who was always called Alfred, never Max – would have liked to study chemistry, for which he had not the smallest opportunity. Instead, thanks to Hy's journalistic connections, he resigned himself to the not very exalted post of bicycling correspondent on a Chicago newspaper. Shortly, however, my grandfather's health began to fail and he entreated one of his sons to come to London and carry on the vanilla business. Hy was always said

Yvonne's parents in
St Mark's Square, Venice

by my mother to have been 'too selfish' to answer this call; yet it seems reasonable that, well-established and successful in his own field and pushing
forty, he should have been unwilling to drop everything and embark upon a
new and uncongenial career as a businessman in an unknown country. So it
was my father who responded and for the rest of his working life ran the
little limited company in what he called Mincing Lane, and he it was who
attended the Summer Exhibition at Burlington House in 1898, to be
married in synagogue in the September of the following year, just before
my mother's twenty-first birthday, when he was twenty-eight.

Looking back, I now think it strange that I was never taken to either of the places where my parents were born. At the age of five I visited the family of my Aunt Florentine in Grünstadt in the Bavarian Palatinate, barely ten miles from Worms, while later I spent several weeks in three consecutive years between the ages of nine and eleven in Kreuznach, no more than thirty miles from my father's native city, yet never did I go there. Nor did I set eyes upon my mother's birthplace until I was over eighty. It must have been assumed by our parents that these scenes were of no interest to their children.

I knew only one of my four grandparents. This was my maternal grandmother *née* Johanna Daus of Hamburg, who, as a widow, lived with us for a few years. She died in 1910 and remains in my memory as the nicest person I knew in childhood. Her daughter – my mother – adored her: it was, indeed, a relationship at the very core, it seems, of her emotional life, far more important than that with husband or children.

Herself widowed in 1948, my mother went back to her native Yorkshire to spend her last twelve years in a small private hotel in Harrogate to which she invited for lunch or tea old women who had been her schoolfellows. From time to time she would briefly revisit London where she had spent almost the whole of her married life and had lived for over fifty years and then she generally stayed with me. On one of those occasions, a year or two before she died, in her eighties, she asked me to take her to Willesden Jewish cemetery where her parents were buried. I had never been there before and it was with some surprise that I read on my grandmother's tombstone the unusual epitaph – a tribute more to the feelings of the bereaved than to the merits of the departed – Tennyson's lines:

> O for the touch of a vanish'd hand
> And the sound of a voice that is still.

My mother, as she stood by the graveside, was not only deeply moved but quite overcome with grief. She wept openly, her old head bowed, and I turned away to let her mourn in private, greatly marvelling that this death of nearly half a century before should still elicit so powerful and poignant a response. Not so had she bewailed my father's dying.

He, my father, had acquired British nationality long before my birth but, with my thoroughbred German-Jewish ancestry on both sides, I shall, for as long as I live, suspect every German national, over the age of eight in 1933 and neither in exile nor in a concentration camp in the course of the following twelve years, of complicity in mass murder. How often have I reflected that there, but for the merest chance, go I, among the millions for whom the lamentations will echo through the world for as long as humanity survives.

2

Of the French connection, the most colourful character was my Great-uncle Michael Mayer whose photograph, showing him in top hat and velvet-collared greatcoat – a handsome man with laughing eyes, an extravagant moustache and large cigar – stood ever in our drawing-room. He was regarded by my parents as the acme of worldly success, though in point of fact his fortunes fluctuated wildly.

Born in 1832 and brought up in Paris, he was a talented linguist who, after many vicissitudes, including a sojourn in America, left France for England at the time of the Franco-Prussian war to live, among many other refugees from besieged Paris and the Commune, near Clapham Common. He was then in his late thirties and worked as a journalist. His interest in and love for the theatre led him to become a drama critic which, in its turn, took him into theatre management. He presented a number of French plays at the Princess's Theatre (on the north side of Oxford Street) and English adaptations of Sardou and Dumas *fils*. But his greatest triumph as an impresario – as it was then called – was to bring over the entire company of the Comédie-Française for a six-week season at the Gaiety Theatre in 1879. Sarah Bernhardt appeared in eighteen of the forty-three performances, including Phèdre, one of her most famous roles, which she performed on 2 June.

Such was the success of her first venture abroad – she was then thirty-five and at the height of her powers – that she decided to sever her contract with the 'Français', of which she was what was known as a *sociétaire*, and work as a freelance. She was sued by the 'Français' to the tune of some hundreds of thousands of francs, but never had any financial cause to regret the breach, entering into arrangements with Michael Mayer and an American named Janet for the brilliant foreign career of her next many years. Whether my great-uncle played quite so important a part in her professional progress as family bragging would have it is open to question.

Michael's wife Adeline, *née* Haes, whom he married in 1862, died in Paris eight years later at the age of thirty-four, when the oldest of her five little sons was not yet seven. Two of those children did not long survive their mother. During the 1880s and throughout the period of his management of Bernhardt, Michael lived in some magnificence at 55 Berners Street, a house with its own private theatre where he mounted splendid performances and lavishly entertained the great actors and opera singers of the day. On his death he was near to bankruptcy. He left his three sons £100 each.

The reason I know quite a lot about him is not only because I was acquainted with those three sons – my so-called uncles who were really second cousins – but also because, as youngsters, they had been cared for by someone who became a very familiar figure in my own childhood, known as Aunt Mary. This was Mary O'Sullivan who had changed her name by deed-poll to Mayer: a very large and lovely pink-and-white elderly Irishwoman who must certainly have been Great-uncle Michael's mistress and a tremendous beauty in her youth. She came to our house once a week as a kind of spare nanny and general helper from the time that I was quite small. Indeed, I cut some of my teeth upon her locket of smooth gold on one side, encrusted with turquoises on the other. She was always dressed in black, had fine, snow-white curly hair and a strong, healthy, distinctive smell when she held me in her arms. She also, as I sat on my po, told me tales of suspense – about puffing and blowing a house down and animals who asked dramatic questions – all unknown to me, for our nanny, called Gertrude, was German and we were nurtured on *Max und Moritz*, *Struwwelpeter* and the like, with no knowledge of English nursery lore. (I may say in parenthesis that since Gertrude came to us before I could talk, so that my first language was German, we were forbidden to speak in that language to our parents or English in the nursery. To grow up bilingual might have been useful had it not been that when the First World War broke out I, as a stout patriot, denied all knowledge of the enemy language so successfully that I could hardly remember a word of German when, twenty years later, I needed it badly to communicate with refugees from Nazi persecution.)

As we grew older Aunt Mary occasionally took us to Brixton where we bought little pretty, fragile toys in the Penny Bazaar under the railway arches. Also her stories grew better and better: no longer about piglets and bears but wonderful tales of Sarah Bernhardt's travels, her wedding, her reckless temper, her tantrums, her prodigal son, her glorious costumes and her dazzling successes in far-flung places with beautiful names such as Montevideo, Santiago, Caracas, Panama and Lima. Aunt Mary, it appeared, had not only always been at her side throughout her travels and varying adventures, but had been a key figure as, for example, when she was able, at the ceremony in St Andrew's church in Wells Street in 1882, to produce, as if by magic, the wedding ring that everyone else had forgotten as they set out from the Berners Street house for Bernhardt's wedding to Aristide Domela. (Aunt Mary did not hesitate to tell us the shocking fact that, though thirty-eight at the time, the bride had declared she was thirty.)

One might have expected that at least one, if not all, of the sons of that father would have shown respect and assumed some responsibility for

Mary O'Sullivan Mayer as she grew old, since she had been as a mother to them. But they did not. Only my father, who owed her nothing at all, saw to it that she did not starve; though I cannot think that my parents did her much honour by employing her – probably for a pittance – as a stopgap servant. For the rest, she and her sister ran a lodging-house for music-hall performers in Talfourd Road, Peckham where, at one stage, my father rented a room to conduct some rather dubious experiments to produce artificially the much-prized crystallization of the vanilla pod.

Something else is connected with that Peckham household – which I never visited – for one of the lodgers was said to have given birth to and at once abandoned a baby girl. The sisters adopted her and, so the tale went, named her after me. I must have been about seven or eight years old when this happened and, of course, that Yvonne had the same birthday as I, so I was never allowed to forget her. I did not take the faintest interest in her: if anything I disliked hearing about her, but I had not only to put aside and send her my discarded clothes and toys but also buy her presents for Christmas and our shared birthday. At heart I detested her, though I did not wonder then, as now I do, whether she ever really existed.

The eldest of Great-uncle Michael's sons was Sylvain, an impassioned mountaineer, who was called to the Bar in the Middle Temple in 1887 and, as a junior to the Lord Chief Justice, Lord Russell of Killowen, accompanied him to Rennes in the summer of 1899 for Dreyfus's second trial (he was found 'guilty with extenuating circumstances'). In 1913 Sylvain took silk. He lived in Carlyle Square, Chelsea, and was married to Aunt Lily who painted miniatures, had bright orange hair and a rasping, upper class voice which periodically gave vent, for no apparent reason, to peals of high-pitched, clattering laughter. They had three daughters and a son, my horrid Cousin Ned, who came to stay with us from time to time and twisted my arm. He grew up to become the bridge correspondent on *The Times*. And serve him right.

The two other 'uncles' were Gaston and Frédéric. Gaston married an

American actress called Maude. They had no children. He had followed his
father into theatre management and for some years ran The Court – Royal
since 1871 – in Sloane Square. Every year, in the Christmas holidays, he
gave us a box for the Drury Lane pantomime. He was tall and slender with
large, dark, melancholy eyes and had a tendency to write poetry of a vapid
nature – *Ode to a Lady's Corsage*, that kind of thing – than which, in my
father's opinion and mine, I had been able to do better when I was ten.

Frédéric had gone back to Paris as an adult and was married to a French-
woman. They, too, were childless. Their flat was in some unfashionable
quarter and sparsely furnished. They were elderly when I knew them and,
rather too obviously, poverty-stricken. This could have been explained by
the fact that Uncle Frédéric spent all his time in cafés playing chess, or
draughts, or dominoes. So obsessive was his addiction to sedentary games
that, although I visited him and his wife only a few times when, at the age
of seventeen, I was placed with a French family in Chatou, he could not
stay away and, on each occasion, far from offering me more suitable entertainment, he took me to his café to watch him at play.

The other branch of my father's family who had become French had
descended in the female line and was not called Mayer but Jonas. The
member of that clan whom I knew best was Edouard, for he came to
London quite often when I was small, bringing expensive, pretty French
toys and, in sequence, his three wives. He lived in the avenue Hoche and
had a rather grand antique shop on the south-west corner of the place
Vendôme. At the end of the First World War he was, briefly, in the government as Minister of Fine Arts. I remember that when he came to see us at
about that time he showed us what must have been a facsimile of the Ver-
sailles Treaty with all its signatures.

His parents lived in an enormous, gloomy flat on the boulevard des
Capucines with their two other sons: huge, gloomy bachelors, Marcel and
Paul. The place was crowded with over-sized furniture of an imposing
nature. I had the strong impression that it was all for sale and the whole

place really nothing but a second-hand store; the begetter, as it were, of Edouard's fashionable shop where only the most rare and elegant pieces were to be seen.

All these people felt they had to do something – though not much – about me while I was being 'finished' near Paris; but I did not care for them. Marcel Jonas was fat and dark and sluggish. Paul, though also large, was at least slim and in every way more personable; but, alas, though he cannot yet have been thirty at the time, he was losing his hair. He sometimes took me to exhibitions at the Grand Palais and other such places, when I felt embarrassed at being out with this bald person. I longed to be seen in the company of some handsome, dashing male. To be sure, I knew nobody answering that description, but Paul might have passed muster had he only kept his hat on.

In the end Uncle Edouard behaved with the utmost treachery, precipitating events that were to change the course of my life. Had I been more sophisticated and mature – though, at seventeen, that is exactly what I fancied I was – I might well have paid him out, for every now and then I was invited to lunch at the avenue Hoche by Edouard's (third) wife, Gaby, who would take me, or rather, make me accompany her to a slightly louche and dimly-lit club where she danced with officers in gorgeous uniforms while I, poor silly young thing, looked on. As it was, it never occurred to me to mention these outings to anyone, let alone Uncle Edouard.

The household of the colonel's widow where I had been placed to learn French and acquire some polish was totally unsuitable and I think my parents – who had interviewed the lady at the Grosvenor Hotel and accepted her credentials – had been largely deceived. The young people with whom I was to consort were her two daughters of round about my age who were not interested in anything nor receiving any form of education. They never rose until half-way through the day, sloped about in dressing-gowns, spent the afternoons playing bridge or feeble games of pat-ball – dignified by the name of tennis – with half-grown boys upon whom they practised a

crude exercise in flirtation. A colleague of the late colonel, an elderly gentleman who was the parliamentary deputy for the Ardennes, lodged with
the widow when he came from his constituency to attend the *Chambre* and
may have been, for all I know, or suspected at the time, her lover. There
were also two lots of American paying-guests – a sharp and domineering
Jewish mother with a music-student son under strict control, and a timid
librarian with a thin wife and two small girls – left over from the war years,
still working for organizations originally set up for the benefit of dough-
boys in Paris.

Once a week Madame took me and her daughters into Paris to attend
some course of lectures, chosen, I rather think, because they were free.
The only one I recall was that given by Michel St Denis, which was fascinating but somewhat remote from the type of instruction an English girl in
my situation might expect to receive. The only other education consisted of
visits to the Comédie-Française where I seemed always to be seated upon a
strapontin. The theatre tickets may well have been a hand-out to the deputy
for the Ardennes.

Most of the time I was so excruciatingly bored and under-occupied that
I read enormously, without guidance or discrimination (I remember chiefly
of that time Bashkirtseff, Baudelaire, Gautier, Maupassant and Louÿs,
though I had a brief austere love affair with Corneille, as one should at that
time of life). I also enrolled at a typewriting school I had discovered in
Chatou and went there each morning for a lesson before breakfast. Then I
would quite often take a train into Paris and saunter about, visiting churches, museums and galleries. I took a great liking for pictures of horses
going mad in thunderstorms. From time to time I stopped at a café and
treated myself to a small *sirop*. One way and another, I managed to enjoy
myself.

It was on one of these innocent jaunts that I ran straight into Uncle
Edouard who immediately asked who was with me. On learning that I, his
jeune fille niece, was wandering about the streets of Paris unaccompanied,

he wrote my parents a stern letter of reproach for entrusting me to such lax care. In response, my mother turned on me in a furious letter, accusing me of 'kicking over the traces', of undutiful and mutinous conduct, the injustice of which so stung me that I retorted with all the considerable insolence at my command and several telling quotations from Oscar Wilde.

Thus was opened the campaign of civil disobedience that was to culminate eighteen months later in my running away from home and cutting myself off once and for all from my family and their way of life.

3

The gratification of chattering about one's childhood, to indulge long-cherished resentments, paranoia, self-pity, self-love and pure swank, must account for the lasting appeal of psychoanalysis.

Dr Meek delivered me on 17 April 1903 at 170 Tulse Hill in south London. He was a heavily-bearded man dressed in black who drove about in a small closed carriage, also black, like a box on wheels. These attributes made him appear slightly sinister, as did his house on the Norwood Road where dwelt his two gaunt, unmarried daughters, hidden behind a semi-circular drive overhung by dark old trees.

I was born with a caul. This, I was later told, had been given to Mrs Gillon who came to our house every week to bake the bread and cakes. She had a sailor son and it was well known that with a baby's caul about your person you would never drown. This simple, credulous old woman, with her long yellow teeth and thin grey hair twisted into a bun on top of her head was for me the embodiment of evil, for I had watched her commit the atrocity of shovelling live, new-born kittens into the flames of the kitchen range. In the ordinary way we were not allowed into the kitchen at all; an exception was made on Mrs Gillon's days so that we could fashion grubby little dough men with currant eyes for her to bake.

That was not in Tulse Hill, which I do not remember because the advent of the German nanny when I was but a few months old was the cause and the occasion for the move to a house not far away where the streets were named – evidently by a feminist with literary leanings – after the novels of George Eliot and Harriet Martineau. Nobody thereabouts had ever heard of either of them or their works; thus the street names were considered rather outlandish, one of them being commonly referred to as Romola Road with the accent on the second syllable. We lived in Deronda Road until I was four years old.

It was during that time that my brother started going to school – in the kindergarten of Dulwich High School for Girls which took such little boys – where he must have picked up what I felt was surely the most brilliant witticism ever to pass human lips. 'What's the difference between a market stall and a tram?' it went. 'One has acetylene lamps and the other a set o'lean horses.' I fell off my chair with laughter. It defines pretty well the kind of children we were and the epoch in which we lived. No part of it would be understood by any child today. (As a matter of fact I recall going with Gertrude in a pea-soup fog one morning to the terminus and boarding a tram that had both attributes.)

It was in those years that I first enjoyed the deep satisfaction of defying authority. This took the tiresome form of saying 'Shan't, so there!' and sticking out my tongue whenever bidden to do anything. Almost every day Gertrude took my brother and me to Brockwell Park. There was the uphill climb to the bandstand, the level path towards the Herne Hill gates, the walk to the pond where the caged birds fluttered and the door to the knot garden. In addition to this great variety one could see sheep safely grazing on a gentle slope and, in the autumn, there was the exquisite pleasure in shuffling slowly through fallen leaves.

It was while so engaged that I met my first moral conflict head on. I had been warned that should I repeat the defiant phrase and rude gesture even once more this would be reported to my mother and condign punishment would follow: I should not go to the Zoo as promised. Three times, on a rising note of exasperation, Gertrude now called me to come along at once. I remained by the keeper's little lodge at the entrance to the park, kicking up the leaves, torn by indecision. Then, having made the choice and fully aware of the consequences, I shrieked, 'Shan't, so there!' and stuck out my tongue. Eventually, of course – but at tilt less than full – I caught up with her. But too late to appease: I did not go to the Zoo.

At about this time I was greatly frightened by the sight of boys wearing masks – probably near Guy Fawkes' Day – and my brother played upon this fear, telling me that a derelict house with dirty windows on the corner of Norwood Road which we had to pass on our way to the park was the home of boys with masks. During that winter when I was pushing three I took my first steps towards literacy. For my father's birthday I had learnt and now recited to him the alphabet. As I stood by his chair at the breakfast table on that dark January morning I handed him the little book from which I had learnt my letters so that he could follow the text. He burst into laughter. I was puzzled, but also mortified: I had not thought this an occasion for mirth and, although my father then listened gravely enough to the recital, I had heard the unmistakable – and unforgettable – sound of derision. However, very soon I was reading fluently within the limitations of a three-year-old's vocabulary and cognizance.

A vivid recollection of those years is of a children's party one winter afternoon, a year or so later. At the far end of the brightly-lit room there was a table laden with glowing jellies, little coloured cakes, trifles, fruits and sweets. I stood behind a sofa, just able to look over it at the brilliant, crowded scene. There advanced towards me a little old gentleman carefully balancing a plate piled high with cakes and puddings. As he shuffled along, his knees slightly bent, he smiled lovingly at his food. A wave of such aching pity for him swept over me that I burst into inconsolable sobs and had to be taken home, quite unable to explain the reason for my distress.

One memory I have of the Deronda Road years is not of winter but of high summer, when there would often be a German band playing in the street. I was to go with my mother to a garden party, freshly prinked out in starched white muslin with many ribbons and an appalling hat to match and I was sent to her room to be inspected. My mother was seated at her dressing-table. She examined me through her mirror. Then she turned round and said in a tone of surprise: 'You look quite pretty today.'

It is a curious fact that whereas my parents, more especially my mother, never ceased drilling us in good manners – interpreted not as consideration for others but, more simply, as the formalities of polite usage – they did not hesitate to insult us to our faces without mercy. Thus my brother was frequently addressed as 'Monkey Brand' – a reference to a soap widely advertised at the time with the picture of a particularly hideous ape – this being among the milder jibes, for he was left in no doubt that he was singularly stupid, gross and dirty. I was perhaps let off more lightly, merely being told in and out of season that I was clumsy, unamiable, graceless and ugly. I could see what they meant: I did not have golden curls nor a pretty tip-tilted nose and it saddened me. Even my dancing classes, which I adored, were spoiled for me when my mother came to look on at one of the sessions and complained to the dancing mistress in my hearing that my curtsies were so ungainly that I looked as though about to squat on a chamber-pot.

(In her old age my mother was once showing some family photographs to friends of hers and produced one of me, taken in Germany when I was about eight, where I am shown sitting on a table wearing my favourite clothes: a panama hat and a plain dress of natural tussore. 'Oh, how sweet!' 'What a lovely little girl!' cried the old ladies. Not in the least abashed by my presence, my mother said complacently: 'Yes, she was a very handsome child.')

In the summer of 1907 we moved to a larger house in West Dulwich so that my grandmother could come to live with us. Here several innovations were introduced for the children. In the first place the nursery was known as the

The photograph taken in Germany, when Yvonne was about eight

schoolroom where we still had our tea though we took our other meals in the dining-room. A telephone was installed here and we had a gramophone with records of the *Nutcracker Suite*, excerpts from Bizet's *L'Arlésienne*, Massenet's *Méditation*, Saint-Saëns's *Swan*, Schubert's *Entr'acte* from *Rosamunde*, Grieg's incidental music for *Peer Gynt* and eventually, of course, the waltz medley from *Der Rosenkavalier*.

But the best thing about the new house – apart from the presence of my loving grandmother and the fact that I could watch the Crystal Palace fireworks from my bed – was its garden. The far end, hidden from the house behind a thicket of lilacs, was shaded by great trees whose branches stretched from the grounds of Sir Hiram Maxim's suburban estate. Sir Hiram himself was a very small man whom we sometimes saw scuttling about the Norwood Road sporting one of those hats favoured in later years by Winston Churchill. Later the trees were felled, his mansion was demolished and the whole site became an enormous tram-shed. This part of the garden was given over to practical as distinct from ornamental purposes: there was a vegetable garden, a glasshouse and a potting shed; there were small beds for the children to grow things; a gravelled area with a swing and a trapeze; a serviceable cricket-pitch and some fine apple trees into which one could climb to find a comfortable perch with a book, to munch and read out of sight and earshot of the adult world. There my brother and I, when not being Mr Sydney Carton facing a furious mob – we took turns and I much preferred to be the mob – played at Dr Crippen and Miss Le Neve (she thrillingly disguised as a boy), making their happy carefree way across the Atlantic until exposed, thanks to Marconi's new-fangled wireless, and arrested on board the liner by a detective, also in disguise, whose part we vied with one another to enact.

We were all tremendously conscious in my childhood of being a seafaring nation. Children, boys and girls alike, wore sailor jackets with sailor collars and lanyards. We had navy blue sailor caps with the names of warships in gold letters on a black ribbon. In spring these caps were transformed with white piqué covers and in summer we wore broad-brimmed straw sailor hats. It is no wonder that my brother, like other small boys, thought it his destiny to go to sea. When he was twelve, since he hated Dulwich College and was doing badly there, my parents tried to get him into the training school at Osborne but, of course, as the son of a naturalized British subject, he was rejected.

When quite little my brother, after a careful inspection of the two ladies, asked: 'Who is older, Mummy or Granny?' It did not seem an unreasonable enquiry for although, like other widows of her day, my grandmother

dressed always in black, with never the sparkle or gleam of a single ornament, she was slender and erect in bearing, had a youthful step and a clear,
merry laugh. A thing immensely in her favour was that, unlike most people,
she approved of me, often calling me, in English or in German, her 'good
little child'. She wintered, as they used to say, in Cannes, sending us boxes
of glacé fruits and crystallized flower-petals. When in London she prepared
herself to walk out on every fine morning and then I would be summoned
to her room. She would stand there and raise her long skirts, revealing
finely-turned ankles, and I would button up her little soft kid boots, earning
a penny for this service. Thus I could be sure of seeing her at least once
each day unless it were too wet for her to leave the house: bad days indeed.

Then my Great-aunt Bella came to stay. This was my grandmother's
sister-in-law, the wife of her favourite brother, Richard Daus who lived
with his family in a splendid mansion in Hamburg with lawns sloping down
to the Ausser Alster. He once sent us a photograph of it on a postcard with
the lines:

Ich wohn' in diesem grossen Haus
Und schick' ein' Kuss, dein Onkel Daus.

Their daughter Daisy was the first woman, it was always claimed, ever to
be seen in the streets of Hamburg at the wheel of a car, and their elder son,
Edgar, the first Jew to receive a commission in a crack Prussian regiment.
We had a photograph of him in his brilliant white uniform looking particularly Germanic and non-Jewish. However, he was cashiered for marrying a
musical comedy actress.

According to my mother, who had spent some of her happiest days with
that family as a young girl, it was the scene and setting for every pleasure.
There she had gone to her first balls, dancing waltzes and polkas to music
composed by her Uncle Richard and played by his own small chamber
orchestra. His wife, her Aunt Bella, had lavished ball-gowns and jewels,
dancing slippers and hair ornaments upon my mother, who was then

suffering the lean time following her father's business failure. She looked back upon those days with nostalgia and retained for the family unbounded gratitude and admiration.

In Great-aunt Bella I had expected to meet someone similar to my grandmother, only, since by all accounts she was very rich, far grander and more beautifully dressed. To my disappointment, she was not. She was short and stout and if, for all a child could tell, her clothes were expensive, they were not at all pretty in my eyes. One way and another I thought her person rather unattractive. However, I was highly recommended to her as a boot-buttoner and on one of the first mornings of her visit I was sent for and bidden to perform. Great-aunt Bella lifted her skirts and to my astonishment disclosed two enormous legs, thick as mighty tree-trunks, the like of which I had never beheld. Startled but enraptured by the sight I cried out: 'Oh, what lovely fat legs you have!' Her face darkened; she let fall her skirts and, pointing to the door, dismissed me, shouting in German that I was a most ill-mannered child.

I remember little else about her stay since, naturally, I was not again called upon to do anything for her. But on the eve of her departure, when I was sent as usual before bedtime, with crisply ironed pinafore and well-brushed hair, to say goodnight, I found the ladies in my grandmother's little sitting-room enjoying a farewell gossip, and Great-aunt Bella, all smiles, told me graciously to express a wish that she would do her best to gratify before she left us. I scarcely hesitated before blurting out: 'Oh, could I see your lovely fat legs again?' It was not well received.

This great-aunt was to figure in one of the great traumas of my childhood; but that was some years later, before which I went through a bad time, being infected by bovine TB.

During my grandmother's last illness she stayed for a while in Westgate, living in a small private hotel facing the West Bay, from where she could watch the sunsets spreading over the sea. On the days when she felt well enough to see us, she would place a sheet of paper in her window. Daily we went past and looked up. There was a leap of the heart when, after many disappointments, the white oblong appeared. Then we rushed into the hotel and raced up the stairs, halting outside her door for a moment to draw breath before entering the room in a decorous manner for fear that boisterous behaviour might harm her. She was always glad to see us, never speaking of her health, nor indeed of herself at all, but ever gentle and interested in what we were up to, though quickly tired.

Exactly when she died in 1910 we were not told at the time. For many months we wore black armbands on our overcoats and all that winter my dresses were of grey and lavender stuffs, known as 'half-mourning'. But it was whole mourning that I felt for the passing of that most lovely old lady. She was fifty-seven.

It was an unhappy winter, for I entered a phase of inexplicable and fearful dread. Although I saw little of my mother as a rule, beyond the ritual goodnight visits, and was by no means in the habit of looking to her for help or comfort, if ever she happened to be away from home when darkness fell I would be seized by an ungovernable terror, convinced that she had been killed, was the victim of some hideous accident or attack and would never come back. I would stand with my head hanging over a basin, heavy pain twisting my stomach, sure that I was about to vomit. I could not be persuaded to go to bed and, although Gertrude enlisted the help of the other servants to calm me, it was no use: I remained rigid and distraught. Nor did the nausea subside until at last I heard my mother enter the front door, when I would rush down into the hall to cling to her, burying my face in her fur coat, cold with frost. I suffered this frantic anxiety throughout the long, bleak winter evenings. I did not connect it at all with the recent death of my grandmother, nor did anyone else. I have sometimes wondered since, given the intensity of the feeling, whether I was suffering not so much from fear of my mother's death but the unbearable guilt of wishing that it had been she who had died.

In that same year, when I was seven, the Turner Wing of the Tate Gallery, donated by Sir Joseph Duveen, was opened. This fired my father's imagination and from then on he would take my brother and me on Sunday mornings to the Tate. What I really wanted to see were the Sargents, in particular *Carnation, Lily, Lily, Rose*, then on prominent display, but I was hurried past it, jerked by the hand: we had come to gaze upon the Turners and upon the Turners we gazed. Today and for many years past I have been grateful for that discipline but at the time, had I not been told – without the slightest foundation – that the seascapes and sunsets were painted by Turner from our favourite beach, I doubt whether I should have enjoyed his pictures at all. On the other hand, nearly seventy years later a friend lent me a cottage on the Farnley Hall estate in Yorkshire. Such cottages as ours were occupied as a rule by retired estate servants of the Fawkes family, descendants of Turner's great friend and patron, so naturally I was not invited to the Hall to see the collection of pictures which, like everybody else, I knew to be there; nevertheless, as I walked about that lovely part of Wharfedale I could not but recognize with delight certain landscapes Turner had loved.

My father's passion for paintings – which later persuaded him to commission portraits of me by a gentleman called Alfred Wolmark and induced him to buy at auction a number of insipid works, vaguely school of Murillo – did less than nothing to moderate the contempt I felt as an adolescent for my parents' tastes.

I recognize now that, in fact, these were perfectly normal and respectable for people of their class and generation, with the exception, perhaps, of my father's lifelong devotion to the collected works of Goethe, Schiller and Heine which he had inherited in stubby little German volumes. His interest in literature increased with age and when he was seventy he confided in me that he had recently discovered Shakespeare and at last understood 'what all the fuss is about'. In music he worshipped Wagner and Harry Lauder, while my mother favoured Puccini and was devoted to comic opera: everything from Offenbach and Gilbert and Sullivan to Lehár and the lightest of musical comedies.

It follows that the first real theatre I was taken to – as distinct from the Christmas pantomime – should have been *The Chocolate Soldier*. Both my parents were ardent admirers of Bernard Shaw and, whatever he himself may have said, they regarded this as a musical version of his *Arms and the Man*. Before we went to see it, my brother and I were required to learn the Oscar Straus lyrics by heart, my mother accompanying us on the piano. (The result is that I remember them and am still word-perfect today.)

In those years we sometimes went to Brighton for the Christmas holidays, staying either in rooms on the front in Albany Mansions, or else in Brunswick Square. There was always a festive feeling in the air; there were parties with dancing in the evening, in preparation for which one had to rest all the afternoon, and we would go to call upon friends of my parents stopping at one or other of the great hotels. We would take them bouquets of flowers or little beribboned boxes of candied fruit or sweets. I rather naturally assumed that these people owned the places where they were living and on one occasion, when the small orchestra in the lounge fell silent, I turned to our host and said would he ask his band to play again.

Those Christmases away were nothing like so good as those at home when everyone was kept out of the drawing-room for several days beforehand and then, ushered in on Christmas morning, we all, children and servants, found our own small separate table piled with presents beautifully set out for each of us. I recall that the servants' gifts always included two dress lengths: material to make their morning and afternoon uniforms, which seemed to me something of a swindle.

4

With the onset of my illness all was changed. For three winters I was sent away with Gertrude to deserted seaside resorts to lie out on a veranda all the short day, muffled up in a fur-lined coat and stuffed into a Jaeger sleeping-bag. Once a week a parcel of books and sweets arrived from the Army & Navy Stores, but the books never saw me through the week. I became an avid newspaper reader, following the progress of strikes in the mines and on the railways with the greatest interest, while I came to know the two *Alice* books so well and turned their pages so often that they almost fell out of their little red covers. From the start of the year I was cut off from the family and everyone I knew; allowed to walk, whether along the wind-swept promenade or the bleak shore, only for half an hour a day. Some-times dreadnoughts – for so they were called – were anchored in the roads and once Gertrude and I joined a party of local residents and rowed out on a choppy sea to be conducted over HMS *Indomitable*.

In all those years I had scarcely any schooling. I underwent two opera-tions to remove the infected glands, suffering the misery no less than the awful disfigurement of bandages wound about my neck and head and the repulsive dressings that had to be done night and morning. An unpleasant concomitant of those days was the recurring nightmare of being pursued and engulfed by a pulsating billow of dark red jam dotted with pink stars. Only much later did I identify this with the throbbing-blood effect of the anaesthetic I had been given for the surgery which took place in my eerily disguised bedroom whose walls had been masked by sheeting while the whole place reeked of ether. Added to all this, I was said to have double curvature of the spine, so that I was made to lie flat upon tables and an ancient masseuse was constantly in attendance. I was, in short, a most horrid mess.

The only good times, in fact, were during my brother's summer holi-days when we went back to the seaside which had been so cheerless a background to the lonely winters and now became the setting for day-long happiness: for sun and rippled sand under bare feet, for blue seas and blue skies and the delicate exploration of rock pools after tea. If the tide were high, we would play cricket on the Green in the late afternoon sunshine, sending in a scratch side of little girls and boys to play against a miraculous family, aged from four to eighteen, who mustered a complete eleven. If unable to go to the beach at other times of the day, we would turn inland – though never beyond the strong tang of the sea – walking between ripe cornfields splashed with poppies; or, on special occasions, for carriage outings to Minster, Sandwich or Pegwell Bay. Then I was allowed to sit on the coachman's box with the driver, watching the curious motion of the horses' rumps.

On one of these blissful holidays our two nannies – known, in true feudal fashion, by the names of their employers – having struck up an acquaintance, we became friends on the beach with Kitty and Dick, the children of Bonar Law. Not long before, there had been a parliamentary election when my brother had pinned a large yellow rosette upon me and said that we were Liberals. Always one to show off, I announced this fact to the young Laws. Dicky looked at me coldly and said: 'But how does your father vote?' I was nonplussed: I had had no idea that grown-ups played this game. (That incident became the subject of one of the earliest short stories I had published.)

My parents were not always with us on these summer holidays. Sometimes my mother would go to Marienbad or Homburg by herself while my father stayed in London, working in the city. On one of those occasions when we were at Westgate-on-Sea, my brother and I set out early one morning to meet some other children and rejoin our nannies on the beach. For some reason these children could not come out with us and my brother, then about ten years old, decided we might as well go for a walk on our own. This was not at all in the plan, but I meekly agreed and we were soon out of the small town and walking along the cliffs. At that point a dapper young man wearing a straw hat caught up with us and said in a friendly way that if we were out walking he would join us. That was at about half past nine in the morning.

We walked all day along the cliff-edge, meeting no one and eating nothing. I grew very tired and my legs ached, but every time I weakly suggested that we should turn back and go home, my brother grew cross and said I was a fool. At one point I found the whitened jawbone of a sheep lying in the short turf and picked it up as a present to take back to Gertrude, any mention of whom enraged my brother still further: he was determined to appear boldly independent in the eyes of our companion.

At about four in the afternoon, when my exhaustion must have been evident to him, the young man sat us down in a bothy on the outskirts of what must have been Herne Bay and treated us each to a bottle of ginger pop. Then he marched us to the railway station, bought tickets for Westgate – all of which we thought very handsome of him – and accompanied us not only on the train but all the way home.

As we turned the corner into Ethelred Road where we always stayed we were amazed to see a large crowd outside our house with, at the centre, Gertrude looking quite unlike herself. We introduced our companion to her and he politely raised his hat, producing from his pocket a visiting card which he held out to her. Thus, at last, we learnt his name: he was Mr Ironsides. Far from responding to these courtesies, Gertrude turned on her heel, delivered a smart box on the ears to my brother and ordered us both into the house and to bed. Disconcerted, Mr Ironsides slunk away and I, certainly, felt deeply ashamed of our Gertrude's churlish conduct.

She, of course, had been frantic with anxiety at our disappearance. Upon learning that the other children had never joined us at all, she had no clue whatsoever to our whereabouts and, as the day wore on, she not only called the police but telephoned to our father in the city. He promised to come down that evening if we had not turned up. She received my offering of the jawbone of a dead sheep with no enthusiasm at all.

The aftermath of that adventure – which I had not really enjoyed – was quite terrible. My dearest possession was my bicycle. An efficient cyclist from an early age, I had been given my own machine on my sixth birthday. I loved and tended it with a devotion beyond the call of duty. Even its oily smell was incense to my nostrils. In the summer, getting up at dawn and stealing out of the house, I would whizz about the lawn, leaving a pattern of crushed silver snakes on the sparkling grass. To the song of thrushes in the lilacs I propelled my mount in ecstasy: a despatch rider on a confidential mission, a horseman galloping to the rescue, a messenger bearing vital news that would sway the fortunes and seal the fate of thousands.

On her return to England my mother decreed that for a whole year my bicycle would be confiscated. She lectured my brother and me in turn as she lay in bed droning on about 'reliability': the word was repeated again and again, until it seemed to lose all meaning. It was a most disagreeable and, in some ways, quite irrelevant wigging; not for one moment did it touch upon the real issues involved: my brother's manly wish to appear his own master, the total lack of consideration for Gertrude who was responsible for us and, last but not least, the potential danger of falling in with unknown men. I did not believe that being deprived of my bicycle – the most severe pun- ishment that could have been devised – would make me more reliable.

It was not many years after – to be precise, in the winter of 1913 – that the great hero of my childhood came upon the scene. This was Captain Scott and, as I lay out in the snow on the balcony, I read every word I could find about him and his companions, news of whose death nine months earlier had just filtered through to the British public. (How strange that seems in these days of instant reporting.) Out of respect for the frightful sufferings of those brave men I took off my gloves to read about them. Later I constructed in cardboard my version of the hut where they had lived and the tent where they had died. A full-page coloured picture of the four-year-old Peter Scott – a supplement, I think, to the *Illustrated London News* – touched me to the point of tears, for I was an extremely sentimental child. I thought there had never been so beautiful and tragic a small figure. All my life I have retained a keen interest in the Antarctic and have read most of the books on the Scott expedition, rejecting with a sense of almost personal affront recent attempts to denigrate the character and motives of the chief protagonists. On that and related subjects I have remained ten years old.

The school I attended in Dulwich was called Oakfield. It consisted of two connected houses and stood at the corner of Croxted and Thurlow Park Roads. In the early days, before my brother was sent away to become a boarder, I walked to school with him. At a certain point other little day boys on their way to Dulwich College Prep School would join us, some with sisters. Then we, the sisters, would fall back and walk behind the boys who were deeply ashamed of being seen in the company of girls.

My school was run by a mountainous lady with bright orange hair who had had a brilliant university career and was a mathematician. Her assistant, who taught French, kept on blushing for no apparent reason. Those two – Miss Westall and Miss Baikie – were supported by a staff of three: Miss Freshwater who, though she looked like a frog, was kindness itself and, being in charge of the school library, could always be counted upon to find another Sherlock Holmes for me; Miss Beebe, the daughter of the local vicar, had a hare-lip and taught the youngest children; and Miss Castle – engaged to be married to someone living far away in a place enchantingly named Valparaiso – with whom I fell madly though not hopelessly in love.

Though I had been a regular pupil at this school, and loved it, from the age of six – when one of the earliest reports bore the general assessment 'Lacks self-control' – I was able to attend very infrequently after my illness set in, and that only in the autumn term. Since I was pronounced 'delicate' – the term always used to prevent me from doing anything enjoyable – it was laid down that on inclement days I should go to school in a cab. This so outraged my sense of the decencies, making me appear a freak to my schoolfellows, that I appealed to my father saying that if I arrived in a growler nobody would speak to me. He was amused, but saw my point and managed to persuade my mother to drop the idea. The upshot was that I must have a pair of Wellington boots to wear on wet days. That sounded rather dashing. I envisaged something in the style of the Household Cavalry, but since nobody in Dulwich had ever been seen wearing Wellington boots, I feared I might be thought even more outlandish than if I turned up in a cab. This fear was much increased when, at the Army & Navy Stores — where, I may say, not only my parents but also my grandmother always did most of their shopping and, in those days, had to be a member and have a number — the repulsive glittering black rubber objects were produced, in no way reminiscent of battle honours or anything of a martial nature. They were no more than glorified galoshes and quite humiliating. So ashamed was I that every time I had to wear them I took them off as soon as I reached the school, hid them under my coat and proceeded on stockinged feet. The children left their outdoor things in a basement cloakroom whose back entrance was approached through a narrow winding little shadowed path bordered by shrubs. It was damp even on fine days; on wet ones it was little better than a shallow stream, so I sat all day with soaking wet feet and the Wellington boots earned a poor opinion all round.

It was not only in the matter of those boots that I was set apart from other Oakfield children. For most of my time there I was the only Jewish girl. Towards the end I was joined by one other, which was annoying as it prevented me from listening through the door to the prayers from which I was excluded. Nobody knows the words and music of *Hymns Ancient and Modern* better than I. A similar effect resulted from scripture being a forbidden subject, thus exciting my keenest curiosity. When that lesson was held I was told to move to a desk at the back of the classroom and was given some undemanding alternative task, with the result that when a visiting cleric came to examine the school and innocently included me, I was able to answer all the questions and came out top. Although Jews were so

rare in that place and time and my Jewishness was thus so unnecessarily
well advertised, I never encountered any anti-Semitism in Dulwich.

My father set some store by his faith – he was *croyant* but indifferently
pratiquant – and in no sense was the household orthodox: we ate such
Jewish delicacies as pleased the palate but ignored the laws governing the
nature and preparation of kosher food. At the same time there was a certain
uneasiness of conscience about the children's upbringing and, while my
parents went to synagogue only on days of high festival, we were taken
quite often from an early age on Saturday mornings to the children's services held in the Norwood Jewish orphanage. There I learnt from the
prayer-book that while boys, who sat downstairs, gave thanks to God that
they had not been created female, girls, who sat in the gallery, could only
thank Him for having made them according to His will. This attestation
from on high of second-class status deeply impressed – and depressed –
me. The Lord's less than half-hearted approval of his female creation
struck me as rather shameful: if he thought so poorly of us, why on earth
have bothered in the first place?

I loathed the orphanage and its inmates – who always smelt cold –
because every winter at Christmas time, which they did not celebrate, my
brother and I were made to distribute presents to them. We sat on a dais
with the headmaster and his wife while the children came up and received
their gifts from our hands. No relationship could have been more degrading to both parties. I dreaded it each year.

Despite my immutable inferiority I was permitted, even obliged, to
attend the Hebrew lessons given at our house by a young rabbi to prepare
my brother for his barmitzvah. I picked up a few words and phrases but
realized that they were never intended to be of the slightest use to me.
However, they enabled me to understand what was going on when the day
of my brother's ceremony came. It took place at the Great Portland Street
synagogue, of which my parents were members, on a beautiful July morning. I well remember how the sun came streaming through the tall windows

of coloured glass and how my brother's sweet clear boy's voice rang out, filling that great place. In the afternoon there was a grand garden party at home; there was delicious food, including ice-cream – then something of a luxury in a suburban private house – and, apart from the obligatory gold watch, presents were showered upon my brother by the many guests who included the Chief Rabbi.

The glory, however, soon departed, thanks to my quite inexcusable misdemeanour. I thought it admirable, even heroic, that my brother, once he was barmitzvah and, so to speak, a grown-up, should not only walk all the way from Dulwich to Great Portland Street on the Day of Atonement but, in addition, should do so fasting. I wished to emulate him and, at last, I was allowed to go without my breakfast on that day. Gertrude took me to the children's service at the orphanage in the morning and, on my return home, I was given a large lunch which I gobbled up greedily. Then we set out for Great Portland Street where I was to join my mother in the gallery and there, dressed in my black velvet coat with lace collar and my fur-trimmed velour hat, all among the starving ladies, with a thumping head which I thought would burst with pain, I was as sick as a dog.

That finished my parents' connection with Great Portland Street. I believe they never again dared to show their faces. They became Liberal Jews, which must be accounted greatly to my credit.

5

Every June during the years of my illness Gertrude had her well-earned holiday while I went with my mother to Bad Kreuznach to take the waters and the baths. It was while we were there in 1913 that Gertrude, after almost ten years with us, wrote from her home town, Hamburg, to say that she would not be coming back: I no longer needed a nanny but her younger sister, Anna, who would benefit by going to England and was fully qualified as a lady's maid, would come to us in her stead. It was there, too, also when I was ten, that Great-aunt Bella came back briefly into my life.

My mother and I were not used to each other's company but, once settled in what she had called upon our first arrival 'this funny little town', I saw little of her, for she allowed me – and I was only too happy – to go about on my own. Each morning, before breakfast, I would go to the Kurgarten where, in a fancifully decorated byre, a man would milk some exceedingly pure cow into a large glass mug. I forced myself to swallow this nauseating cow-warm liquid, encouraged by the presence of an immensely tall and handsome park-keeper wearing a uniform of forest green with scarlet piping who also drank the beastly stuff with every sign of relish. I did not wish to appear a weakling in his eyes. He, however, ate a slice of delicious rough black bread to help it down which I was not allowed. The mornings were taken up with my 'cure' – the waters and the baths – as well as exercises on a battery of apparatus in what was known as the Zander Institute. It was not as a rule until I joined her for lunch on the terrace of the Hotel Oranienhof that I saw my mother. After the meal she rested and I, too, lay down and read *Three Men in a Boat*. We occupied adjoining rooms and sometimes, after I had gone to bed in the evening, I thought I heard people talking to my mother on the other side of the communicating door; but, try as I would, I never managed to hear what they said before I fell asleep.

As often as possible I went roller-skating on the outdoor rink; generally I was the only skater there. I had been a confident performer since the age of five, so I was able now to practise the most elaborate gyrations without fear of being laughed at if I failed or fell over. For the rest, I wandered about the streets, gazing into shop windows, particularly those of the many small jewellers where ornaments of amethyst, aquamarine, topaz, garnet, opal, agate, onyx and amber were displayed.

It may sound somewhat desolate but the truth is that I was intoxicated by my unaccustomed freedom. An over-protected child, seldom out of the nanny's sight – the happiest day of my life to date had been that of King Edward VII's funeral when the entire adult household, save for a harum-scarum cook called Violet, was out of the way from the break of that sunny morning until long after my usual bedtime – I enjoyed every moment of my Kreuznach liberty. Besides which, I was not always alone, for I struck up acquaintance with many other children – Russians, Americans, Germans – in the hotel grounds where there were seesaws, swings and tennis-courts. Some children I met, too, in the Kurgarten and was given leave to have tea or play games with those living in other hotels once my mother had looked them over and approved of them, their parents and their governesses. No doubt some of those parents and those governesses thought not too well of my mother, while I daresay the children envied my independence.

Only towards late afternoon, when I was rigged out in my detested 'best' dresses, horrible, frilled confections run up by the gentle little dress-maker who lived amidst great clutter in Norwood and was called Miss Budden, did my mother and I go out together, to the park where a band played and children danced while the grown-ups sat or strolled about. My mother would chat with a few people, in particular a large, imposing couple whom she joined in egging me on to dance with their overgrown son, Ernst-Otto von Something: a huge boy of about thirteen who wore a white sailor-suit with trousers that came to just below his knees revealing his tremendous calves. This grotesque creature, it seems, had watched me skating and, though maddened with admiration, had not dared speak to me until he had induced his parents to meet my mother – which they did rather reluctantly – and, not knowing my name, he had taken to calling me, of all sickening things, Süsschen. I was invited to go on drives in the countryside when Ernst-Otto and I would sit with our backs to the horses, facing his cold and stately parents who cannot have much liked their son's infatuation with a small Jewish girl whose mother did not look after her properly.

Apart from that, my Kreuznach life was entirely agreeable; and then calamity struck. One night the voices heard through the communicating door were more persistent than usual and I recognized, or thought I recognized, the doctor's voice. I immediately felt left out. I liked the doctor and resented his visiting my mother so late. The next morning when I came downstairs the hall porter, a good friend of mine, said he had a message for me: I was not to worry, my mother had been taken to hospital in the night and an aunt of mine would arrive later in the day.

It was bewildering and rather frightening. When Great-aunt Bella arrived from Hamburg that afternoon I expected her to tell me what was wrong with my mother and to take me to see her. Nothing of the kind: Great-aunt Bella pursed her thick lips, refused to answer my questions, said I should know all in good time and, in short, made a first-class mystery of an already puzzling and, in some ill-defined way, threatening situation. I roamed about the hotel grounds in a state of troubled uneasiness and came to the conclusion that, behind my back, as it were, my mother was having a baby. It seemed the only rational explanation for that, of course, was a subject too delicate to be openly talked about. But why had I not been fore-warned? Why was I kept in the dark? Babies did not happen overnight. I had, naturally, penetrated the great secret of where they came from long before and had been given to understand that, until their birth, they 'lay under the mother's heart'. It sounded cosy, even enviable; and all this time some unborn brother or sister of mine had been lying under my mother's heart and she had never told me. I felt betrayed and, at the same time, a feeling I had never before experienced, an emotion so powerful and so violent swept over me that I thought it must destroy me. There was a strange tightening in my belly and a dreadful weight or terror and hatred of I knew not what.

This anguish, now fastened upon me like some gnawing animal, was intensified by the blazing heat of those days from which, like the pain, there was no escape. What I went through then, concentrated into little more than a few days, was a lifetime's savage and ungovernable jealousy of a younger sibling. That torment remains in essence indescribable, but it poisoned every waking moment. I did not know, of course, that it was jealousy, but I did know that in some horrible way my feelings were shameful and this added an overwhelming sense of guilt to my burdened spirit.

At last my great-aunt announced that in the afternoon she would take me to visit my mother in hospital. I must be very good and not bother her with much talk. The hospital was peaceful, even soothing. Pale blinds were drawn against the glare of fierce sunshine, nuns wearing white head-dresses and long white robes moved quietly over the polished floor. My mother lay on a high bed looking pale. She put out her hand to me and squeezed mine, but she was plainly too tired to speak. There were no signs of a baby.

Driving back in the carriage Great-aunt Bella said that she would be leaving in the morning. 'And your father will arrive in the afternoon. You may go to the station to meet him,' she added and told me the time of the train. The next day a sullen, clouded, dusty heat had settled on the little town, blotting out the sun at last. I met my father as he came off the train and while we drove to the hotel I told him I had been badly frightened by my mother's sudden removal to hospital. 'There was no need,' he said. 'They had to act quickly, you see, and operate at once because she had acute appendicitis, but there wasn't any real danger.'

I might have protested: then why wasn't I told? Why was it kept a secret from me? Instead I said, 'I thought she was going to have . . .' I halted: I could not for the life of me pronounce the word 'baby'. It told too much, exposing the heart of the fear, the guilt, the hatred – 'going to have a child', I finished. My father gave a low, amused chuckle. He made no attempt to probe the wound.

Those reminiscences of my disagreeable Great-aunt Bella, for whom I felt no affection at all, should not be recorded without a postscript relating the fate that overtook her. And not only her, of course, but also my Great-uncle Richard who, unlike his wife, was of a genial and warm-hearted disposition, always ready with a joke, always sending us volumes of the nursery songs he had written for his own children, and always pouring out his apparently inexhaustible wealth. Much younger than his sister – my grandmother – he outlived her by many years. Two of his three children – his elder son and his daughter – married non-Jews; and, as I was told the story, in 1933 his daughter's son, then a boy of fourteen or fifteen, joined the Hitler Youth, no doubt in self-protection, and went one step further by denouncing his grandparents. Everything they had, including their house and all its contents, was confiscated and in their last years my father was sending his cast-off suits and overcoats to Great-uncle Richard while parcels of underclothing went to Great-aunt Bella. Their children left Germany but they were too old to emigrate. They were utterly destitute and, I believe, died from starvation.

6

In my description of life in Kreuznach, where I went for three consecutive early summers, I have somewhat telescoped the years which were much alike and followed the same pattern in 1911, 1912 and 1913. However, on the second occasion, when I was nine, my mother took me as soon as we left Kreuznach to stay with the family of my Aunt Florentine, my father's sister, in Auerbach, Hesse-Darmstadt. My mother left me there and went off to Homburg where, after the tedium of being in Kreuznach with me, she planned to have rather a jolly time on her own.

Aunt Florentine was a large, dark, handsome woman married to a large, blond, handsome man: my Uncle Sigmund. They had three children: my two big cousins, Helene, then sixteen, named, as I was, after her Mayer grandmother; Eva, thirteen; and their small brother, aged seven at that time and my inferior, as I judged it, in all respects, being not only younger, but slower, and much, much fatter. These young people went to school each

day in the neighbouring town of Bensheim and my aunt was at first concerned that I should not feel lonely and bored. She need not have worried: I
found plenty to do and was entranced by it all. In the first place the family,
whose name, was, oddly, Nahm – a most un-Jewish name and, indeed,
nobody could have looked less Jewish than Uncle Sigmund who would
have been taken for a Bavarian peasant – lived on the premises of and
across the courtyard from the small factory, more a workshop, where blue
plums were treated in vats that produced a most heady, pungent scent.
Once conserved, they were packed into pretty little wooden boxes for
export. It was an exceedingly small-scale enterprise – which, I may say,
failed in due course, whereupon my father rescued his brother-in-law, not
for the first time, by restarting him once more in a similar business – but it
presented infinite possibilities to a small girl. There were a couple of jovial
workmen, delicious hot syrup to taste, little trolleys to shunt about and,
when tired of what the factory offered, I could walk a few steps to the
nearby railway station where I soon made friends with the keeper of the
level crossing.

The village lay beyond the station: in fact, the Nahms' house and factory were almost the only buildings on the other side of the line. It was surrounded by open country, by fields and orchards, so when I was not at the
station, I would help with the haymaking where I picked up and entertained
my cousins by using the local dialect. However, it was the level crossing
that became the centre of my life. I took to going there as soon as breakfast
was over and stayed all day long. I learnt how to work the barriers: you
turned a great handle and the heavy red and white striped wooden beams,
tilted skywards on either side of the tracks, slowly descended shaking out
their curtains of thin metal rods with a silvery tinkle. It was a highly
responsible job and, properly executed, ensured that the bars would come
to rest in their sockets with a little bounce and a satisfying clunk. Raising
them was heavier work, but not beyond my strength.

The crossing-keeper, when not in action, sat in a small rather stuffy little

wooden cabin with a look-out window. He lived in a cottage across the line
with his wife and many small boys with shaven heads like dirty eggs. I soon
became so proficient that he would leave me to it and go home. At such
times I would wear his cap of office. It was on the large size for me but a
smart affair with a shiny black peak, a red top and a protruding knob, like a
strawberry, on the front. I would sit in his cabin, wielding his little leather
fly-swat to while away the intervals between trains. I knew the timetable
precisely and would be punctually on the spot to work the barrier for an
arrival from the left where the train would round an invisible curve and
puff slowly to a halt or, more interestingly, I would tell myself that the tiny
black blob on the horizon to the right, where the rails stretched away to
infinity, was not a train at all and then watch it grow ever larger in the shimmering haze above the permanent way. When no trains were due I would
sometimes go into the station booking-hall and, for five pfennigs, extract
some rather unappetizing caramels from the one automatic machine – the
only customer, I think, for many a year – or else, lying stretched out on the
grassy bank bordering the line, eat the rough-hewn chunks of rye-bread I
had persuaded my aunt to put up for me, as befitting a person engaged in
heavy manual outdoor work. Aunt Florentine, though no doubt she
thought it a curious career for her nine-year-old English niece to adopt,
was infinitely tolerant and kind. She saw that I was contented and uttered
no word of criticism.

Then one day there came a letter from my mother enclosing a five-mark
note. Had I been a little less thick-skinned I might have thought of buying
something for my generous hosts. As it was, the only thing that occurred to
me was to give my mother a present. On my cousin Eva's next half-holiday
I coaxed her into going with me to the shop across the railway line that sold
everything likely to be needed in a village. Its dark interior had a strong
and rather exciting smell but it did not seem at all likely that I should find
anything fitting for my mother among the bootlaces, soaps, corn-plasters
and sacks of dried peas and lentils on display. At last, however, I spotted a

plain gold bar – probably intended as a man's tie-pin – on a plain white card. I thought this had a certain severe chic about it. It was a pity that it should cost the whole five marks, but there was nothing else in the least suitable, so I bought it and sent it off to Homburg.

A week or so later there was a letter for me on the breakfast table. As I picked it up I felt the unmistakable shape of my gold bar-brooch. Quickly I slipped it on to my lap so that nobody should catch so much as a glimpse of it, ignoring the fact that someone must have handled it before I came to table: I did not, of course, open it until everyone had gone: the children to school, my uncle to his factory, my aunt to the kitchen. Then I went into the bedroom I shared with Cousin Eva. There I opened the letter and read my mother's baneful words: artificial jewellery, she explained at some length, was vulgar. She was returning my gift. I put the letter and the brooch back into their envelope and hid it inside the empty trunk under my bed. Then I sat down on the bed and cried.

An excursion was planned for the following Sunday to visit some beauty spot with a monument in the neighbourhood. We were to take a picnic and walk in the woods. I had always enjoyed such outings, but when I said I had no wish to come, nobody queried my decision. I cannot too highly praise my aunt for her tact and loving kindness since, before dispatching the brooch, I had displayed it to every member of the family, showing off my restrained good taste and reckless prodigality. She must have known very well what was going on. Yet not even her children were allowed to exhibit the faintest curiosity or pass the slightest remark upon my behaviour. Once all of them had left the house that Sunday, I took the envelope out of its hiding-place, went into the garden, found a spade and dug a deep hole in a corner under a shrubbery. There I buried the shameful thing. Although I have never been able to forget the precept – to which I do not subscribe – that artificial jewellery is vulgar, this episode led me to the conclusion that the ultimate vulgarity lies in humiliating another human being; most particularly a child.

It was my dear, good, reliable Aunt Florentine who, in 1913, when both Great-aunt Bella and my father had left Kreuznach and my mother was out of hospital, joined us there to spare my mother, I must suppose, the not very arduous task of looking after me during her convalescence. My trust in and respect for Aunt Florentine were badly shaken by my mother's irritable, even rude way of speaking to her. She did not exactly sneer, but she commented unfavourably upon her sister-in-law's clothes, which were serviceable rather than smart, in keeping with her usual way of life, though she had brought with her on this visit what I recognized from the year before as her formal dark grey coat and skirt, her plumed hat and her best dress of lilac silk. She was noble looking but clumsily built and had the simple ways of a countrywoman. She treated my mother's ill manners with quiet good humour. I think she looked upon her little brother Alfred's wife as a slightly exotic creature made of some rare and precious material, certainly not to be bound by the ordinary courtesies between human beings.

To the ten-year-old looker-on, it was all extremely unpleasant, for it was to my mother that I felt I owed my loyalty and I assumed the treacherous role of affecting to see Aunt Florentine as a figure of fun, which did violence to my true feelings.

Here I may say that the whole of my acting career was crammed into these early years. It gave me no taste for the boards. Selected to lead a bevy of flitting persons who, to Mendelssohn's incidental music, would grace the open-air, end-of-summer-term performance of *A Midsummer Night's Dream*, I wrote to my mother – as usual abroad at this season – to ask 'May I be a fairy?' Never one to miss an opportunity to ram home my lack of elfin grace, she replied, 'Yes, if you can.'

Unfortunately Anna, who was to fashion the fairy costume, being German, failed to understand the instructions so that when all the others came tripping across the greensward in glittering tinsel, I at the head wore plain white with some paltry silver trimming. In my mother's absence my father, correctly dressed in morning coat and top hat, attended this production. He, of course, was unable to appreciate these finer points and saw nothing amiss.

At that point real life took a dramatic turn: on returning home from the play we found that Anna had fled. She left a letter saying that she had heard that day from her family bidding her to come home at once as war was imminent. She had not wished to upset everyone on this special end-of-term day so we must take this as her farewell. The startling development was the signal for my father to go at once to the rescue of my mother who was at some foreign watering place: Marienbad, I believe. My brother's school had also broken up that day and my father decided at a moment's notice to pack us off to stay with the Hynes – Bradford friends of my mother's now living in Herne Hill – and he gave us each a shilling, which was twice the going rate of our pocket-money in those days.

Thus the outbreak of World War One is forever associated for me with the most frightful act of gluttony. No sooner had we been taken to and then left in Herne Hill than I went out with my brother and spent my shilling on twelve bars of Fry's chocolate cream. That night I lay in bed and scoffed the lot. It does not speak well for giving people freedom combined with wealth.

My father caught the night boat. His dash across the continent, in the throes of mobilization everywhere, was an alarming adventure. The trains were constantly shunted into sidings to allow troops to go through; the taxi-driver who was supposed to take my parents from the hotel to the railway station had been called up and abandoned them with their luggage before they reached their destination. The journey took many days and they arrived home exhausted to tell us the tale on Sunday, 2 August 1914.

7

We left the house-and-garden life of the south London suburbs in 1915 and moved into a flat in St John's Wood. I was not told the reasons for this but they must have included the increasing difficulty, if not impossibility, of getting and keeping domestic servants during the war.

My mother had never been very good at this. There was a touch of the Queen of Hearts about her – the 'Off with her head' proclivity – and in her dealings with inferiors, servants and children alike, she showed all the makings of a colonial governor. It was sad – particularly for the inferiors – that her despotic sway should have had to be confined to the domestic sphere: it needed larger fields of operation. In earlier years, it should be said, and for a brief period, she had joined the women's suffrage move-ment, going on marches and to meetings with a green, white and purple sash slung across the bosom. That must have provided a constructive outlet for her redoubtable qualities, but it did not last.

Another motive for the move away from Dulwich that may have weighed with my father was that, as a naturalized German, he could well have suffered from the spy-mania and rampant jingoism of those times. Perhaps he wanted to get away from a neighbourhood where he had never made a secret of his background. Not that my parents had many local friends: those they had were for the most part either Yorkshire families who had known my mother in her youth and, like her, moved south, or else the parents of children at my own or my brother's school.

Looking back, I realize that in truth my parents had a restricted circle of acquaintances. They were not on visiting terms with any of their near neighbours and when, from time to time, they entertained people for dinner-parties (followed by songs at the piano in the drawing-room – guests always brought their music), they generally came from far-distant parts of London, including the area where my parents now proposed to live.

Yet another reason for the move – and perhaps its justification – was that we had, so to speak, come up in the world: my father's business, moderately successful in its small way, had suddenly expanded as a consequence of the war. With the diversion to the Port of London of merchandise previously sent to or through France from its colonial possessions, my father, as the principal British importer of vanilla, had become, almost overnight, a small monopolist: a little war-profiteer through no enterprise – or fault – of his own.

While the flat-hunting and the move were in train, my parents put up at the Regent's Palace Hotel off Piccadilly Circus, an exciting place where I joined them on Sundays, meanwhile boarding at school for a term. This gave me exceptional opportunities for furthering my love-affair with Miss Castle. My brother, who had been a boarder in one of the Dulwich College houses for some time past was never seen between holidays and was scarcely affected by the move.

Once settled in Abbey Road I was sent to the South Hampstead High School for Girls where I was continuously unhappy for a whole year. I was pushing thirteen whereas almost all the other pupils had been there since they started school: they were old hands, they knew the ropes. I was not and did not and, after the agreeable atmosphere of Oakfield, with its friendly staff and small classrooms, the High School was a bewildering institution. I have no recollection of the names or faces of any of the teachers, let alone anything they taught, though I do remember learning the details of the Battle of Jutland shortly after it had taken place (at the end of May 1916), when the whole school assembled in the Great Hall to hear the Headmistress, with map and pointer, give a rather untruthful and vainglorious account of that engagement.

On most nights during that year, I cried myself to sleep, dreading the next day. My utter misery finally became too noticeable to ignore and I was allowed to leave the school. I then went to Queen's College in Harley Street where I may not have learnt much but enjoyed myself immensely.

What little I learnt there was most precious, for the lecturer in English – we had 'lectures', not lessons – a Reverend Dr Kendall, and in French, Professor Emile Cammaerts, the Belgian poet, were inspired teachers with so deep a love for their subject and for literature in general that the imagination of even the dullest pupil must have been fired.

It was assumed at Queen's College that no one would ever need to pass an examination – and I never have – or work for a living. This is rather curious, for the place was originally founded in the mid-nineteenth century to provide young governesses with a modicum of learning which would improve their status in society. The founder, the Reverend Frederick Denison Maurice, was indeed a Christian Socialist whose advanced views, not only on the education of women but on a whole number of social questions, would have been anathema to the high-ranking families who now sent their young daughters there.

Although I was not myself made conscious of class distinctions, the school was acutely alive to them. Discreetly I was steered towards consorting with the daughters of doctors, businessmen, lawyers and writers, rather than those of peers of the realm or admirals and generals. However, I did strike up a friendship with the daughter of a minor South American diplomat – rather small beer, it may be thought – through the fortuitous circumstance that we two had sat the entrance examination together: a perfunctory affair which had really nothing to do with our educational attainments save to demonstrate that we were averagely literate. That our fathers could afford the fees would not necessarily have guaranteed that qualification.

While I had been so deeply unhappy and a fish out of water at South Hampstead – among the children of professional people, merchants, shopkeepers, journalists and artisans, predominantly Jewish and wholly middle- or lower middle-class, to which categories I belonged – I was divinely happy at Queen's though I had so little in common with most of my schoolfellows. I was like them in only one respect: all of us were fetched every afternoon by a maid or governess. Considering that I was at Queen's until over the age of sixteen, this was a mortification endurable only because it was the accepted thing at that time for that school.

My governess was called Miss Yates, an amiable character whom I could twist round my little finger. As I was supposed to be in her charge I called her my charger, and she was ever ready to plunge into action in my defence against less lenient authority. Instead of going straight home for tea, as I was supposed to do, I made her plod after me – she was very large and somewhat heavy-footed – to the Poetry Bookshop in Devonshire Street off the Theobald's Road, unknown territory to us both, to hear Harold Monro and others read their poems by candlelight. I was then, at the age of fourteen and fifteen, enthralled by the Georgian poets and the anti-Georgian Wheels, though I believed such names as Sacheverell Sitwell, Lascelles Abercrombie and Sherard Vines so beautiful as to be, quite obviously, assumed.

There were definite advantages to living in a flat. For one thing, while in Dulwich I had been obliged to practise the piano immediately below my parents' bedroom so that whenever I stopped to read a little something I had propped up on the music-stand, or had a go at playing a snatch from the swing song in *Véronique*, rather than scales or Czerny exercises, my mother would thump on the floor with a stick. Here, however, provided my mother was out of the way as she usually was, I could intersperse my practising with *Don Juan*: one of the great discoveries of my adolescence. I had no idea that revered and celebrated poets could be wildly funny. (At the same period, *Venus and Adonis* also came as a great though different surprise.)

Making people laugh had ever been my aim in life and being funny my idea of social success. I had been writing comic verse from the age of seven (illustrated and clumsily bound in coloured paper as birthday presents for my parents) and I never had the smallest doubt that I would continue all my life to be a writer, either in the manner of Gilbert's *Bab Ballads* or, if reduced to prose, in that of Stephen Leacock, both of whom were among my favourite authors. Until an absurdly late age, when I should have known better, I cherished the illusion that everybody was at heart a writer, prevented only by unfavourable circumstance from obeying this natural, human urge: something on the lines of I write, therefore I am.

At the age of eight or nine I began writing school stories which were not merely inspired by but in puerile imitation of Angela Brazil. These Works in Progress I generally read aloud to my ancient masseuse while she was at work on me, hiding the manuscript behind the covers of a real book so that she might obligingly pretend to believe that she was listening to extracts from some popular publication.

At twelve I embarked upon a preposterous war story called *Battery Five* which I sent to a magazine. I could not know that the letter enclosed with its return, inviting me to submit anything else I might write, was a singular mark of favour and would be the precursor to an entire corpus of rejection slips containing no such civilities.

In early adolescence I tended, like most people, to produce whimsical, sentimental or lugubrious verse until, as I neared the end of my teens, I ceased to versify altogether but for an occasional lapse, marked by no talent, in later life when under the influence of love or loss. My largest output was between the ages of eleven and seventeen and the first money I earned by my writing was at the age of fifteen when a weekly journal published a slightly cynical and exceedingly short story of mine, paying me half a guinea.

It was at this stage that, as many another priggish youngster with literary pretensions, I wrote off my parents as philistines of the lowest order. They, for their part, snubbed my callow preciosity until a fair state of mutual disparagement prevailed. I had reached the second phase in Wilde's dictum: 'Children begin by loving their parents, after a time they judge them; rarely, if ever, do they forgive them.'

August 1914 had, of course, brought to an abrupt close the Victorian way of life in which my parents had been born and bred, married and brought up children. I was eleven at the time. The generation gap, much

Yvonne aged about
fourteen (1917)

talked of in the years after the Second World War was as nothing compared with the chasm that opened between the young and their elders during that earlier conflict when all values and assumptions, even behaviour patterns and social norms, were in flux. If that is the situation which forms the background to the usual rebelliousness of adolescence, a truly explosive mixture of reciprocal intolerances is brought into being. One does not need to be especially 'headstrong', as the contemporary expression had it, nor one's parents peculiarly repressive, though I dare say both descriptions fitted my case, for antagonism to erupt violently.

8

I have said that my brother was never seen during term time, but that did not last. Expelled from his public school for climbing out at night to visit some ladies in the neighbourhood whom he knew, or had heard about, he was quite inevitably caught by his housemaster upon trying to climb back. Thereupon he came home in disgrace but, being just under conscription age, was entered in the Inns of Court OTC. As part of the training it seemed, there were frequent field days, many weekends of manoeuvres and what he called night ops. He had reckoned without my mother's compulsion to go through our personal belongings: I would sometimes come home from school to find my drawers emptied upside-down on the floor because they were untidy. Now, among my brother's socks and shirts, she had come upon letters of assignation making only too clear the nature of the field days, the manoeuvres and the night ops.

She was not, however, the only one to be outraged: the authorities also took a poor view, for it appeared that, while he had for his own ends grossly exaggerated the number of his military duties, he had also on far too many occasions ignored those he was genuinely under orders to perform. This had evidently gone a bit too far and he was summarily dismissed from the corps as unsuitable officer material at the very moment when he reached the age of eighteen and was thus called up. Since the Armistice was declared almost as soon as he was drafted, he saw service in the devastated regions of France as a private in the Pioneer Corps, scavenging among the corpses in the mud throughout the bitter winter of 1918/19.

This harsh experience was thought in my parents' terminology to have 'taught him a lesson', perhaps several lessons, though whether of an improving nature is another matter. Be that as it may, once my brother was demobilized my father decided to article him to a business associate in Holland, preparatory to taking him into the family firm, for which he was not yet fitted in his parent's view. He was furnished with a number of introductions to Rotterdam families of worth and respectability and kitted out for the new life. On the day before he was to set sail he came home in a state of agitation saying that his gold watch had been stolen. My father wanted to know all the details: where, when, how and so forth, upon which information he based his call to the police, only to be telephoned a couple of hours later by a pawnbroker demanding that the watch left with him earlier that day be immediately redeemed since it was being circularized by the police as stolen property and he wanted nothing to do with it. Seizing his hat in one hand and my brother by the scruff of the neck with the other, my father set out to return some hours later with the watch, having learnt from the pawnbroker the precise nature of the transaction. The upshot was that, at the last minute, the arrangements for his apprenticeship were cancelled, the letters of introduction withdrawn and he was sent abroad, as planned, but to fend for himself.

Much of this history is accounted for by the fact that from earliest childhood my brother had wanted to be a horse. While he was causing ever more anxiety to my parents – without getting any nearer to being a horse (or even acquiring horse-sense, for that matter) – I, too, was giving trouble, 'getting ideas into my head', as they expressed it. I asked whether it would be better to have porridge there instead, which impertinence was treated with disdain.

I had shaken my father badly by concluding (like Boswell's daughter) that God did not exist. Then thirteen, I was not only going regularly to the Liberal Jewish synagogue in its ramshackle premises behind Upper Gloucester Place (though for the high festivals in those war years the services were held in the Wigmore Hall) and attending its Sunday School, but I embarked upon my first essay in biography – or was it fiction? – by writing a brief lecture on the life of the prophet Hosea which I delivered from the pulpit to my startled classmates one Sunday morning.

My father, though greatly troubled by my declaration of atheism, was unable to summon up any but a lame expostulation to my argument that no deity worthy of human worship could possibly be claimed by both warring factions to be on their side, nor permit the atrocious slaughter to which the daily casualty lists bore witness. Even within my own direct knowledge there was scarcely a girl at school who was not sent for by the Head sooner or later to learn that her father or a brother had been killed.

If spared that experience – my father being too old (forty-one when the war broke out) and my brother (whose age marched with the century) too young to be conscripted – I felt as though life were passing me by in those war years: that I had no part in them. I yearned to mix with people like the groups of splendid, laughing young subalterns who filled the auditorium when I was taken to see *Chu Chin Chow* and *The Bing Boys are Here*. My brother and I saved our pocket-money to treat some half-dozen wounded soldiers in their bright blue suits and red ties to a matinée performance at the Coliseum. But apart from that and the Zeppelin raids we had, as a family, almost no direct association with the events of the time.

Never was the sense of being 'out of it' more acute than when the Armistice came. The entire population, it seemed, rushed out into the streets, dancing and singing in a frenzy of rejoicing, while I drove with my parents in staid solemnity and considerable boredom to Spithead to see the fleet lined up for review. As it happened, the ships were invisible through the dense fog. The car turned and we were driven back to London. The fog and the frightful pointlessness of that excursion seemed to typify my life.

It is impossible to forget, however old one grows, that – apart from jealousy – there are no pains so agonizing and corrosive as those of adolescence. The suffocating sense of injustice, of being misinterpreted, one's newly discovered values decried, one's tentative opinions snubbed or derided by parents who, nevertheless, demand love and respect. There comes a great boiling-up of rage against what one sees as their mean-spirited, small-minded inability to envisage a whole world of beauty, courage, generosity and passion. A tiny incident brought these feelings of stifled protest to a head.

I must have been about fifteen, helping my mother to put things away into the great linen chest one Sunday morning, and arguing some point or other with great force. She brushed my words aside impatiently and I cried out: 'But can't you understand?' to which she replied, 'I don't *want* to understand'. I was stunned into silence. It had never before crossed my mind that sane people did not wish to understand each other. From that day on I deeply mistrusted my mother and never again placed any reliance upon her.

Being my mother may not have been altogether easy I will admit; but she never really tried. In 1914 Bernard Shaw wrote (in 'Parents and Children', the Preface to his 1910 play *Misalliance*):

> On the whole children and parents confront one another as two classes in which all the political power is on one side; and the results are not at all unlike what they would be if . . . one were white and the other black, or one enfranchised and the other disenfranchised.

9

It was now, coinciding more or less with my brother's latest misdemeanour, that a matter of real contention cropped up. Queen's College, as I have said, did not prepare its young ladies for public examinations or higher education nor, indeed, for anything that might lead to a career. I desperately wanted to go to university which, I was convinced, was essential if one was to be a writer. I therefore needed to matriculate though there was not the slightest hope of doing so as long as I remained at Queen's.

In that summer after the war – 1919, when I was sixteen – this matter was being debated, with heat on my part, with only desultory interest on that of my parents. At that point we went on a motoring tour of Scotland, starting in Edinburgh, travelling over the Cairngorms and by way of Cawdor as far north as Elgin and Nairn.

The acrimonious arguments about my future, which often ended in my mother dissolving into hysterical tears, were finally concluded in a compromise: I was to be allowed to leave school and go to crammers in Baker Street. But it was too late: I sat the exam a year later and even before the results were out – though my failure was a foregone conclusion – the plan to which I had reluctantly agreed was acted upon and I was placed in a finishing school in Lausanne that summer.

My mother and I stayed overnight at an hotel on the lake and, after a delicious breakfast on the balcony, she deposited me at the school which by then had broken up for the holidays. A skeleton staff was about to take the permanently resident pupils – of whom there were a round dozen or so – to a chalet in the mountain region of Plan de Frenières above Bex and I joined them.

It was 1920. The entire Swiss population – its hoteliers, restaurateurs, shopkeepers and commercial entrepreneurs of every description – was bent upon recapturing its pre-war clientèle from among the contending nations. The owners of this school had concentrated on the Allies, since more of those were solvent and might have declined to let their children hobnob with the ex-enemy so soon after the end of hostilities. I was the only English girl and for the most part the others who did not go home in the holidays were the daughters of Russian, Belgian, French and Dutch diplomats or consular officials. They were used to being trailed from country to country according to their fathers' postings. As small children this had probably done them little harm beyond depriving them of settled – in some cases, indeed, of any – schooling while turning them into little polyglots. Now, in their teens, they presented something of a problem: too old to be kept in the nursery, not old enough to appear at social functions, in need of a little polish to gloss over the lack of education, the obvious and most convenient thing for their families to do was to abandon them to the care of a so-called finishing school.

I, who had arranged to have the *London Mercury* sent out to me regularly and saw myself as of a most superior intellect, thought them a pathetic crew: semi-literate in half-a-dozen languages, they seemed to me as ignorant as mud. Passively they sat doing silly little bits of needlework while *Quo Vadis?* was read aloud in French. They made sudden forays to the piano to thump out scraps of Chopin and they played timid games of pat-ball on the tennis court behind the large chalet that we occupied. They took exceedingly short walks in the meadows from time to time and the nearest thing to teaching was when one or other of the mistresses embarked upon some elementary aspect of geography – the one subject on which they were moderately well-informed from experience – or what passed for history of the kings-and-queens order.

Admittedly it was a holiday period; but the narrowness of their interests, the futility of their pursuits – teachers and pupils alike – excited my deepest scorn. The staff, when not in the hearing of their employer, spoke ceaselessly of Gabbitas and Thring: names, one might say, to conjure with, being those of the scholastic agency through whom they one and all were striving to get better jobs. In addition, the food was atrocious – I remember well an apparently inexhaustible barrel of fermenting cherry jam – and we were all permanently hungry.

Although I was quite determined not to remain in this environment, where I could learn nothing, and wrote saying so in no uncertain terms to my mother who had retreated to the Palace Hotel in Bürgenstock for the summer, the truth of it was that I was having a heavenly time. I was writing a great deal of verse, and played some good, fierce tennis with the only other English person: a young pupil teacher who, upon the advice of her family, had returned to the school where she herself had been 'finished' before the war in order to help her to get over the loss of her fiancé, killed in one of the last battles of 1918. She was a tall, slender young woman in her early twenties, with heavy honey-coloured hair arranged in an unfashionable style. With her I went for long walks in the lush valleys and climbed the mountains, with her I watched the afterglow of sunset fade on the Dent du Midi and with her, naturally, I fell in love.

I had always been infatuated with someone or other from about the age of eight. I first experienced this rapturous state of being when there was among the fellow-guests in Kreuznach a beautiful young Romanian lady with her little boy of three or four. She was small and neat with a fragile porcelain complexion and lilac eyes. She wore pretty things; her hands were soft and pink and bejewelled, her tawny hair shone in the sunlight and she smelt delicious. She inflamed me with a desire for I did not quite know what.

My next overwhelming passion was for an army bandmaster with the honorary rank of captain who was called Neville, though I cannot remember his surname. This was at the seaside and I would ride my bike about the town in order to cross his path again and again until he really could not avoid noticing me. Of course I listened to all his concerts in the outdoor bandstand, leaning against my bicycle and admiring his slim, belted figure in ceremonial uniform. He was not only a conductor but also in my view a wonderfully gifted composer. We did in the end strike up a sufficiently odd friendship – adoration on my part and amusement, probably, on his – for him to present me with the autographed piano score of one of his compositions; and on my birthday (I became nine) I was allowed to go to an evening concert indoors where this fine piece was performed and, after acknowledging the applause, he turned to where I sat in the front row and accorded me a special bow. My cup ran over.

At the outbreak of war I lost my heart to a private in the London Scottish Regiment whom I encountered daily on my walk to school. We never spoke but exchanged smiles of great significance and I recognized the authentic thrill of love as, having dawdled or hurried to make sure I should not miss him, I saw him stride into view, kilt swinging.

Then, of course, there was my infatuation with my schoolmistress at Oakfield who, after we had left Dulwich, continued to see me and to nourish my passion. She also invited me in the holidays to stay with some relatives of hers near Woking. There I went down with chickenpox and was comforted by a thirty-five-year-old major in the Royal Engineers with a bristly moustache who was stationed at Sandown Park racecourse. He visited the household nearly every day and spent most of his time sitting on my bed and kissing me in a quite intoxicating manner. Though I can hardly have expected him to marry me, for I was not yet thirteen, I was disconcerted to learn that he had a wife. Thus before I was well into puberty I totally accepted that people of either gender could arouse the strongest emotional and erotic response. Throughout adolescence I had charming affairs with schoolfellows, unwittingly fostered by our parents who knew each other and liked going on motoring, golfing or seaside holidays together, pleased that their young daughters got on so well.

Although men played a predominating part in my life as I grew up, this other love never ceased to exert its attraction. Of the women with whom as an adult I fell in love, some had children while those who had none naturally wanted them, so that all but the constitutionally barren eventually did well, if not perhaps entirely as wives, then certainly as mothers.

In the nature of things, all such affairs have to end. One of my oldest and most trusted friends, a looker-on, remarked: 'Yes, you get a teeny, weeny bit bored and, hey presto, you are left.' But that was not the truth, which is that to be Forsaken for Another is always a painful experience. However, there was but one instance (coinciding with the year of Munich, a time of dishonour) where the betrayal was so gross, the suffering so atrocious, as to inflict a permanent wound and instil an implacable rancour.

Another wove her enchanting way in and out of my life for close on three decades: the gentlest, wittiest, most engaging if also the most airily inconsequent human being I have every known. She had in addition what André Breton so aptly called *'ce petit rien de "déclassée" que nous aimons tant'*. At one stage when we were young I took a *chambre meublée* in the rue Cambon on the second floor with two long windows overlooking the courtyard. The trouble was that the *chambre* was not really *meublée*: it had nothing but a bed, a bidet, a washbasin and a soiled rug. I hired a piano and provided a table, chairs, a corner cupboard for drinks and glasses, a pretty carpet and a well-filled little bookstand that included *The Travels of Marco Polo*, the poetry of Villon, Donne, Marvell and Verlaine, *Albertine disparue* and *Nadja*. For reasons I cannot recall, we pinned a large ornamental map of Africa to the wall. The place looked, we said, like a whore's school-room. There we played Ravel's *Pavane pour une infante défunte* (originally dedicated to one of her aunts) and spent rapturous hours from five till seven and sometimes overnight.

In a different time we would meet at the end of the day in the Deux Magots and drive out to Maisons-Laffitte where she had rented a little house for the season. There we would linger over a delicious meal and drink still champagne in the quiet of the sweet-smelling summer night garden before going to bed. It was in every way the most perfect sensual experience, for her beautiful use of her beautiful language was such that, even now, some of her turns of phrase come back to me in all their rare felicity and elegance to cause a *frisson* of delight. Ultimately she returned to her childhood faith, renounced me, albeit with perfect grace and, for all I know, went into a nunnery.

To revert to 1920 and my Swiss finishing school; or, rather, to that school's finish as far as I was concerned, for, upon its return from Frenières to its Lausanne base for the autumn term, I rose on the very next morning in the early hours and stole out of the house, together with my beloved. We boarded the train for Lucerne where we were met by my mother who, I must say, took it rather well, treating my partner in crime as a chaperone to be graciously received and greeting me with the exclamation, 'Oh, darling, your hair looks frightful!' After the hairdresser and delicious *pâtisserie* we took a steamer across the lake and then went up in the funicular railway to Bürgenstock.

It was a heavenly fortnight in glorious weather. The luxury of the great hotel and the splendid food after our school fare gave us pleasure which was in no way diminished for me by the arrival of my trunks with letters of recrimination and a bill for the term I had not attended. Then my love left for England and I stayed on with my mother who had no intention of changing her plans or curtailing her holiday merely because I had turned up. I found plenty of young people to dance and play games with as the late summer passed. There followed a brief period in London, during which the French colonel's widow was interviewed, before I was packed off to her house near Paris for a second shot at being 'finished'.

My tedium at Chatou – and its consequences – have been related. In the course of the sour correspondence with my parents I made it clear that I would not consent to remain in this household for a whole year and, if not allowed to leave, I should simply run away, as from the Swiss establishment. The quarrel reached an *impasse*, but I took it as a victory when, shortly before Christmas, my mother and father came to Paris to take me home.

We stayed at the Hotel Edouard VII and the atmosphere on both sides – we were barely on speaking terms – could not have been more icy. This struck me as rather silly and unreal so I went to my parents' room and, quite sincerely and humbly, apologized for the frightful insolence of my letters. My mother, as I might have expected, was entirely unmoved: she might not have heard me and scarcely turned her head, but my father remarked that had his son ever spoken in similar terms he would have been glad to forgive past misdemeanours. How my mother took this rebuke I cannot tell, for I then left the room, but a truce was tacitly declared and my mother could then embark upon the delightful task of rigging me out in

Paris for what she hoped might be my more tractable future. She would have envisaged this as taking the form, once I had 'come out', of my getting engaged to and speedily marrying some young businessman, preferably of good Jewish family. Certainly she must have been impatient to get me off her hands. (As it turned out, she did not have long to wait, though it hardly accorded with what she would have wished.)

There is no doubt that, having failed so signally to turn me into the kind of daughter they desired, my parents tried their best to accept me and to make me accept them. For my eighteenth birthday they arranged a 'surprise party' at the Savoy Hotel where I arrived, thinking I was to dine there with my parents alone, to find a dozen or more of my friends already assembled at a festive table to celebrate the occasion, which we did by dancing the night away. Dancing was, indeed, the great thing in those days and hardly an evening had gone by that winter when I did not go to a party in a private house, some public ballroom or a dance club with one or other of the young men I knew. These were often invited to dine at our flat before taking me to the dance and, as the year went on, I was growing quite accustomed to spending my time doing little else but playing tennis and dancing. But it did not last.

During all this time I was writing secretly and I began to feel a most urgent desire to work at it for which I needed to learn more. The year was 1921 and the University of London, I found out, was admitting people without the usual qualifications for entry. This was, of course, intended for men and women returning from the armed forces to civilian life, but through that loophole I managed to slip in and when the academic year began in the autumn I was enrolled at King's College in the Strand as a student for a course known as journalism.

I do not know whether, even had I stayed the course, it would have provided me with a diploma – certainly not a degree – nevertheless, it gave me the opportunity to attend lectures on English literature and language, which was exactly what I wanted. Also, I was elected by the Students'

Union to become the editor of the College magazine so that, one way and another – including the fact that, since most of the men in the medical and engineering faculties had lately been demobilized and were thus no mere boys but what we should now call 'mature students', that is, in their late twenties or early thirties – I had a most wonderful time.

My mother had, not unnaturally, disapproved of the whole move. She thought it not only wrong and a diversion from the main purpose of my life – namely, to marry – but she was convinced it would – as indeed it did – introduce me to entirely undesirable types and social circles. My father, on the other hand, while doing his best to appear to support her disapproval, showed that in fact he was rather proud of me.

Looking back on those heady days I realize that I was beginning to see my parents in an entirely new light. The furious, inarticulate anguish of my earlier adolescence seemed futile now; the rebellious attitude of my Chatou days jejune and rather silly; I had been striking a blow for the quite frivolous right to trot about on my own and go wherever I chose. Now, on the contrary, I aimed at an altogether more rational and serious freedom, one that represented human values other than those put forward as models by my parents.

Recently I read that the centenary of Katherine Mansfield's birth was being celebrated. It seems an unimaginably long time ago and yet is not in fact so very far from my own. I never knew Katherine Mansfield but her name and work played a significant small part in my life, for at a party in the autumn of 1921 I met for the first time the man I was to marry. Our talk on that occasion, when I fell instantly and wildly in love with him, was entirely about Katherine Mansfield's *Bliss* and Dorothy Richardson's *Pilgrimage*, which at that time I was devouring with tremendous admiration. This lovely man seemed struck, even surprised, at finding a young woman with such enthusiasms.

The party was at his parents' house and I had gone to it with two young

men, at that time my suitors, one of whom – the more devoted and per-
cipient – was not slow to diagnose my symptoms, calling upon me the next
day to declare that he realized he was out of the running and would probably hold the coats of his old rival and the new. I made it plain that what he
called his 'old' rival was never in question and need not trouble him.
Within a matter of weeks, Edmond Kapp had become my lover.

Then and for some time past Edmond, still called Eddie by his parents,
was known to his friends as Peter. He had adopted the name, he openly
admitted, in tribute to *Peter Pan*, an early production of which, with
Pauline Chase in the title role, he had attended again and again as a youth.
Whether the significance of the nickname ever dawned on him is unsure,
but not until he had reached his eighties did he try to persuade people to
call him Edmond. It was too late.

He also explained to me that when, still living at home, he had begun to
get correspondence he wished to keep private he had inserted the letter X
in his name, since he shared the initial E with his father, called Emil. It was
simply a distinguishing device and he never, save in jest, claimed that it
stood for anything; but as Edmond X. Kapp he appeared publicly for the
rest of his life (including in *Who's Who*) while remaining Peter to all his
intimates, not excepting his wives and his daughter.

10

That winter I went with my parents to Germany to renew contact, broken
by the war, with our relatives. We first stayed in Frankfurt from where we
visited the Nahm family and my cousins, Eva and Helene, both now
married, came to see us. From there we went to Hamburg to be with the
Daus family and, leaving my mother with her kin, my father and I travelled
overnight to Berlin on New Year's Eve.

This was the first and last time for many a long day that I was to enjoy a friendly relationship with my father. The ugly conflicts of the recent past were forgotten and, relieved of my mother's goading, he ceased to quarrel with me, reverting to the easy-going camaraderie that had characterized our morning walks through Regent's Park to Baker Street in my school-days. We stayed at the Hotel Bristol in Berlin. Never shall I forget the piercing cold and penetrating wind that threatened to knock me off my feet and the breath out of my body as we struggled along Unter den Linden that New Year's Day. We visited the main tourist sights and recently vacated Imperial residences where, to my father's vast amusement, the guide drew particular attention with pride to every item of furniture and decoration that was '*stark vergoldet*' or lavishly gilded.

As though to set a seal upon my grown-up status, my father took me to a night club: an extremely daring move, though I didn't know and I don't suppose my father knew that the Berlin of that time was thought to be the most wicked city. It was a dimly lit place where, on a low gallery surrounding the tiny dance floor, the patrons sat at little tables, each with its telephone on which you could be rung up by any stranger asking you to dance. No one, of course, rang me and I had the familiar sensation of not being a part of what was going on, with this difference: that it no longer mattered for not only was I ecstatically in love but for the past many weeks I had known the delights of having a clandestine lover of great experience.

So friendly was my father on this Berlin jaunt that I was tempted to confide in him. Prudence dictated that I should not. How right I was became only too clear a few months later.

Once back in London and entirely absorbed by my blissful love affair on the one hand and the exciting everyday life at King's College on the other, the conflicts at home grew ever sharper. Peter and I invariably made love before, or more usually after, going to a concert, or a play – in the case of the Chelsea Arts Ball, during – which in no way impaired the virtuous indignation we felt when my father, who had waited up, reproved him for bringing me home too late.

It so happened that he proposed to take me every evening for a whole week to hear the Léner Quartet perform all the Beethoven quartets at the Aeolian Hall in Bond Street. On the third or fourth evening my father was standing in the hall as we arrived and, nodding a curt good-night to me — tantamount to sending me off to bed — said he wanted a serious word with Peter. It was not particularly late but my mother was conspicuously absent and it was fairly plain who had planned and contrived this situation.

What then transpired was faithfully reported to me the next day. My father objected most strongly to his daughter going out with the same man every evening. Reasonably, Peter advanced the fact that not he but the Léner had elected to give Beethoven concerts every evening for a week. He and not a variety of others had invited me to share what many would consider a rare musical treat, even an education. Determined not to be tricked into any kind of rational argument, my father blustered on, for his heart was not really in it, and he ended by declaring in a rousing non sequitur that he intended to put his foot down. This provoked Peter's unwise but prophetic retort: 'Well, if you do, you'll find she's gone.'

So it turned out. Breakfast and, if I were at home, dinner became the occasions for ever more acrimonious discussions and furious clashes of opinion. The dictum that so long as I remained under their roof, living at their expense, I must conform with their rules of conduct had long since spent its force. Again and again I replied that I should be only too happy to leave their roof if they did not like what I was, what I did, what I said. Again and again my father advanced the rather abstract view that 'daughters don't behave like that', to which I could only retort that I was a daughter and — look — that was how I was behaving.

When one is eighteen the threat of material deprivation has no effect whatsoever, most certainly not upon those who have never known hunger or hardship. On the contrary: I welcomed the idea of earning my own living and being independent and felt I was being pushed towards ridding myself once and for all of the chafing yoke of people for whom I had lost respect. I told my lover that I must get away from them but he was so entirely opposed to this that I decided not to let him or anyone else know my plans. In the warm dusk of a late evening in May I simply left home, running away, beating the pavement with my feet in counterpoint to my pounding heart.

Such events never end tidily. I had elected to go to the home of respectable people known to and trusted by my parents. Upon my unexpected arrival I made it clear that they must allow me to stay with them or else be the last people to have seen me. That settled it: they agreed to say nothing to my parents that night and I, on my side, was willing that they should inform them of my whereabouts next morning – when, presumably, my absence would have been discovered, thus alleviating any real anxiety.

I went to King's College as usual, rather expecting some melodramatic development, but nothing happened and I returned to my parents' friends that evening. Not at all to my surprise my mother and father turned up there a few hours later. The scene that then took place had the effect of hardening my resolve to leave home for good.

My mother took me aside and, once alone with me, made a tearful speech, appealing to my compassion and claiming that I was breaking her heart. I steeled myself against the rank sentimentality of all this, but as she went on and on, heaving with convulsive sobs and holding out her arms to me most piteously, I did feel I had to try to pacify her. She held me against her breast and at that moment someone – I could not see who it was – opened the door and made to enter. Totally in control of herself, my mother waved them away without releasing me from her embrace and, behind my back, as it were, made a gesture that said as loudly as words: 'Keep out: I'm doing nicely.' I was repelled by the unpleasant play-acting element and my mother's calculated emotional blackmail.

Of course I went back home that night, but on the plain understanding that I would pack a few of my belongings this time – though nothing of theirs – and then clear out for good. Before breakfast next morning I went to my parents' room to say goodbye. Neither of them responded, but on the hall table I found a cheque for £10 made out to me. I took it and returned the sum to my father within a month.

I believe that I should never have had the pluck to run away from home had I not had a lover, however much he disapproved of that action. My parents, of course, thought – or at least asserted – that he had prompted it and egged me on, which led to a grotesque little incident, a very low comedy indeed, when my brother – never known before to have taken the smallest interest in my affairs – called on Peter with a horsewhip.

Far from having encouraged me to leave home, however, Peter had been so opposed to it that, once I had taken the plunge, we quarrelled bitterly and, shortly after I had settled in to the West Hampstead flat belonging to absent parents of a girl I knew, we agreed to part. He even went so far as to send me, by special messenger, one of his drawings as a farewell gift, until we realized that we could not in fact bear to live without one another and a little later that year – on 2 August 1922 – we were married at Marylebone Registry Office from his studio in Clifton Hill.

Part Two

Married Life

I

Edmond Kapp was born in Highbury, north London, on 5 November 1890 and was named, romantically, after Dumas's hero, Dantès. His parents were of German-Jewish origin. His maternal grandparents had emigrated to the United States where his mother, Bella Wolff, was born, though her English accent bore not a trace of American but remained steadfastly German-Jewish to the end of her days. It is uncertain when his father, Emil Kapp, a wine-merchant in a small way who came from the Rhineland, established himself in England or where he met his bride.

Edmond was the eldest of three children born at relatively long intervals. His brother Harold died of meningitis at the age of thirteen when the last child, a girl named Helen, born in 1902, was five or six years old. Despite the age gap between them, these two, Edmond and Helen, were devoted to each other, enjoying an exceptionally close relationship throughout their lives. Indeed, the emotional shock of his sister's death on 13 October 1978, no less than the strenuous duties laid upon him by her will in his eighty-sixth year, probably hastened his own end, for he died before the month was out on 29 October. What she had meant to him was expressed in the very last letter he wrote to me in that short interval: 'Helen's going will leave a great gap, blank, emptiness in my daily living, thinking, dreaming...'

A creditable pupil at Dame Alice Owen's School, he left at the age of seventeen having won three open scholarships: to Paris, Berlin and Cambridge. After a year spent at each of the two universities abroad he went up to Christ's College, Cambridge, where he read modern languages, graduating in 1913. Apart from Dr Arthur Shipley, the Master of Christ's, with whom he long remained on excellent terms, he made lasting friendships with a number of his fellow undergraduates. Two in particular, Emmanuel Miller of St John's and Alfred Bacharach of Emmanuel, were introduced to his family and came regularly to the convivial Friday evenings at his parents' house. While Edmond did not marry until he was well over thirty, these two contemporaries of his did so even later in life so that they formed a kind of bachelor group. Another close friend dating back to his Cambridge days was Miles Malleson, also of Emmanuel, who became a much-married man.

After coming down, though he had begun to draw and had even held a small amateur exhibition of his caricatures in Cambridge, he took a job teaching at a boys' prep school. He had his own strongly-held ideas and methods, not entirely well received, for he believed that education should be literally interpreted as a drawing out, an elicitation of the young mind, rather than a process of cramming in knowledge. He never lost his interest in teaching, nor in the young. In the most unpretending way, but with the enthusiasm of the true pedagogue, he furthered and broadened the culture of each of the many youthful women who figured in his life at every age; while his delightful manner with children, whose company he vastly enjoyed, made one regret that he did not father a large family.

With the outbreak of war in August 1914 he enlisted at once, was commissioned as a subaltern in the 11th Royal Sussex Regiment and was soon sent to the front. Thus, when not yet twenty-four he was, as he later put it, dragged, or threw himself into those 'five long dreadful years that I had planned so gaily and so differently'. For nearly three of those years he was in the trenches. He did what he could amid unspeakable horrors to retain a hold on civilized values. He had with him a stout leather-covered gramophone and, like others of his kind, arranged for small luxuries to be sent out to him, including expensive scents to smother the all-pervading stench of death.

That he had not lost his sense of fun or capacity for enjoyment by the second year is attested by Edmund Blunden who, in 1916 at the age of twenty, was drafted into the company of which Edmond was now in command at battalion headquarters in Festubert. 'Here we were amused by the skill of Kapp,' he wrote in *Undertones of War* (1928)

> who made charcoal drawings, no doubt scarcely proper, but as clever as anything he had done; nor was he artist alone; he also tried to popularize rounds and catches, as 'Great Tom is Cast', 'A Southerly Wind and a Cloudy Sky', 'Go to Joan Glover'. The intellects of the others scarcely rose to his magazines from home, among which was *The Gypsy*, a frolic in decadent irreverence published in Dublin . . . Kapp was a lively hand to have in a dugout; his probably imaginary autobiography, peeping out at intervals, and enriched by other versions, was also a diversion.*

Elsewhere Blunden speaks of how Kapp would 'philosophize, scandalize, harmonize and anatomize among us', and in less lighthearted vein:

> One night, Kapp went out to study a suspected sniper's post in a ruin. He stayed out too long, and when at last he scrambled back from the

---

* These extracts are reproduced from *Undertones of War* by Edmund Blunden (Copyright © Edmund Blunden 1928) by permission of PFD on behalf of the Estate of Mrs Claire Blunden.

hurrying light of day to the Island where I awaited him, one of his
men had been badly wounded. Poor Corporal Mills was carried down,
and died later. But (at this cost) Kapp's patrol had been remarkable,
and he sent back a long precise report, full of suggestive information.
The Olympian comment was, 'Too flowery for a military report'.
Our chieftain could not encourage anything that bore the semblance
of the mental method of a world before the war.

These fitful glimpses of Edmond at a certain stage of life in the front line
reflect the high spirits he managed to maintain. But his platoon was wiped
out twice over; he saw whole units reformed with fresh cannon-fodder
from home and it scarred him for life.

The first draft with which he had gone to France was largely made up of
young Sussex farm-workers and in after years he often described their
physical beauty: the strong, fair bodies, shapely feet, blond heads and the
natural grace of their movements as they dived and swam in a river behind
the lines. None of them survived and he, who did, never quite recovered
from the hideous crime of that slaughter.

Life in the trenches was bad enough; but then worse befell. Because of
his fluent German he was sent forward into No-Man's-Land, alone, in
order to interrogate prisoners as they were brought in. The intention was
that he should stay there, sheltering in a dugout, for a couple of days. At
that juncture the front was a fluctuating line: a few yards of ground would
be fought over, won, lost, regained, in a matter of days. The fighting
shifted; no prisoners were taken on that sector and the churned-up roads
were under such heavy bombardment that the man sent up as relief was
killed before he reached the advance post. Then, as the battle raged,
Edmond was forgotten by his commanding officers at the rear. For weeks –
it may have been three, it may have been six, nobody will ever know – he
stayed in that dugout, his only food the tins of bully beef lining its walls,
under continuous shelling and, the last thing he remembered, a poison-gas

Edmond (Peter) Kapp, photographed around 1917

attack. When eventually he was rescued he was deaf, almost blind, delirious and his bodily functions had altogether ceased. He was invalided back to England to spend months in hospital.

He had a moderately distinguished army record and had been mentioned in dispatches on several occasions – not always uncritically: he relished and often quoted one of his superiors' comment: 'His zeal sometimes outruns his discretion' – so that as soon as he was sufficiently mended, though no longer fit for the trenches, he was seconded to a newly-formed Intelligence Unit attached to GHQ to write stories from the Allied point of view for the press of neutral countries, for which, as Blunden put it, 'his remarkable facility for languages would be needed'. The idea was, rather late in the day, to counter the endless flow of well-organized German propaganda in those neutral countries.

From that time on until the end of the war, Peter – the nickname he adopted and as from now on I shall call him – enjoyed life as a staff captain, living in extreme luxury with a small band of colleagues, headed by the artist Neville Lytton who had earlier joined Peter's own company at the front and was himself wounded in 1916. They travelled about in splendid motor cars, were furnished with passes that allowed access to any part of the front; frequently, in the last weeks, they overshot the retreating German troops, while they occupied fine chateaux for their nightly billets and, in general, conducted themselves as befitted privileged brasshats.

'I was 21 or 22 before I ever drew a line,' Peter wrote. 'I was over 28 when I came back to it, tired, nervous, sick . . .' Nevertheless, even if only to amuse his brother officers, he had continued to draw while in the army and he now, in 1919, newly demobilized, submitted some of his work to and was published by illustrated magazines. He began to be widely commissioned for this type of work, and, what was more, he had the blessing of Max Beerbohm who wrote an introduction to the catalogue for a one-man show he was given at the Leicester Galleries. In the same year, he brought out his first volume of twenty-four collected drawings, *Personalities*, beautifully produced in a limited edition by the Pelican Press under his supervision, and published by Martin Secker.

He took a studio in old Hampstead and, pushing thirty, seemed well on the way to a successful career when he threw everything up and vanished for nearly two years. This was one of the most significant periods of his life. How the first few months were spent is not clear. He recorded that he approached Professor Tonks at the Slade, asking to be enrolled as a student. He felt a great need to acquire the basic academic training his work lacked; but Tonks rejected him on the grounds that, if taught, he would lose such originality as he had and gain little by way of compensation. He says that he then went to the Lake District, but what he did there or how long he stayed, is not known. Certain it is that he then went abroad and, still determined to get the schooling he sought, applied to enter the Vienna Academy of Arts. Again, upon showing his drawings, he was turned down, and for the same reasons. That he never accepted this judgment became plain, and with some bitterness, a few years later; but at the time he had no alternative and he left the cities bent on seeking some discipline, if not in art, then in his interior life, to which he could submit.

This retreat from London, from women, from social and professional success and easy money-making may have been his way of trying to exorcize the nightmare of the war years. In this it did not succeed, for they had left him permanently damaged, which could be said of many of his contemporaries. Two quite small incidents were symptomatic of the deep injury done to this one of the survivors of that tragic generation.

One evening in the early 1920s at a concert in the Albert Hall Peter was accosted in the interval by a pleasant fellow who greeted him with every show of friendliness and respect – calling him Sir – and held him in conversation. 'Who was that?' I asked as we went back to our seats. 'I haven't the faintest idea,' he said. About a week later, he suddenly slapped his forehead and exclaimed with something like horror: 'Good God, I've just remembered. That chap was my batman for over two years. A splendid man. I do wish I'd recognized him. We went through hell together every day of our lives and I never even asked him how he was getting on and what he was doing because I simply couldn't think who he was.'

The other symptom showed itself when we were living in a small Italian mountain village where, to mark every saint's day – an event that occurred at least once a week since the whole social life of the inhabitants revolved around the church – an ancient artillery piece was fired. At the sound

Peter's face would be drained of blood and he would start shaking uncontrollably from head to foot. For several minutes he stood palsied, white and trembling, as if in torment.

But though he could never lay the ghosts of the war, even by amnesia, he did in this time of solitude lay the foundations of a personal if slightly homespun philosophy of life and, not being a profound thinker but of a highly intuitive intelligence, he arrived at certain principles that were to govern his life henceforward. He became an avowed pacifist – until 1939 – a lifelong health and food crank, a truly religious agnostic and something of a Tolstoyan in matters of sex: that is to say unbridled indulgence in practice combined with an almost mystical faith in the virtue of celibacy. (This faith was not new. While still at Cambridge, suffering some disquiets, he had consulted Dr Eder, a psychologist friend, who, on learning that, at nineteen, Peter was still a virgin, firmly advised him to enjoy a woman. He was outraged and disgusted by this advice but, having once followed it, he never looked back, save perpetually to bemoan his happy-go-lucky and indiscriminate fornications as a fall from grace.)

At the end of some months of an ascetic existence in the Austrian Alps, he tramped across Europe to Count Keyserling's *Schule der Weisheit* in Darmstadt. There he found exactly what some part of his being needed: a slightly fanatical, strict regimen that required him to spend his time if not exactly fasting and praying, then at least in solitary and critical self-contemplation, in penning a kind of spiritual curriculum vitae and in mortifying the flesh. These exercises entailed keeping an obsessional tally of the incidence of masturbation, nail-biting, over-indulgence in food and other transgressions against the self-imposed ordinances.

Among other austerities he practised hardening his body until it was impervious to the elements. This gave rise to some alarm when finally, arriving back in England to be met by his family, he alighted on the platform at Victoria Station on a particularly cold and dismal late autumn day in 1921, clad only in a thin, open-necked shirt and exiguous cotton shorts whose whiteness set off to great advantage his deeply bronzed face and limbs. That is how I first met him towards the end of that year. But on that occasion he wore evening dress at a party at his parents' home in West End Lane, Hampstead, to which I had been invited by his sister Helen, a year older than I, whom I knew as a fellow member of a tennis club.

I had not witnessed his startling arrival a few weeks earlier but, as he came towards me across the crowded room, nothing could have been more striking than the sun-tanned face – darker far than his great thatch of crinkly light brown hair – in which eyes of pale green, the colour of grapes, sparkled with fun. I fell in love on the spot.

2

Immediately upon leaving home I had got in touch with Alec Waugh, the author of *The Loom of Youth*, a novel about English public-school life – the first of its now familiar kind – which had so impressed me that I had written a gushing letter to the author and received a gracious reply. He was my one tenuous link with what could be called the literary world since he worked in the Strand offices of Chapman & Hall, the publishing company of which his father was the chairman, and there I went to see him. I told him that I must have a job and he promised to help me. He was as good as his word: within a day or two I was employed at £4 a week as assistant to a Miss Hogg, the editor of the women's page of Sir Edward Hulton's *Evening Standard*, to be seconded almost at once as dogsbody to the editor of the *Sunday Herald* which was produced in the same Shoe Lane building. He urgently needed someone, almost anyone, it seemed, because overnight and without warning he was obliged to enlarge his paper by no less than eight pages to keep up with a Northcliffe Sunday rival that had stolen a march on Hulton's by taking this unannounced step. In those days there were evidently few Fleet Street moles.

My tasks were as ill-defined as they were various. I made the tea and learnt to sub-edit copy; I checked facts and counted words; I bought sandwiches for the editor's lunch and held the fort while he went to the pub; and on Saturday mornings I went down to the compositors' room and helped to set up type. This I enjoyed best of all, for the compositors were jolly men who wore aprons and brought me little bunches of flowers from their gardens while teaching me about formes, slugs and matrices.

Another job to which I was assigned was that of errand girl: I was sent to pick up articles from our contributors wherever they lived in London. That was how it came about that I went one day to a flat in Kensington. Usually I was left standing on the doorstep while a maid fetched the packet I had come for, but in this instance the writer herself answered the door, invited me to come inside and, quite as though I were a welcome guest, made me sit down beside her and encouraged me to talk about my present work, my hopes and my ambitions as a writer. This was my first and warming encounter with Rebecca West. Though a cocky little upstart with an altogether false opinion of myself, I was not so stupid as to be insensible of this rare and charming kindness.

Someone else who gave me much encouragement at the time was Mrs Dawson Scott, an untidy lady with fly-away hair and a generally blowsy appearance, then in the throes of founding her PEN Club which she pressed me to join. Since I could not claim to be a poet, essayist or novelist, I did not see how I could. Also, although by no means a sceptical young person, I somehow felt that anything Mrs Dawson Scott launched would instantly sink once her inflated fervour no longer buoyed it up. That shows, if any proof were needed, how little the prescience of an eighteen-year-old is to be trusted.

Such encounters helped to make life on the *Sunday Herald* tolerable for, try as I would, I could not get on with the editor, my boss, who had a repulsive way of clicking his false teeth and, since he was a man of little education and no manners – though I believe he was a brilliant editor of this popular newspaper – I thought it my function to put him right whenever possible. He objected one day to my failing to cut what he considered a long-winded and high-flown passage in an article I was supposed to sub-edit and I took occasion to point out in no uncertain terms that it was a quotation from Shakespeare and could on no account be changed. Mounting my tiny high horse I refused to give in and the argument ended, as one might have foreseen, by my walking out before he had reached the point of towering exasperation and sacked me.

By this time I had begun living in Peter's studio; thanks to his help and his Fleet Street connections, I started to write articles on a freelance basis which were occasionally accepted. It occurred to us both, almost simultaneously, that we might as well get married and, after much discussion of the pros and cons – my pros over-riding his cons – we agreed to do so.

My wedding day was an occasion of mixed emotions. I was ecstatically in love with Peter but my parents had put a ban upon our marriage. Before the Family Law Reform Act of 1969, girls under the age of twenty-one (still legally minors) were not able to marry without parental consent, parents – in most cases, inevitably, the father – not being obliged to give any reason for the veto. My father had formally lodged an interdiction upon my marrying any one of some dozen young men whom he named: everyone, it seemed, with whom I had ever gone to a dance or played tennis or spent time in other innocuous pursuits, one of whose proposals I had already turned down while the very notion of the others – except for Peter – as possible husbands had never remotely crossed my mind nor, I was quite sure, theirs. It was simply the product of my father's overheated imagination. However, when we went to the Registry Office in Marylebone – where later stood part of the Polytechnic of Central London – to confirm the day and time for the civil ceremony, we were told that it could not take place and were advised to consult some high-ranking law officer of the crown in Somerset House. There we learnt of my father's bravura. The list of husbands not-to-be was read out to us and, thunderstruck, I could only say that it must have been compiled in a moment of aberration. The law officer of the crown showed some interest in this remark, pointing out that if my father were insane his objections could be over-ruled. Though I advanced the view that he must have been mad indeed to carry out this coup, that was not good enough and we left without having come any nearer to removing the ban.

We consulted a lawyer and explored various possibilities: we believed, for example, that the captain of a ship twelve miles out to sea was authorized to perform the nuptial ceremony, but discarded the idea as impracticable. We then resorted to indirect attack. A friendly person, known to me since childhood and called, by courtesy, aunt, who had also long been acquainted with Peter and his family, was perfectly aware that we had been lovers for many months. She did not really approve of this and was greatly in favour of our getting married. She proposed, when we approached her with our problem, to send a telegram to my parents then on holiday in Switzerland. She appealed to them to lift the veto on what she termed 'this highly suitable match' and added, regardless of expense, that, should they fail to do so, we had decided to give the fact that we were living together and their refusal to let us marry 'the fullest publicity'.

That might well have been an empty threat but, as it happened, Peter's recent exhibition at the Leicester Galleries, whose catalogue again carried an introduction by Max Beerbohm, had won him some small celebrity. The press considered him newsworthy at that juncture; and my parents knew it. Several further telegrams flew to and fro and, finally, my father gave in. Once he had put in writing his formal withdrawal of the ban on his daughter, a minor, marrying Edmond Kapp, the wedding could take place. How right my aunt had been was proved by the fact that the occasion was widely reported in the papers and the actions of the wicked parents, forced to relent, blown up to sensational proportions.

My mother, however, could not climb down with grace. I do not know why anyone should have thought she could. She wrote me a letter of such calculated unkindness, to arrive by the first post on my wedding day, that I was reduced to tears, arriving at the Registry Office in that damp condition. There the friendly aunt and my new sister-in-law were the witnesses.

Once restored by the happiness of being with Peter and in the highest spirits we sauntered along Jermyn Street to spend the £25 of which we were, jointly, possessed in buying each other presents. This included ordering a glorious silk dressing-gown for Peter to be sent, on approval, to the Piccadilly Hotel where he had booked a room for one night. We dined at the Savoy and, as he smoked his after-dinner cigar and we emerged into the Strand, we bought all the evening papers to read the reports of our wedding. He then hailed a taxi and when I objected that we were merely going as far as the Coliseum in St Martin's Lane he said: 'You don't expect to walk, do you?' What we saw that night was *The Three-Cornered Hat* with Leonide Massine.

After the performance we went, again by taxi, to the Piccadilly Hotel and there, in our room, sister-in-law Helen had strewn the pillows with summer flowers. The extravagant silk dressing-gown was laid out for Peter to wear the next morning. After we had breakfasted on our favourite food of kippers and raspberries, sent up to the room, he arranged for it to be returned to the shop, presumably as not approved. Later that morning we went back soberly to the studio in Clifton Hill, now completely broke, to start from nothing in frugality and hard work: he at his drawing, I at freelance journalism. (That was ever to be our way of life: cheese-paring austerity punctuated by bouts of glorious if rather irresponsible extravagance to celebrate the sale of a picture.)

As a rule we stuck to kippers and raspberries for dinner. We ate them every day for weeks and then I came out in an unsightly rash. Peter decided that we must bathe in the sea, so we went to Birchington and stopped at a small hotel where, since there were always kippers on the breakfast menu, we kept up our usual diet and, despite constant sea-bathing, my rash spread alarmingly. On our return to London Peter, reluctantly – for he had no faith in conventional medicine – took me to a doctor. 'Here,' he said, 'is this new wife I have and she is covered in corrugations. How do you account for that?' The doctor examined me carefully and then asked: 'Have you been eating much fish lately?' 'Oh, yes, every day,' we cried. 'Well, that's it,' pronounced the doctor, 'stop it at once.'

Soon afterwards we left Clifton Hill and rented from Adrian Allinson, a painter of Peter's acquaintance, a fine, dilapidated, rambling old place – long since demolished – in Maple Street, off the Tottenham Court Road, called Thackeray House. It had a magnificent studio where Peter entertained his friends and patrons for, in some mysterious way, following his second one-man show in 1922, he had acquired a number of these. They were rich men who enjoyed his lively company and liked his work well enough to subsidize him in return for taking their pick of his drawings.

The most faithful of these was a Scot called Vernon Roberts of Dalpowie, who had inherited *Old Moore's Almanack* which bizarre legacy, owing its prosperity to the sale of 'Pink Pills for Pale People', yielded an unbelievably large income to its owner. Once a year, Vernon Roberts visited the poky little offices in the city where the Pink Pills were packed and dispatched to every corner of the United Kingdom where the credulous pale people dwelt. Vernon Roberts himself was free to expend his energies and his fortune in whatever field he chose and he collected everything. Whether he ever displayed Kapp's drawings on his walls is unknown. It is a fact attested to by Mrs Vernon Roberts, a very patient, good Scottish lady, that the cellars – or dungeons – of their great mansion were crammed with unpacked crates of *objets d'art* from all over the world.

The subventions from such people did not amount to a maintenance allowance but they did to a large extent make Peter independent of Fleet Street and enabled him to choose his own subjects. This relative freedom of choice, far from making him indolent, so stimulated his zest for work that he would often stay up more than half the night to finish a drawing, coming to bed stiff with cold, for Thackeray House was incurably draughty and

quite unheated. To warm up in the morning we would (in those days jog-
ging was something you did to your memory) run round Fitzroy Square;
and it was now that I made my first ignominious attempts at cooking. (Up
to now Peter, who was very good at it, had prepared all our meals.) So disastrous were my early efforts that I had to throw the resultant mess into the
dustbin before Peter had a chance to smell, let alone taste it. We took to
having lunch – an innovation – at a small Swiss restaurant in Charlotte
Street frequented mostly by shop assistants from Heal's (when they did not
go to Shearn's vegetarian restaurant in Tottenham Court Road) and also by
Matthew Smith, who shyly got off with one or two of them.

In those first few months of married life, Peter took me to many parties
and introduced me to his enormous circle of friends, people of a kind I had
not met before: poets, sculptors, actors, writers of every kind, and, above
all, musicians, many of them world-renowned. He was keenly interested in
early music and a great admirer of Arnold Dolmetsch whose portrait he
drew, settling the gentle face against a background of one of his pretty
clavichords with the characteristic axiom '*plus fait douceur que violence*' let-
tered on the inside of its lid. Dolmetsch and his family, who made as well as
played these replicas of ancient instruments, lived in Haslemere where we
visited them quite often. I used to sit, amazed, to see the huge spread set out
by Mrs Dolmetsch on the tea-table disappear in a matter of seconds as the
four gifted children and the young craftsman-assistant tucked in. Dolmetsch gave Peter one of the four (numbered) first recorders ever produced in his workshop, a fine tenor of boxwood; while later I, too, had one
– an ebony descant – and we learnt many duets. These recorders played a
significant small part in our fortunes.

This happy, exciting life was occasionally shot through with remorse at
the thought of my poor, pathetic, parents, their cheerless way of life and
implacable hostility to us both. I confessed to Peter that such thoughts
made me miserable and I wished we could mend the breach. He proposed
that we should ask the advice of a rabbi his family had known and revered

since he was a small boy. We called upon this wise and kindly man who listened to my tale and then offered to go to my parents – out of respect for the cloth, if for no other reason, they would have to receive him – and put it to them how much better we should all feel if there were a reconciliation. This he did and then asked us to come and see him again. 'Your mother,' he reported, 'is quite adamant. A hard woman who leads your father by the nose.' There was nothing to be done, he advised. 'Leave them alone and, like Bo-peep's sheep, they'll come home in the end.' It is strange that I have never forgotten the exact words he used; perhaps because they were so singularly depressing at the time.

We made many new friends now, both by joining the 1917 Club in Gerrard Street (founded by Ramsay MacDonald), and by going to the cabaret held near us at the drill-hall in Charlotte Street, known as The Cave of Harmony, where Elsa Lanchester – who was also a member of the 1917 Club – satirized the old sentimental music-hall songs, accompanied by Harold Scott at the piano. It was as a result of Peter introducing Nigel Playfair to The Cave of Harmony to hear Elsa sing – she, of course, enchanted him – that she was given a part in his production of Čapek's *Insect Play* (for the translation of which Playfair himself was partly responsible) at the Regent Theatre (formerly the Euston Music Hall). This really marked the start of Elsa's professional career.

After the performance at The Cave of Harmony the audience would freely mix to talk and dance. That is where and how I got to know Kathleen Hale, of *Orlando* fame, who was to be a lifelong friend, not yet then married to Douglas McLean, who danced with me to confide how much he loved her; also Dora Black, not yet then married to Bertrand Russell. I grew very fond of Elsa, with whom I had the greatest laughs and met her mother – Miss Lanchester, known as Biddy – who, despite a tumultuous early history, was now a mild old lady with pink cheeks, dressed in handwoven garments of ineffable dowdiness.

Among our closest friends at the 1917 Club, apart from some old

THE CAVE OF HARMONY

(103, Gower Street, W.C.I.)
84, CHENIES MEWS.

ELSA LANCHESTER and HAROLD SCOTT

announce the beginning on September 7th of the Autumn Season.

There are vacancies for a few half yearly members (at £1 11s. 6d.) and they will be pleased to receive cheques or applications from now onwards.

Membership dating from the end of October.

The Cave of Harmony is open every Sunday.

Dancing from 10 o'clock. Performances at 11.30,

The guest fee for all dances is 5/-. Members may purchase any number of tickets for the use of their friends. These are undated and can be used when desired, but should be obtained beforehand.

AUTUMN PROGRAMME.

Two dialogues by Franz Molnar.

"'Tis a pity she's his wife" by Mrs. Congreve

A Play by Ernest Milton.

A Hindu Travel Lecture with Lantern Slides.
Produced by Dorothy Massingham.

HARRIET COHEN.   JOHN GOSS.
The KAPPS with Recorders.

Revivals.

"The Man with the Flower in his Mouth" by Luigi Pirandello.
" Di Chi Sei il Bambino " by Mrs. Congreve (as produced by the Turtle).
"Sicilian Melodrama."

A 1925 programme for The Cave of Harmony

Cambridge chums of Peter's, were the Meynells, Francis and Vera, then about to launch their Nonesuch Press. Over the years, whenever I made a flying visit to London while domiciled abroad, I always stayed with the Meynells in Great James Street when they would take me to see such things as *Blackbirds* – for whose cast they gave a wonderful party – and the sparkling Cochran revues at the London Pavilion. If they were on holiday in Paris or the south of France when we were living there, they, too, would spend most of their time with us.

During the 1929 General Election I drove their car about the Holborn constituency, its back and sides plastered with Labour posters, causing a foreign acquaintance to stop me to say: 'It looks parr-tic-u-larly capitalist.' (It was the same opulent-looking car that, during the 1926 General Strike, had enabled the Meynells – that handsome, well-groomed pair – to deliver quantities of leaflets to the headquarters of the strike committees in the midlands and the north; in this, they were helped by the police who kindly directed them to the areas they were seeking by warning them of locations to be avoided.)

In that same year of 1929 Elsa Lanchester married Charles Laughton. She told me that he was wonderful but, though prepared to believe her, I found that he seemed to quench her fiery spirit and mocking wit. An adoring wife, she kept the best of herself – like the choicest morsel of food and the heart of the lettuce – for Charles. He, to my irritation, could not so much as order a cup of tea without playing the part of a man ordering a cup of tea. Though he came to be acclaimed a great actor (and I did, indeed, admire his Angelo in *Measure for Measure* at the Old Vic), I thought he was a great ham, both on and off stage and screen. Gradually I saw less and less of Elsa until, once she and Charles had gone to America, coming but rarely to England, she became a virtual stranger. Many years later I came to think that, because her private life had not turned out too well, she deliberately avoided friends from the past.

As for the Meynells, in 1936 I quarrelled bitterly with Francis over whether to demonstrate against Mosley's provocative Fascist march through the East End as I proposed – and was urging others – to do, or to ignore it. By that time he had been having an affair for some years with 'Bey' (Alix) Kilroy, who was to become his third wife a decade later. But I always remained on affectionate terms with Vera though, by force of circumstances, I saw little of her during her last melancholy years which ended with her suicide in 1947.

The one constant fixture in our social calendar in those early days was the Friday evening at my parents-in-law, who kept faith with this and other orthodox Jewish observances, but had the knack of turning them into festive occasions for their agnostic children and those children's friends. The hospitable board was presided over by Mrs Kapp, a woman of singular warmth and sweetness, while her husband, a kindly man of sterling insignificance, celebrated the short rituals of the Sabbath eve. There were generally half a dozen regular guests, including Alfred Bacharach, Harriet Cohen and Emmanuel Miller. The talk and the laughter of all these young people gathered round the glow of the candle-lit table generated an atmosphere of happy, free and easy family life such as I had never known. It hurt Peter that I resisted the blandishments of that homeliness: he wished that I could love his mother as he did. But I was on my guard and in terror of being drawn into any but the most formal relations with parental figures.

We lived in Thackeray House until January, during which time Peter's second book of twenty-four drawings, *Reflections* (dedicated to me), was published by Jonathan Cape with introductory comments by Laurence Binyon – not perhaps often enough remembered as the author of 'They shall not grow old, as we that are left grow old' – and W. H. Davies, much admired by Peter, both as man and poet, whom we visited in his unlikely lodgings over a pub in Bruton Street. Then, undeterred by the advice he had earlier received, and determined to get the instruction he needed, Peter resolved to drop everything to go abroad and to enrol in an art school.

3

On the eve of our departure from England, to embark upon what we called our honeymoon walk – although six months after our wedding – along the French and Italian Riviera we gave a huge fancy-dress party at The Cave of Harmony. During the early part of the evening Peter, wearing a false nose and moustache, a peaked cap and doorman's voluminous greatcoat that touched the ground, stood at the door to usher in the guests. Later, when all had arrived, he discarded the disguise to reveal his old staff captain's tunic with red tabs worn with scarlet tights, and was taken to task by some slightly tipsy chauvinist who challenged him to a duel for insulting His Majesty's uniform. The music and the dancing went on into the morning when, as winter dawn broke, the half-dozen or so remaining guests, our most intimate friends, tottered back with us to Thackeray House and slept on the floor for a few hours so that, later in the day, on 11 January 1923, they could see us off at Victoria Station on the first leg of our journey to Rome. We had amassed £120 and were determined to make it last as long as possible.

We spent the first week in Paris where we were joined, as was to be my fate throughout our married life (though I did not then know it), by Peter's sister Helen. Our entire luggage consisted of one rucksack apiece, Peter's considerably heavier than mine, to which disproportionate weight he added enormously by buying *Ulysses* in Sylvia Beach's bookshop. From Paris we took the train to St Raphaël, sitting up all night on the wooden slats of the Paris–Lyon–Mediterranée third-class carriage, to arrive, all traces of fatigue obliterated in the clear winter sunshine and pure light of a Mediterranean morning.

It is hard to realize nowadays that we were able to walk hour after hour along that coast road without meeting or being overtaken by any but the occasional car or lorry; that we could, and did, stroll in the middle of the road, stopping to enjoy the view, sitting by the wayside to eat a picnic

A photograph from The Twenties *by Alan Jenkins (Heinemann, 1974), captioned* 'Edmund *[*sic*]* Kapp, the artist, and his wife about to set off on a walking honeymoon'

lunch, or on the terrace of some small café. We spent our lovely nights in little hotels or *pensions*, and stopping on our way: in Cannes, as a journalist, I interviewed Suzanne Lenglen whom I had met that summer in Wimbledon, while in Juan-les-Pins we called on Peter's friends, the dancer Margaret Morris and her partner, the painter, J. D. Ferguson. From there we went to the Cap d'Antibes to visit George Davison, a former Director of the Kodak company, to whom Eugene Goossens had given Peter an introduction. Davison had turned his magnificent villa into a kind of luxury orphanage, or enormous family, by adopting some half-dozen children as companions for his own small daughter, so that it was known at the Château des Enfants. The oldest of these was now five or six, while there were several baby newcomers. There was a full complement of Norland nurses and qualified infant teachers. These little children had everything that love and money could provide. The whole household revolved round them and their rituals of walks and paddles, meals and swims and siestas. The highlight of the day was the hour before bedtime when they would all come from their playrooms and nurseries to the immense *salon* to play games, sing songs, listen to tales read aloud, dance to the gramophone – all in different parts of the room – to end by being given, the youngest first, a cuddle from one or other foster parent and, if of a suitable age, an 'evening sweet' for going off to bed.

We stopped again in Beaulieu where, among other acquaintances, we ran into Sybil Colefax who recommended us to make a detour to see such places as Castellane on our way, which we later did, picking oranges and lemons from trees on the roadside. Our next port of call was Monaco. Peter who, under my parents' disapproving eyes, had taught me to play poker, was in truth an irredeemable gambler and we made straight for the Monte Carlo Casino but were refused admission on the grounds that Peter was not wearing a collar and tie. We went at once to buy a stiff white collar and a black bow-tie, which looked particularly silly worn with an open-necked blue linen shirt, corduroy jacket, old army breeches, knee socks and stout brown walking shoes, but, technically, the authorities could not debar him. They therefore turned their attention to me, asking how old I was for, although I was quite as unsuitably clad, there were apparently no hard and fast rules about female attire, only a convenient one about age. I claimed, with but slight inaccuracy, to be twenty, which I thought was the right thing. Bowing low and in a very nasty manner the official said: 'Mademoiselle must have meant twenty-one.' That gave us the clue: twenty-one might be the correct age for *demoiselles*, but I was a married woman.

However, proof had to be produced, passports fetched and examined after which, though still obviously undesirable customers, we were at length allowed into the gaming rooms.

Peter played roulette all that evening until the early hours and the whole of the next afternoon and night. How undesirable we were only transpired as time wore on, for he never stopped winning and when at last, on the second day, we left the Casino to walk back to our hotel, it turned out that he had won enough money to cover every penny of our expenses since leaving London. Peter gave the white collar and the black tie to our waiter before we took to the road again.

After a memorable meal at Rumpelmayer's in Menton, we hired a carriage – for expense was now no object – to the frontier at Ventimiglia on 26 January and then took a train to Genoa. Once across the frontier things were a little less easy for neither of us spoke Italian. However, thanks to Peter's great facility in languages and his astonishing aptitude for imitating accents and the rhythms of speech, he very soon picked it up, to sound as though he had spoken it all his life.

Above all else Peter wanted to visit Max Beerbohm, so we put up at a small hotel and, next morning, walked to the Villino Chiaro. It was a pretty house, slightly austere, even monastic in feeling, with dead white walls, sparse, elegant ornaments and a general air of luxury and calm but certainly no *volupté*. You felt that you should not speak too loudly nor move too precipitately; that really you were rather too gross to be there at all.

Max, however, could not have been more genial. He was full of jokes, at which he himself chuckled quietly, paid me the compliment of instructing me in the use and abuse of punctuation and took us up to his roof-top studio to show us his wickedly defaced book-jackets and frontispieces, as well as his unpublishable caricatures of members of the royal family (such as Lord Lascelles standing rigidly to attention to inspect a toque for his mother-in-law, Queen Mary). Although Max was then about fifty and most decidedly master in his own house, Mrs Beerbohm – Florence – was,

almost too obviously, nanny to this elderly, brilliant and mischievous child.
Another, different, Max emerged when, together with the Beerbohms, we
lunched with the Granville Barkers who had rented a *castello* on the
promontory of nearby Portofino. After lunch they proposed taking a walk
to the end of the high, wild headland, for which very short excursion Max,
carrying an elegant walking stick, put on a bowler hat of outmoded design
but immaculate condition and a pair of yellow gloves, as if to stroll down
St James's Street.

By contrast with the Villino Chiaro, the neighbouring household of
Gordon Craig and his family at the Villa Raggio was bustling with life and
activity and permanently untidy. Mrs Craig (as we called her, though she
was not) was never much in evidence, for she seemed to be always busy in
the kitchen, but daughter Nellie and son Teddy (privately we referred to
him as 'the unshorn lamb', for he had just started to sprout a light fluff on
his youthful face) were pressed into service as apprentices to their father.
Craig himself had a magical effect upon me – as I believe he had upon most
young people – for he was, indeed, a magician: his passionate and fascinating obsession with the theatre, his wonderful designs for stage sets and
lovely wood engravings, not to mention his personal beauty, quite bowled
me over. We were tremendously pleased when, as we prepared to tear ourselves away from Rapallo and move on, he decreed that he and his family
would follow us to meet again in Sestri Levante.

We, of course, walked and it may be – I cannot recall – that the youngsters also came on foot, but their parents arrived by *carozza* and the whole
family appeared to have ransacked their theatrical wardrobe for this excursion. While Craig himself wore his usual broad-brimmed Borsalino hat
and flowing cloak, his wife and children were rigged out in motley, giving
immense pleasure to the inhabitants of the small town, who followed them
about for they looked as if they would tell fortunes or give some type of
unusual street entertainment, not to be missed.

It is not too much to say that in those few days I fell in love with Craig –

Gordon Craig (courtesy of
V&A Picture Library)

that is to say, I worshipped him, and, throughout my time in Italy, as also later in England, I kept up a thrilling correspondence with him. When my child was born, I begged him to be her godfather. He consented and the name Gordon was incorporated in hers but, apart from sending her some Victorian fashion plates when she was a small girl, his rôle as godfather was one he never in fact played. One evening at the theatre I was taken to a box and presented to his mother, the glorious Ellen Terry, then in her mid-seventies. I told her of the baby who was her son's godchild and she said: 'Oh? A baby. Aren't they delicious? Like velvet.' I remember little else of that brief encounter, only that she was surprisingly small, still extraordinarily beautiful and wore a lace cap with little ribbons.

It may be that all this social life had undermined our characters, or perhaps the gambling gains had gone to our heads; at all events, when the Craigs turned back to Rapallo we sybaritically went by train to Pisa and then to Lucca where, in the rain, a rather glum carnival was in progress: people, as I recorded at the time, 'gravely throwing confetti at each other'. To add to that rather depressing scene, Peter now suffered a strange and even alarming complaint: he could not open his jaw. After an uneasy night, we went back to Pisa to catch the connection to Rome. We had bought our tickets in advance and had checked the train most carefully; but in fact it did not exist. (It was then that we learnt about the *pezzo coloro*: the way that Italians will always say the right thing and tell you what they think you would like to hear.) However, the matter was taken out of our hands in so spectacular a way that it caused Peter's jaw to drop. He was cured.

We were sitting in the lounge of our seedy little hotel, downcast at having to wait until the next day, when it turned out that one of the other guests was the chauffeur of an American car, a Pierce-Arrow, which he was driving from Paris to rejoin his employers in Rome. He had heard from the hall porter that we, too, were on our way there and, deadly bored on his solitary journey, he wondered if we would give him the pleasure of our company. We tried (unsuccessfully) to get a refund on our railway tickets, and promised the chauffeur that we would be ready at five o'clock next morning to set out with him.

He was a pleasant, talkative Frenchman who rightly assumed that English travellers who stopped at the same cheap hotel as he did must be pretty hard up (and not at all stuck up); but when he discovered that we carried all our belongings on our backs and had come on foot the length of the French and Italian Riviera, he thought we must be either truly on our beam ends or else insane. He inclined to the former view and, genuinely sorry for us, would not let us pay for anything or buy him so much as a drink, flatly refusing the *pourboire* Peter tried to press upon him when we parted.

We drove all day. Despite the magnificent vehicle in which we travelled, it was not a comfortable ride, for in those days, long before such words as *autostrada* had been invented, Italian roads were so abominably rutted that, being something of a lightweight, I was bounced up and down, to crack my head on the roof of the car every few miles until Peter devised a crash helmet for me, stuffing all our socks into his old beaver hat, which I had adopted, to cushion the impact.

Our journey ended with the unforgettable first sight of Rome in the glow of an early February sunset.

4

After a couple of nights lodging in the piazza Venezia while we looked around for something we could better afford, we moved into a back room on the top floor of the small no-star Hotel Dragoni in the largo Chigi. (I believe it later came up in the world.) Our room had French windows leading on to a narrow balcony that overlooked the piazza Silvestro, then a terminus where trams squealed in and out of the square by day and night. Without question, we had picked the noisiest spot in Europe.

It should be recalled that 1923 was an era when horse-drawn carriages rattling over cobbles were still an integral part of Italian street life and not just a tourist trap. Moreover, this was the year of Mussolini's so-called 'March on Rome' and his bully boys made a practice of tearing about the city late at night in screeching cars with blaring horns, shouting and singing at the top of their voices. Sometimes Peter would get up and empty a jug of water on them from our balcony. The Italians have always been extremely fond of noise but at that particular era the *fortissimi* seemed to have reached their climax: even the chambermaid who cleaned the corridor outside our room at dawn each day went in for a special line of *crescendo* activities which entailed banging together heavy metal utensils. We called it clattermania.

After a brief period of sampling various *trattorie* – from the quite horrible to the horribly expensive – we bought a little methylated spirit stove which occasionally blew up and frequently set the room ablaze, but on which, once I had mastered the art of firefighting, I prepared our simple meals. The Dragoni had no bathroom so we went to the imposing public baths in the corso Umberto from time to time; but the worst thing about the place was that the pitch-dark little water-closet on our corridor was furnished with a catch that, when fastened, switched on a dim light and simultaneously administered a severe electric shock.

In the very first week Peter had enrolled as a student at the Lipinski School of Art in the via Margutta where he went punctually each morning and again from six till eight in the evening, drawing from the plaster cast or, which he much preferred, attending the life class. Meanwhile I stayed in the hotel room writing articles which I hoped to sell to English papers. At lunch time I would fetch Peter, doing the shopping on my way. This was not a pleasant experience, for it was impossible for any young woman to walk about unaccompanied without being not only verbally accosted, but pawed and pinched every few yards.

Since we were here for the one purpose of enabling Peter to pursue his studies, nothing was allowed to divert him. Our social life was naturally restricted because we did not know many people in Rome. We never did any sightseeing as such, which had the advantage that we would come upon the noblest monuments, the loveliest fountains and most beautiful squares, not to mention the glories of the Forum, almost by chance, as it were.

One indulgence Peter allowed himself and that was to go every Sunday afternoon to the St Cecilia concerts in the Augusteo and, when invited, to private recitals given at Oscar Browning's flat. These were attended by ancient British ladies and very young Roman boys. The ladies affected a style of dress not seen for perhaps half a century. Browning himself, then eighty-six, appeared indeed to have surrounded himself with people who recalled the mid-nineteenth century: even the boys had a strangely out-moded look. It was we who were the anachronism.

Our money had to be stretched as far as possible, and it was not only for the fun of it that on mild evenings we would go to out-of-the-way bars and cafés not frequented by foreigners, to play our recorders. We played *Greensleeves* – not then the hackneyed little tune it has since become – and a number of traditional Italian airs we had picked up. At the end of our short performance Peter would go round with the cup in which we made our coffee *filtre* and generally we collected enough *soldi* to cover next day's subsistence.

However, as the spring advanced there came changes: visitors from England began to arrive; among them many acquaintances and, as always used to happen in the past to the English abroad – though it could not, of course, nowadays – even if you did not know them at all well, upon meeting them in a foreign country you hailed them with an enthusiasm you would not have felt at home. Among these was an old schoolfellow of mine from Queen's College, one of those girls of 'good family', who made me all at once aware and ashamed of my shabby, down-at-heel appearance. She, too, was clearly conscious of it and, in the nicest possible way, despite my protests – for it was of course acutely embarrassing and a kind of implied criticism of my husband's and my way of life – insisted, for her own pleasure, as she said, upon buying me a dress at an expensive shop in the piazza di Spagna.

I soon had reason to be glad of it for, shortly after, in April, one of the most welcome arrivals was Albert Coates, a friend of Peter's, who had come as guest conductor of the St Cecilia orchestra for a series of concerts lasting ten days. Our lives underwent a total change, for we were swept by Coates's exuberant personality into a ceaseless round of festive luncheons and dinners given in his honour, persuaded to come to rehearsals when

Peter should have been at his school and, in cortège, were driven in the company of distinguished Italian musicians, writers and artists to visit such places as Tivoli, Frascati and Villa Adriana in the environs of the city.

These incursions from England were unsettling and I began to feel homesick. It was agreed that I should pay a brief visit to London, travelling as far as Paris with Coates when he left. Before I went I gave Peter a single pink carnation.

I stayed in Paris for a few days, made memorable by Coates taking me to hear Chaliapin in *Boris Goudonov*, before going to London where I crammed into a few short weeks brief reunions with my friends. I was more than ready to return to Rome at the end of that time and there I found that Peter had made his first oil painting and formed a new friendship that was to be a lasting pleasure.

The painting was a still life of three books – yellow Tauchnitzes and the brilliant blue 'Greek flag' cover of *Ulysses* – upon which stood a toothglass of water holding the pink carnation. This tentative and delicate first effort, which could not fail to move, marked a turning point in Peter's working life, for he became fascinated by the techniques of oil painting, enjoying every moment of even the stretching and preparing of canvasses.

The new friendship was with a young South African painter, Edward Wolfe, known as Teddy, who said he was twenty-three which pleased me immensely as I did not meet many people so near to my own age (though he was in fact twenty-seven). He now attached himself firmly to us and we three became inseparable.

Peter and Teddy designed for me a most beautiful dress. The full skirt was of rich Roman silk with horizontal stripes of many colours on an emerald-green background, while the tight-fitting bodice that came down to a peak on my belly was of fine emerald-green silk, lined with lemon yellow, of which the narrow sleeves were also made. This bodice fastened at the back with countless little silk-covered ball-buttons that slipped into silken loops, impossibly difficult and time-wasting to do up. At every fitting Peter and Teddy would lie on the floor giving contradictory instructions and opinions to the confusion of the dressmaker who, when she finally came to the hotel to deliver the finished creation, was horrified to find all three of us resting on the bed.

There were not many occasions when I could becomingly wear so spectacular a garment, but now and again after a long evening, Peter, who wanted to be up and at work early next morning, would go to bed, whereupon, having changed, Teddy and I were off to a dance-hall known as the Bal Tic-Tac, frequented only by Italians, where my dress excited amongst the women the utmost admiration and all the men insisted upon dancing with both Teddy and me.

5

With summer the city heat became oppressive; Peter's school closed its doors and we retreated to Anticoli Corrado, a mountain-top village in the Sabine hills renowned for the beauty of its men and women, many of whom went down to Rome for the winter when they were much in demand as models in the art schools and studios. Whether they were in fact better endowed physically than the inhabitants of other like villages, or had acquired their reputation thanks to the artists who, with the coming of the railway in the nineteenth century, had taken to frequenting this picturesque and accessible summer station, it would be hard to say. However that may be, there was scarcely a man, woman or child in Anticoli who was not willing to sit for the visitors.

At the summit, towering above the main square and narrow, winding, unpaved streets, stood the rather grand but decaying *castello* which had been rented for the whole season by an American couple, Ned and Peggy Bruce. The owner, an impoverished gentleman of the minor nobility, as decayed as his property, was accustomed to letting the best part of his ancestral home every year, taking up his own residence in the servants' quarters on the ground floor at whose windows he could sometimes be seen of an evening, unshaven and resting his shirtsleeved arms on the wide stone frame, gazing out at the dusty street with a melancholy expression.

Ned Bruce was a retired merchant – an old China hand – and Sunday painter; Peggy a modest woman, devoted wife and splendid gardener who turned the vine-clad roof terrace leading out from the *piano nobile* into a flowery retreat. They had invited Maurice Sterne, a Russian-born American academic painter (the former third husband of Mabel Dodge) to stay with them for as long as he pleased if he would but give Ned lessons.

It could not have fallen out more happily for Peter: Maurice Sterne had not one pupil but two. For better or worse, his influence on Peter was lasting. All that summer he worked under Maurice's tutelage, sometimes elated, more often discouraged, but ever persevering in a ramshackle studio – a mere shed – that stood in a rough field on the slope of the hillside at the bottom of our garden. We had taken a small house, recently built, which was among the few to have piped water. Most of the village women still carried their pails and jars on their heads to and from the fountain in the piazza, which accounted for their superb carriage and their majestic gait, their ample skirts swaying. In the cleanly tiled, shady kitchen of our little house I learnt to cook on charcoal: the perfect fuel whose embers, covered the night before with their own soft white ash, I would revive each morning by waving a fan of cock's feathers.

There was a peasant's son in the village, a young boy, who, talented but quite untutored, was painting scenes familiar to him in field and village, making his own colours from plants and earth. Ned Bruce was most interested in him, gave him every encouragement and promised to arrange an exhibition of his work in New York.

Forty years later, in the early 1960s, I spent the winter in Rome with friends living there who, one Sunday, after hearing my reminiscences of Anticoli, drove me to revisit the place. It had not greatly changed, though now – but only since the end of the war – the houses had both piped water and electricity. We strolled about and then went into a dark little *cantina* filled with acrid smoke from a sulky wood fire. A few men who came in from hunting, heavily wrapped up (for it was cold), rested their guns against the wall and tossed down small glasses of spirit, while an old woman with a kerchief drawn tightly about her head sat by the hearth and stared at me. After some time, describing an oval in the air with one hand and pointing at me with the other, she said: 'I remember the face.' I was astonished and rather moved. In my halting Italian I told her that many, many years ago I had spent a whole summer here. 'Yes, yes,' she nodded. 'I remember.' I then asked her about the peasant painter, wondering whether he had remained in the village, given up painting, or what had become of that promising boy. 'Is rich, rich, rich,' declared the old woman. 'We are proud of him and his fine house in the piazza. Go to see him, he will be pleased.'

We went. It was not hard to identify the house for it was the newest and the largest in the square, built upon the site of what must have been several small dwellings – of the kind that still adjoined it. Here we found our peasant, now a thickset ageing man, too stout and too florid to be recognizable as the comely lad I had known, though he still had a mop of curling black hair. He was delighted to welcome us into his handsome living-room where we were made to sit through a display of repellent pictures: his latest productions. There were simpering madonnas, the child Jesus in various mawkish attitudes and suchlike subjects, badly drawn, crudely coloured and oozing false sentiment. His youthful work had been clumsy and, in the true sense, artless; it had honestly tried to depict what he saw and knew. This hideous rubbish with its blatant bid for a market of gullible pietists made a most uncomfortable impression. We sat there, smiling and nodding, as he recounted his successes at home and abroad: yes, he had had exhibitions in the States and all over Italy, bringing great prestige to his native village which he would never, never leave. All manner of important people came here to see him. His parents were dead, but his many relatives had greatly benefited by the glory of his fame. Indeed, Anticoli Corrado itself was renowned thanks to his achievements. Nothing could have shaken his self-satisfaction nor marred his pleasure in the tribute we were paying him by our visit: it was the one entirely innocent thing about him.

In that far-off summer of 1923, the *fascisti* came to Anticoli and held a day-long ceremonial of flag-waving and swearing-in. They promised – then – water and electricity for every household and they shaved the heads of all the small boys. They departed, leaving for the local band the score of *Giovinezza*. Every evening thereafter the strains of this rather banal tune were wafted on the still mountain air as, from all parts of the village and in a great variety of keys, the musicians practised on cornet, flute, fife and bassoon. On Sunday mornings they came together in the piazza and performed what they fondly supposed was a unison rendering of the anthem.

The Bruces entertained lavishly and gave splendid parties in the vast *salone* of the castle, lit by a hundred candles in sconces on the bare, whitewashed walls. There was a magnificent celebration when, in July, Maurice Sterne entered upon his latest marriage to a fair-haired and very young dancer from the Isadora Duncan school in Vienna, for which occasion Peter and I went to Rome to pick up the elaborate wedding-cake and other good things ordered for the banquet.

We, too, had our guests. Naturally my sister-in-law came on a prolonged visit and Teddy joined us for a while, though neither of them stayed long enough to interfere with our very regular way of life, with Peter painting in his studio every day while I, after washing the tiled floors and tidying the little house, sat at the open French windows overlooking the garden, trying to write. At the height of the summer heat our good friend Edgar Mowrer, then stationed in Rome as the correspondent of the *Chicago Daily News*, came out to see us, bringing with him Tennessee Anderson, the second wife of the writer Sherwood Anderson, and a young girl recently arrived in Italy to study art. They came early in the morning and we spent a leisurely day with them, swimming in the swift-flowing river in the valley, lying on its bank to dry in the sun, eating and drinking under the vine-clad arbour in our small garden and generally enjoying each other's company until dusk when, so reluctant were our guests to return to the heat and dust of the city, that they remained with us until they had missed the last train. Since there were not beds enough for all – and in any case the atmosphere of the sunbaked little house was still close – when the moon rose, we carried blankets and pillows up to the newly harvested fields above the village and spread them out on the stubble. As we lay there, I between Edgar and Peter, I became aware of a fumbling and a wriggling and realized that Peter was trying to make love to the young student.

Naturally I knew that he did this to every girl he met, everywhere, and he had taught me that it was idiotic and petty-minded to object or take it seriously. But I had never before been present when it was actually going on and I found myself overwhelmed by anger and disgust. Slipping out from under the covers I walked about the fields in a turmoil of what I knew to be these base feelings. An hour or so must have passed when I saw Tennessee's tall figure striding towards me in the moonlight. She had come to look for me and now, taking my arm, she said: 'You're furiously jealous, aren't you?' I was ashamed to admit it, but she would have none of that, even when I said that of course it was silly and childish, but I could not help it. She proceeded to tell me of a disastrous experiment in communal living conducted by Sherwood, her husband, which had more or less wrecked the marriage of every couple involved. The silly, the childish part, she said, was that played by the immature personalities of those who professed to think it was all a huge lark, in order to hide from themselves that they were incapable of shouldering adult responsibility. In such matters my only teacher had been Peter, releasing me from the fetters of my conventional background. Now Tennessee posed an entirely different view: marriage, she pronounced, was to be respected – I think she used the word 'honoured' – or it would wither and die, if not, which was worse, degenerate and putrefy. Yes, of course, possessiveness was ugly, since no human being should or could try to possess another without the loss of dignity for both; but, though she was not claiming that strict sexual fidelity was a prescription for conjugal happiness, she was absolutely certain that, if a relationship were not to become almost worthless by being held too cheap, it must be 'jealously guarded': the words, she said, were no accident but well-chosen.

All this was startlingly new to me. Could Peter have got it wrong? I could not bear to think so; yet as Tennessee went on talking and my rage began to subside I faced many unanswered questions. At last we stole back to where the others were now fast asleep. I lay down in the darkness before dawn, pondering deeply. When it was light we all trooped back to the village and had breakfast. Our guests caught the early morning train to Rome while Peter and I went back to the house and to bed where we made love. It was different from anything I had ever experienced before, in that it was complete fulfilment. Something of profound importance had happened to me overnight. In an indefinable way I had been liberated.

I never told Peter of Tennessee's talk, nor referred to that night in the fields; but after a few days I announced with total conviction that I wanted to have a baby. (Until then I had practised the current methods of birth control, having been instructed by Maria Huxley.) Our daughter was conceived a few weeks later on the occasion when we spent the night in the Mowrers' flat in Rome – said to be in the house of Torquato Tasso – on our way to stay with them in Capri. We had an enjoyable time with Edgar and Lilian and were given hilarious entertainment by Cerio, the *sindaco* (mayor), who took us about, introducing us to such histrionic characters as d'Annunzio, Axel Munthe and others whom, we felt, Cerio had himself conjured into being – unless it was that the Tyrrhenian air had bewitched them – so wildly eccentric did they appear.

It was Cerio who had ordained that a notice be put up on the Tiberius beach: 'Undesirable nudity is not permitted.' (Would that there was such a rule on other strands.) When he wished to rid the island of a particularly unpleasing couple of American dipsomaniacs – refugees from Prohibition – but could not persuade the shopkeepers to let them leave before they had paid their bills, he made them deposit a piece of jewellery as a pledge while they crossed to the mainland, simply, he claimed, to replenish their funds. He then gave out that Peter was a famous London jeweller who had valued the object at a sum far above the debts incurred – and Peter gamely sat in public places gazing at things through a jeweller's lens – so that, though Cerio well knew the object to be worthless, he thus placated the tradespeople into letting the couple depart, though not before the native Caprese, carrying their luggage down to the landing-stage, tossed it into the sea. Cerio, indeed, acted as a mixture of impresario, circus-master and magician – a Prospero on his island – who extracted the maximum of fun out of his own performance and that of those whom he had manipulated, often with their knowledge, into playing certain rôles.

Edgar was now called away to report the Italian attack on Corfu, so we left the Mowrers' villa and moved to a small *pensione* on the *piccola marina* kept by a mad old German. It was, of course, perfectly possible that Cerio had cast a spell on him, but he certainly behaved like a lunatic. He put it about – and was widely believed – that, as a youth some seventy years before, he had been washed up, unconscious, on this shore in a rowing boat, with no recollection of where he came from, to be found and restored to life by the young girl he then married. It was a story that fitted well into the romantic landscape. He was now in the habit of writing what he called a poem every day. He would then scramble up the footpaths to the principal café in the piazza Umberto to pin this offering on the wall. The next day he would remove it and replace it with another. These runes, sometimes of no more than a few words, were of a surrealist nature. His compositions were not always confided to paper. I well remember one that was inscribed upon his espadrilles: on the right foot it said: *'Badate!'* and on the left: '*Oggi Potate*'. (Watch out! Potatoes today.)

It was now beyond doubt that I was pregnant and Peter decided that I should stay on in Capri while he went back to clear the house in Anticoli and collect our belongings, and that I should then rejoin him in Rome preparatory to our return to England where we wanted the baby to be born. As soon as his message came I set out for Naples, where I was met by friends who showed me the sights, took me to the National Museum and gave me a meal before putting me on the train for Rome, where a most Italian scene was enacted.

The train was full and I had to stand in the corridor. There I was shortly surrounded by a gang of youths who, at first in playful mood but with an increasing undertone of menace, pressed around me, firing ribald questions at me and bellowing with laughter at my replies until I felt real apprehension. One of them wanted to know how many children I had and while they cackled and jeered I was inspired to say that I had not been married for very long and was now pregnant. Immediately the whole situation changed. They dropped their mockery and offensive gestures and assumed grave expressions of concern, while one of them went off to return with a sheepish young man who had been unceremoniously turned out of the seat to which I was now conducted and where, for the rest of the journey, I was plied with solicitous attentions, including food and drink. Upon arrival in Rome, my former tormentors escorted me along the platform in a protective posse until I was delivered into the safekeeping of my husband upon whom they showered extravagant congratulations, bowing respectfully to us both as they took their leave. 'And what was all that about?' asked Peter, much puzzled.

We were in no great hurry to leave Italy and spent almost three weeks in Florence, most of the time with Teddy, looking at pictures; but we were also invited to stay and make our temporary home in the delightful pavilion Carlo Loeser had built in the grounds of his villa to house the Rosé Quartet when they were not on their travels. Off the gallery surrounding the central music room were four separate small apartments. There the Rosé lived and could relax and rehearse between tours. It was a most tempting offer, but we felt we must decline.

We booked our tickets on the night express to Paris, having ascertained that we could break our journey and join the train in the early hours of the morning at Rapallo where we wanted to pay a last brief visit of a few days to the Beerbohms and the Gordon Craigs. The night of our departure we rested for a few hours in our hotel room and then made our way to the station. The express train for Paris came rushing in, slowed up and, as we made to board it, the Pullman guard, clinging to the handrail, waved us away and refused to let us on. The train gathered speed, the guard disappeared, and our *wagon-lit* vanished into the darkness, leaving us stranded on the platform. This spelt disaster as the last of our money had gone to pay for this luxury. Indeed when, next day, we took the slow train to Paris we were remarkably lucky to find friends aboard who were willing to lend us enough to pay for food on the journey.

The sequel to this misadventure was that, later, Peter wrote to the chairman of the International Wagons-Lits Company in London claiming the most enormous compensation: we had been misinformed; our money had been taken on false pretences; he himself had missed an appointment with an important client at the Hotel Crillon in Paris where he had reserved rooms, while his pregnant wife had suffered extreme distress, if not irreparable damage. The recipient of this audacious letter invited Peter to come and see him. He went and a good-humoured interchange took place. The chairman, making it clear that Peter had not a leg to stand on and knew it, dismissed his extravagant claim while acknowledging that some inconvenience and a good deal of annoyance had been sustained, though he did not for a moment believe that we were booked in at the Crillon. He now proposed, however, in salute to an ingenious try-on and the amusement it had afforded him, that Peter should do a portrait of him which he would purchase for the price of our railway tickets. The deal was merrily concluded.

We reached London in late November 1923, having been in Italy for the best part of a year.

6

We went straight to my parents-in-law in West Hampstead. They received us warmly but we knew that, although penniless and with no immediate prospect of earning anything, we must find a home of our own. Since we had no idea where the rent was to come from this was not going to be easy. Nevertheless, Peter answered advertisements for places to let which were quite plainly out of our reach. One such was a studio flat in Mulberry Walk, Chelsea, where we went and, as one might bring some particularly treasured *objet d'art* in order to judge how it might look in such surroundings, we had brought our recorders and now tried them out in the empty premises. The owners, who occupied the upper part of the house and had come down to show us round, were so struck by this singular behaviour on the part of prospective tenants that they invited us to come upstairs for lunch and to continue the performance. Before the meal was over they had decided that they did not really need the money, would much prefer the flat to be occupied and would welcome us if we would care to take it, rent free, until the baby was born in June, provided we would sometimes play duets to them.

Once installed – though it was a very cold, lofty studio with a north light and, of course, entirely unfurnished until, bit by bit, we assembled a few rather wretched second-hand pieces, a minimum of crockery, and at least a good bed for the otherwise bare little room off the studio – we began seriously to try to earn some money. I was employed for a brief period by Dodie Todd, the editor of *Vogue*, then housed in the Aldwych, and was able to sell some of Peter's drawings to her; but that did not last. (When I asked whether I had been dismissed because of my condition Miss Todd replied, non-committally: 'My staff is not in the habit of becoming pregnant.') I then broadcast once a week from Savoy Hill in *Women's Hour*. This was a good thing for by now my pregnancy made it more suitable that I should be heard rather then seen.

There could be no question of Peter painting – apart from anything else it entailed too much expense – and, having lost his former connections with various periodicals by reason of his year-long absence from England, he bowed to necessity and followed a somewhat catchpenny course, drawing portraits of people who happened to be in the news, some of whom were merely passing through London and left too soon for him to complete his work, so that it was I who sat for Dr Coué's hands and Professor Einstein's hair. He did, however, allow himself to do some drawings for his own pleasure, notably several of D. H. Lawrence (one of which is now in the National Portrait Gallery) who, regardless of the cold, sat for him again and again in the icy studio.

Over the years I have often been asked: What was Lawrence like? And I have had to say, to the surprise of my questioners, that he was one of the kindest people I had ever met. Here was I, a vulnerable, self-conscious and ungainly-because-pregnant twenty-year-old whom he went out of his way to hearten, showing an unobtrusive, unsentimental tenderness for my condition, taking the trouble to talk to me about writing as though I were an equal, to reveal an entirely unexpected sweetness of character.

Also, to keep his eye in, Peter persuaded a grizzled, old, out-of-work actor with a splendid torso to become his model. This ageing, alcoholic but engaging fellow struck poses of an ever more dramatic nature while reciting Marlowe by the yard. His 'divine Zenocrate' ricocheted off the walls of our bare studio with wonderful resonance. There was also, of that time, a drawing of me in the bath which now hangs in my room.

One mid-winter evening we went to a concert in a private house to hear Mrs Gordon Woodhouse play the *Goldberg Variations* on the harpsichord. The drawing-room was already packed when we arrived so that we could not sit together and Peter took one of the small gilt chairs in the row behind me. At the end of the recital, as the audience began to disperse, an august lady of great beauty, wearing a sable coat and ablaze with tremendous jewels, buttonholed Peter. She had been watching us throughout the performance, she said, and it was clear that he could not take his eyes off me; he was obviously head over heels in love, so why did we not marry? Assured that we were an old wedded couple the lady, with truly patrician insolence, shot a fusillade of personal questions at us, demanding to know where we lived; and having introduced her husband, a tall, quiet gentleman of great good looks and a slightly melancholy cast, she declared that they must call on us, now, this very evening, at once, to continue our talk. There was no way of parrying her inquisitiveness; she was an imperious person accustomed to command and to be obeyed. The room was emptying and as Peter, hatless and coatless as usual, began to draw on his huge fur gloves – relic of army days and his only concession to the climate – she took it for granted that we were driving home. We hastened to catch our bus, faced the problem of inadequate household crockery in a bold spirit, put on a kettle and had made some decent coffee by the time this strange couple arrived. In view of the shortage of chairs, they stood about most of the time looking at Peter's pictures, ignored completely the obvious deficiencies of our surroundings and gave us the feeling that they, not we, were dispensing hospitality. Before they finally left, the lady, having pumped us pretty thoroughly, decreed that, since our tenancy here would expire when the baby was born, and since we had no other accommodation in view and, as far as she could make out, no regular income, we must come and live in a cottage in the grounds of their estate on the outskirts of Slinfold, near Horsham. We could occupy it as long as we liked: indeed, it could be ours for good. In the meantime we must come down the following weekend to inspect it. Her husband would fetch us.

Once our whirlwind visitors had gone, leaving us rather limp, we came to the conclusion that so much impulsive behaviour was unlikely to have any sequel: we were pretty sure that the whole episode would have been wiped from the memory of the impetuous lady by the next day. That is where we were wrong: on the Friday morning, at the appointed hour, there at our door was the husband in a powerful open touring car, a Daimler, and we were whisked off to join a rather grand house party in Slinfold Manor.

If we regarded our hosts as eccentric, they apparently looked upon us in much the same way. The other guests – beautifully dressed, with elaborate manners, distinguished names and such high-bred voices that you could not always understand what they said – regarded us with the fascinated attraction owed to objects of curiosity, collector's items, as it were. I did not find this rôle at all comfortable, though Peter, it may be said, was always at ease in any company, however well- or ill-mannered. That first week-end set the tone for what was to follow.

In the spring, Peter had his third and most successful one-man exhibition at the Leicester Galleries and, on 5 June, our daughter was born in Queen Mary's Maternity Home for the Wives of Soldiers at the top of Hampstead Heath, facing the Whitestone Pond. This maternity home was maintained on the ample funds left over from the wartime Royal Needlework Guild under the direct patronage of the Queen, who continued to take a personal interest in its running and had decided on that, of all days, to make a tour of inspection. Having been examined by a doctor early that afternoon and told to come in, I was unable to find anyone to admit me as all were busy preparing for the royal visitation. So Peter and I went off and, after sitting for a while on the bench outside the Home, had a pleasant ramble over the Heath and then, in a teashop, drafted a notice for *The Times* as the best way of acquainting my parents with the news that they had a grandchild. (It was to be Joanna for a girl, Jonathan for a boy.) Not till after that did we stroll in a leisurely way to the Home while I made Peter swear that he would on no account come back with my belongings that evening: the baby would almost certainly not yet be born, and it was such a tedious journey to and from Chelsea – wait till tomorrow, I advised.

We were confronted by a furious Matron who had made arrangements for me as the one and only sitting-up patient to greet Queen Mary and, although Her Majesty, with consummate regal tact, had made no comment upon being ushered into an empty room but had kindly left a copy of some rather splendid publication for the patient, should such happen to turn up, the Matron was beside herself with rage when she found that I had gone absent without leave. She was in no mood to be trifled with. When, in obedience to my nods and becks, Peter said, yes, he would come next morning, she rounded upon him in draconic style: 'I'll have no more argument, Mr Kapp. You will go at once, Sir, and return with your wife's things as fast as you can.'

I gave birth swiftly, easily and without the benefit of much obstetrical attention, for it was now supper-time and the entire staff was at table, engaged in exchanging impressions of the day's thrilling event which was not, of course, the birth of my baby. When Peter returned at about nine o'clock, our Joanna had arrived and was fit to receive him. I stayed in the Maternity Home, learning from experts how to feed, bathe, dress and generally handle my baby, for nearly three weeks – unheard of nowadays following an uncomplicated parturition – during which time, whatever else he may have been up to, Peter wrote to me every day, even when he was to visit me later. Sometimes his letters projected an imaginary future, picturing our little daughter, whom he thought we should be calling Jo, busy in all manner of exciting pursuits. (In point of fact, from the earliest weeks and ever after, she was known as Janna.)

7

We now went to live in the Slinfold cottage. It stood in a great field, known as Half-Moon Meadow, with an immense old oak tree at its centre to which we attached the clothes-line. My mother-in-law had generously lent us for the first few weeks the help of her good and friendly maid, Amy, who in my memory is always to be seen pegging up clouds of snowy napkins to wave and flap in the summer breeze. I cooked on a Calor gas stove which had a movable oven with a transparent window at eye-level, so that one could watch meat roast and cakes rise. Water had to be drawn from a well at some little distance from the cottage, but in fine weather that was no great hardship. Admittedly the dwelling was primitive, furnished with bits and pieces from some lumber-room; but they were adequate and we were perfectly contented. Peter did his full share of fetching water, washing nappies and – because we thought the baby must miss the perpetual motion of prenatal existence and should not be left just lying about – he gave her bumpy rides in the decrepit old pram, partly held together with string, which, lent to us by the local vicar, had seen punishing service with generations of needy young parents since the turn of the century.

It was now that I started to write my first book: twenty-eight short pieces in differing styles to go with drawings by Peter. In a prefatory note he explained:

> The drawings . . . were not made for the purpose of illustrating the letter-press with which they appear. Rather do the text and pictures stand side by side in mutual accompaniment.

For the most part the pictures were of musicians, or of subjects connected with music. They had been done when, on first returning to England in 1921, Peter had arranged with Edwin Evans, the editor of a small music journal, to contribute a series of drawings in return for two tickets to any London concert he chose to go to. He loved to work to the sound of music, sometimes drawing the performers, sometimes the listeners, and I, in our earliest days together, had shared in the pleasures of this payment-in-kind, starting with the famous week of Beethoven quartets that had precipitated my parents' first outspoken objections to Peter. I did not finish the book in one go, and it came out only in 1926, published by Faber and Gwyer, as

Pastiche: A Music Room Book; but it was then and in that connection that, thinking it would look silly if it appeared under the names of two people called Kapp, and since I refused to use my parents' name, Peter invented the *nom de plume* Cloud, which I used for the eight books I had published before 1939.

All that summer while I was happily breast-feeding and writing, the Manor was the setting for a continual social round: there were weekend parties and tennis parties and dinners and dances, to many of which Peter, the gifted artist, sometimes with his dear little wife and their adorable baby, was invited as, more or less, an entertainer. He would be pressed to do sketches of other guests, to sing Lieder and folk songs in his pleasant light tenor voice, or we would be asked to play our recorder duets to the assembled company. I found all this faintly distasteful and, as with the Chelsea studio, was not at all convinced that the world owed us rent-free housing, for which a mortifying return might be exacted, but was unsure whether such thoughts were not generated by the false values of my upbringing. It was something of a relief to me when we were able to escape for one weekend by going to stay with the Heron-Allens in Selsey Bill.

Edward Heron-Allen, whom Peter had first met in Bruges during the war when both were staff intelligence officers, was a strikingly handsome old polymath in his early sixties. He was a Fellow of the Royal Society, the Geographical, the Zoological and almost every other learned society, as well as President of the Royal Microscopical Society. He was an expert on violin-making, foraminifera and meteorology, on all of which subjects he had written the standard works of the time. He had also translated *Omar Khayyám* from the Bodleian manuscript, gave lectures on protozoa and, when not otherwise occupied, practised as a lawyer. In his early forties he had been told that he was suffering from a fatal illness and had no more than six months to live. He resolved to spend the brief time left to him by going on a world tour, during which he met and proposed marriage to a very young lady on the understanding that she would shortly become his well-endowed widow, free to remarry. He then remained alive and well for decades. Peter had renewed his acquaintance when, in 1923, he turned up in Rome – where he was an honorary member of the St Cecilia Academy – with his permanently bewildered wife and two strapping daughters in their late teens.

That I was doing the capricious lady of the manor no injustice was made plain when, as the year declined and the grand house-parties ceased, we were simply dropped as of no further interest. This spelt something like isolation, for although many of our own London friends had been glad enough to visit us for summer weekends, they, too, ceased to come as autumn advanced, at which point Peter was commissioned to do a series of portraits of notable members of the legal profession for Butterworth's, the law publishers. This meant his going to London, where he stayed at the Savage Club and attended the Law Courts during the day. (Later I accompanied him a few times and was present at the trial of Horatio Bottomley, that of a most sordid murderer and, in the Lords, the case of the Russell baby whose legitimacy – long before genetic printouts – was in question.)

With the onset of winter, and Peter away, life in the cottage became less and less agreeable. Oil lamps had to be trimmed and lighted earlier each day; to heat the place meant sawing wood and lugging in coal, while the preparation of bottles for the baby, now weaned, entailed breaking the ice on the well to fetch the water that had to be boiled and filtered before use. I was lonely and miserable but I stuck it until, one bitter cold day in December, I decided I would put up with it no longer.

We had been in the habit of seeing something of Anthony Bertram, the art critic on the *Spectator*, then living in Horsham, who had occasionally given Peter lifts in his car. Now I wheeled the pram to the nearest public telephone and asked him to pick me up the next time he went up to London, which he did quite often for he was the official lecturer at the National Portrait Gallery. He would come the next day, he said; whereupon, packing up a few things for immediate needs and with the baby in her crib on the rear seat, I was driven away without a single backward glance or pang of regret.

I went straight to my parents-in-law – where else could I have gone? – but though they were happy enough to put us up and, indeed, beside themselves with joy at having the baby to cosset, I knew we must find a home of our own and, as certainly, that it should not be another spongers' tenancy. Thanks to the lawyers, this was not necessary. What we then found was one of the most attractive places I have ever lived in: above an enormous double studio there was a small, well-designed flat – previously occupied by a successful prostitute – on the top floor of a house on the corner of Orange Street, off the Haymarket. Its bright living-room had wide windows on both sides opening to the north on a skyline of housetops and chimneypots – no Post Office Tower or high-rise blocks and, of course, not a TV aerial in sight – receding far into the misty heights of Hampstead, while to the south one overlooked the roofs of Central London to spires, domes and Nelson on his invisible column.

It had a narrow walled parapet outside the south-facing window, just wide enough to take the baby's wicker basket, and there, every morning in fine weather, I would put her down to sleep. From time to time I took her in her pushchair – not then called a buggy – to be weighed at Boots, the all-night chemist, where she was known as the Piccadilly Baby and was a great popular favourite, being something of a rarity among the customers in that neighbourhood. She practised her first uncertain steps, to come down with a square bump at intervals, and rolled her first ball in St James's Park where I wheeled her on most afternoons, often accompanied by Desmond Bernal whom we had recently met and who had taken to spending a good deal of time with us.

Sage, as Desmond was known to his friends of that era, was then living in a small flat somewhere off Guilford Street and one of his unforgettable stories arose from the tram rides he regularly took at night from Gray's Inn Road to Hampstead. Waiting at that terminus for his return journey, he approached a young woman also standing there and asked if he might talk to her. In those days of all-night trams and relatively little gratuitous street violence, she was, despite his wild appearance, not in the least frightened, but, clearly a person of common sense, wanted to know why. 'Because I'm unhappy,' he told her. 'Why are you unhappy?' she wanted to know. 'Because my wife's in bed with another man,' he explained. 'How disgusting!' she cried and turned her back upon him. 'And what did you make of that?' I asked at this point of his tale. 'I realized,' he said, 'that some people are worse off than I am.'

We naturally saw a lot of Teddy, now temporarily in London and living with his mother, whom he called Agatha though it was not her name, in Notting Hill where she ran a lodging house of an informal character for those of her son's friends – young writers and painters for the most part – who could not afford to live elsewhere. Another of our welcome visitors was Noël Coward though, unlike Teddy and Sage, both of whom remained friends for life, we were never to meet him again after this period when he was acting nightly – I believe it was in his own play *The Vortex* – at the Comedy Theatre whose stage-door was almost next to us in Orange Street. Coward would drop in almost every evening before or after the performance to chatter and sometimes, when I knew that we could offer him a decent supper, I would go to fetch him from his dressing-room.

We were also seeing something of Ernst Toller, recently released from jail in Germany, who was in London primarily to meet Vera Meynell, one of his translators. She – and I am sorry to say most of those among whom she spread the task of entertaining him – found this noble fellow, for such he undoubtedly was, a terrible bore. He made the rounds of our circle, telling the same not very amusing stories again and again in the kind of accent everyone enjoys imitating. We often saw Mark Gertler at this time too for he was, briefly, engaged to the sister of one of Peter's friends: a young Jewish girl who took her fiancé to meet all the members of her extensive family, which so frightened him that he broke off the engagement. It is not possible to think of the people we were seeing at that time without mentioning Gerald Brenan, a charming man, but one who in an evil moment offered Peter the loan of his house in southern Spain.

Conveniently near to us was the New Gallery Cinema in Regent Street where, that winter, the newly-formed Film Society gave its first Sunday afternoon showings. The audiences always seemed to be entirely composed of our friends. I used to say: 'Have you seen anyone you don't know?' and, indeed, it was more like a private reunion than a public function. Many of those friends would be spending their evenings dancing at the Gargoyle Club, but I went rather seldom, for baby-sitting was not yet a common practice and, anyhow, who in that part of London had ever heard of helping out young mothers? Not that we were without domestic help: a very nice Welsh woman came daily to clean, while her husband, a commissionaire at the Carlton Hotel across the road, gave us a roll of the most beautiful red carpet whose provenance we did not dream of ascertaining.

That April we gave a great party in the two large studios below the flat to celebrate my twenty-first birthday (a year late, for at the proper time I had been too gravid and we were much too hard up to do anything about it). To perform at the party we invited the Punch and Judy man with his little dog Toby who gave his regular show at the corner of Orange Street and the Haymarket; John Goss sang for us; and a professional jazz pianist, the star turn at some night-club, played for the guests to dance. Most of them came in fancy dress. The whole thing was very gay and lively. At the height of the fun Vera Meynell – whose only concession to *travestie* had been to powder her hair with gold-dust – said to me: 'This is a very good party.' 'I'm so glad you're enjoying it,' I said. 'I'm not,' she replied, 'but I can see it's a good party.'

8

Before I left home I had never, of course, known women who clothed themselves in homespun fabrics, professed Socialism and were married to like-minded men padding about in the type of sandals designed for five-year-olds. There were many such couples to be met at the 1917 Club, mostly Old Bedalians now living in the country – almost always in certain parts of Surrey – who used the Club as a port of call when in London to attend political functions or shop at Heal's.

We became friendly there with the Clifford Allens who, in that early summer of 1925, invited us to spend a weekend at their house in Abinger Hammer. Clifford Allen was then in his mid-thirties, the Treasurer of the Independent Labour Party and a director of the *Daily Herald*. He had a splendid, indeed an heroic record, as the leader of the No Conscription Fellowship, and had been imprisoned three times during the 1914–18 war under the government's cat-and-mouse policy on conscientious objectors. This treatment had ruined his health; he was even now suffering from TB and forced to retire from active political life only a few years later, to die in 1939 at the age of fifty.

While Peter was to come down later that evening, I arrived at midday to walk from the station through the woods. My baby was slung in a shawl supported on my hip, making a comfortable hammock in which she derived drowsy pleasure from the warmth and movement of my body. It was a lovely day and I lingered in the dappled sunshine, in no hurry to reach the Allens' house, Lemon Cottage. When I arrived I found that, in addition to Evelyn Strachey, later known as John, whom I had not met before, our fellow-guests were the Meynells who, though undoubtedly Socialists – and Francis had been a conscientious objector of the most courageous stamp during the war – did not go in for advertising their beliefs in their style of dress. On the contrary, both of them were, in my eyes, models of sophisticated chic and I longed to be exactly like them.

That first evening after dinner they proposed a game of poker. Peter, the inveterate gambler, eagerly agreed and the five of us started to play. Clifford had gone to see Mr Attlee while our hostess Joan (her name was in fact Marjory but for some obscure reason she preferred the equally banal Joan) refused to join us. The game went on, as games of poker will, for many hours; we were all in high spirits and enjoying the fun when suddenly, without any warning, Joan flung herself face down on a sofa, burst into muffled sobs and accused us of 'turning my lovely home into a gambling hell'. We were struck dumb; but in view of her distress we naturally stopped playing at once and slunk off to bed, much subdued, with our quaint oil-lamps. (The house had perfectly good electric wiring of course, but it was thought more in keeping with real country life that we should use this thoroughly inconvenient form of lighting.)

There were other even more unexpected and embarrassing signs of incompatibility. For example, Clifford, who had returned home the previous night, went into his small daughter's nursery on the Sunday morning with two fingers upraised in benediction and greeted her by saying: 'God be with you, little one.' That shook us; not because we should have preferred a display of militant atheism but because we could not endure any form of display and most particularly not that of a mawkish nature.

During the rest of our stay we spent the evenings, as we were to spend many others at that time, suggesting items for the *Week End Book* which Francis Meynell was to edit and publish, including Peter's clerihew contribution:

When Augustus John
Puts it on
His price is fourpence
More than Orpen's.

We remained friends with the Allens and, later, Joan was often to be met at London parties where she generally turned up without her husband and had

cast off not only her taste for peasant costume but also some of her puritanical attitudes. She seemed, in truth, though still quite serious, rather racy.

I was now pregnant again. I reflected with pleasure that my second child –
for I hoped to have a large family – would be less than two years younger
than the first. It came as a shock when Peter declared quite firmly that we
'couldn't afford' another baby. I went for an abortion to a doctor friend of
ours, known to me as a fellow-student at King's College, who had since
come to stay with us in Slinfold. I liked and trusted him but, though certainly I lost the foetus, things went horribly wrong and septicaemia set in.

We were in the country for the day, visiting Catherine Carswell in Buckinghamshire, when I began to feel extremely unwell. Peter persuaded me to
stay on, putting up at a small, friendly pub in the village near the Carswell
cottage, where I was soon in such excruciating pain that I could not get out
of bed. As soon as I was able, I went back to London and was rushed into
hospital for a life-saving operation. The consequences of this episode were
far-reaching.

Its most immediate upshot was that my parents, informed by the house
surgeon – the son of friends of theirs – that I was on the danger list, threatened to come and see me. That would have been the first time since I had
left home three years earlier. This sudden awakening of family feeling
struck me as macabre: they had not shown the smallest interest in, had not
so much as acknowledged, the birth of their first grandchild – a joyous
event – but now, when I was at lowest ebb physically and morally, too weak
to defend myself against their intrusion, they sought to re-enter my life.
I begged my own surgeon to protect me, on medical grounds, from so
unwelcome a trauma, which he did. It is a fine irony that, at this of all
moments, my parents should have been reconciled with Peter, inviting him
to dine with them while I was in hospital and treating him for the first time
as an accepted son-in-law. Once I was at home again and out of danger,
they came to see me and an armistice, if not a peace treaty, was concluded.

We went to the seaside – Kingsdown – for my convalescence when I was still so infirm and had lost so much weight that I tired easily and Peter, to my amusement – but not without my gratitude – hired a bath-chair to take me and the baby about. He was of the view that it would be a good thing and a help toward my full recovery if I avoided the London winter and went to the south of France for a few weeks after Christmas. I fell in with this plan and set off in January with the pleasant young girl whom Peter had picked up somewhere and then brought home to help with the baby. We travelled overnight – the baby sleeping in a hammock slung between the luggage racks in the railway compartment – to Pardigon where we stayed at the one small hotel. Teddy came out to join me there and, later, Vera Meynell. It was not a particularly happy time, but at least I did a good deal of writing.

By now I knew from Peter's letters that I would be going back to a bleak prospect: he had given up the second studio in Orange Street – splendid for parties but he did not really need it – the communicating double doors had been sealed and it was let to Oliver Messel. He had also let the flat for, as he explained, he longed to go abroad, alone, to paint. This meant that we must save as much money as possible and, in his absence, I would be able to live on the rents we should be getting. The thought of living in the one large, chilly studio with no proper facilities for the baby filled me with misgiving. So, while still in Pardigon, Teddy and I took the baby by train to Antibes where I left her with the Davisons at the Château des Enfants, telling myself that she would be far better off in the sun, surrounded by every care and luxury, than sharing my solitary, penurious and uncomfortable existence in winterbound London.

That was in February and I came home just before Peter set out in March for Gerald Brenan's house in Yegan, Ugijar, near Almeria. He planned to be gone for six months. On his way he called at the Cap d'Antibes to see the baby and then went on to settle down in Spain to a regimen of early rising, painting for long hours, taking systematic exercise before and after work and following an altogether well-regulated programme. At first he relished this and loved the house with its roof garden, enjoyed the enormous choice of books it offered and was well pleased with everything. But it did not last. He began to feel more and more, as he expressed it in his almost daily letters to me, 'cut-off, unhappy, empty, helpless, hopeless'. The idea of staying away for half a year appeared entirely wrongheaded, foolish and even iniquitous; he was lonely and wretched, he wrote, his wife was lonely and wretched, his little child was exiled among strangers and for what? He felt profoundly dissatisfied with himself, his work and his whole life.

By the middle of April his unhappiness touched its nadir. In an immensely long letter which reached me on my birthday – the most miserable one I could remember – he analysed his past: he had started to work seriously only after he had come down from Cambridge: the best things were still those he had done in that one year before the war claimed him. Slowly, after it was over, he had tried to revive something that had been dead in him for over four years; but in truth it had never come to life again and it was then that he made what he called his 'big, irreversible, irremediable mistake': he had not had the wisdom or the fortitude to apply himself to 'exercises and scales', to spend all the seven years since the end of the war in 'grind and obscurity'. There should never have been exhibitions with 'yards of press-notices'; he hated what he had produced – 'stunt books of freak drawings' – that had commanded 'false prices and a press reputation with its false values'. The work was meretricious: 'Clever, good-taste trash.'

He went on to decry the way in which he had 'shirked difficulties' so that there was no solid knowledge nor honest apprenticeship behind him: he had merely 'invented a trick or two' and now, naked to this self-examination, he knew he was too old to start afresh when he no longer had the innocence and humility of the beginner. He had tasted success too early: it had come too easily and he had enjoyed its rewards which had destroyed his integrity. It was too late now to expiate the wrong of having allowed

A portrait of Janna by Edmond Kapp

himself to be led astray – by Tonks, by Max Beerbohm, by the Vienna Academy – in the early years of his career. Only in Italy had he begun, falteringly, to take the right path; even that had been too late. It was sheer effrontery to suppose that he could produce anything of worth without having studied the great masters, without having so much as made a single copy of a drawing or painting he admired. Where Holbein and Ingres had shown the way he had not troubled to look and learn. He had never been through the mill; never slaved away until the use of brush and pencil had become second nature as the only reliable foundation for any serious creative art. Lack of money might be the excuse but was no exoneration. And now, too old and still too poor, what use could these few little months be? It needed years: years that had gone. 'I don't know what I'm doing here,' he wrote in his despair. For days he had not touched a brush; his will to work was paralysed; he felt he had become 'just nothing at all', and the savour had gone out of his surroundings. He could not even be bothered to go walking 'alone in this landscape which so far doesn't interest me much, which I find hard and cold and unsympathetic and whose people I don't understand'.

It was in the pain rather than the analysis that the creative artist in him was now crying out (in Wilfred Owen's sense that 'the poetry is in the pity'). In his self-disgust, combined with missing us, he played with the notion of going into commerce, providing security and, perhaps, a permanent home in Old Hampstead, which he had always loved. While he now spoke of having more children, not for one moment did he castigate the purely selfish considerations which had prevented the increase of family I had so dearly wanted. It was pure fantasy and he knew it. But what was clear and real was that this escape from marriage, if such it was, had failed to satisfy and, after barely six weeks, he abandoned it.

In the first week of May he met me in Paris and we travelled south to reclaim our little daughter and to settle nearby.

9

For me, despite the misery caused by Peter's letters, these weeks were not entirely unhappy. For a start, my closest friend at the time was Iris Barry, then married to Alan Porter, and newly appointed to be the film critic – an innovation – on the *Daily Mail*. (Iris Barry was an assumed name. I do not remember what her first name had been, but I do know that her surname was Crump, so it is hardly surprising that she had adopted another.) I shared her passionate – though not of course her professional – interest in the cinema and went to many film shows with her, both public and private.

Thanks to the repaired if formal relations with my parents over the past few months I was invited to join them for a fortnight in Biarritz where I had rather a good time. Upon my return I saw a good deal of Sage Bernal who, on the eve of the General Strike – and of my departure for France – gave me my first real lesson in politics by explaining that whole situation to me. It was to be many years before the lesson took effect: at the time it led to nothing more than an argument with my parents and a denunciation of my brother who, I learnt, had volunteered to drive strike-breaking public transport.

I arrived in Paris a few days before Peter and spent most of my time in the Dôme, the Rotonde or the smaller, brighter, Select Café in the company of three couples of young men – painters and dancers, later to win fame – who, subscribing to Yahveh's view, informed me that women, often amusing and sometimes decorative, were not to be taken seriously. I was disheartened by the news; but as, in the course of those few days, at least two of the young men screeched at their partners, sulked, flounced and behaved in an altogether pettish manner, I wondered whether I should really take it so much to heart.

Reunited with Peter, all this became totally irrelevant: as we travelled south to retrieve our little daughter, we faced the fact that Peter's Spanish interlude, no less than the consequences of my terminated pregnancy, had left their mark upon our marriage: it had no longer quite the happy-go-lucky gaiety of our first few years together. I had been made conscious that I wanted children whom I would probably never have, in much the same way that Peter knew he would not attain to the inner peace and salvation of the humble, obscure life of study he yearned for. Those desires were, at bottom, incompatible, representing a latent, undeclared conflict. An additional factor in this complex of our changed relations was that, while Peter and Teddy between them had trained me to look at paintings with a little understanding (and I had also heard Roger Fry lecture, with slides, on Significant Form), Peter's ruthless disparagement of his work and savage contempt for its superficiality made me, for the first time, consider it critically. Certainly I did not set myself up as a judge, and I knew that in its skill, its wit, the often beautiful and always sensitive lines of his draughtsmanship no less than its manifest integrity of purpose, it was far from being the vulgar rubbish he branded it. I was nevertheless able to discern its weaknesses and, in particular, those of his paintings; but felt ashamed of doing so.

We stayed at first in Juan-les-Pins where, in those days, the almost empty beach was ideal for small children. Along the whole coast we found people we knew and, as the summer wore on, more and more of our friends and acquaintances turned up, including the Meynells. (I shall always remember Francis Meynell, who took part in the physical jerks on the *plage*, describing our tiny sun-browned daughter as like 'a grain of sand between the instructor's toes'.)

We spent many of our evenings in the little casino where one could dine on the terrace and afterwards dance or play a nursery form of roulette, known as boule, for low stakes. On one such evening we were invited by friends to join them at a neighbouring table. We were introduced, inaudibly, to their companions. Opposite me sat a handsome woman who leant forward and said: 'Weren't you Yvonne Mayer?' 'Yes, I was,' I said brightly, 'and who are you?' 'Rebecca West,' she answered to my undying shame.

She never held this appalling gaffe against me and over the years, she did me innumerable kindnesses which included taking me to see Paul Robeson and Peggy Ashcroft's *Othello* at the Savoy Theatre in 1930; and from her review of my first novel until her last broadcast interview, she never failed to speak well of my work. I do not now remember whether or not it was she who suggested that we should move into the guest-house, the Pension Josse – mid-way between Juan and the old town of Antibes – where she was living with her twelve-year-old son, Anthony, and his governess. At the time she was writing a novel: I now know that it was *Sunflower*, which she later abandoned.

Among the other guests were the American writers Glenway Wescott and Lloyd Morris, the young Maurice Sachs – unconvincing seminarist in *soutane* and shovel hat – and William Gerhardi (as he then spelt his name). Though we all thought his behaviour distinctly bizarre, we admired his novel *The Polyglots* in whose recent success he was basking. I recall his declaring one day that he would 'never *speak* to anyone who did not admire Margaret Kennedy's *Constant Nymph*,' to which Peter rejoined: 'That's a very good idea.'

We went to the bathing parties – where I learnt to balance on a surf-board lashed to a speed-boat – and the dances given by such villa residents as Lloyd Osborne (the stepson of R. L. Stevenson and co-author with him of *The Wrong Box*, *The Wrecker* and *The Ebb Tide*); and we were glad to meet again Ernst Toller, now much happier, nicer and in the company of a most beautiful young girl. Among our other acquaintances was Walter Fuller, a former editor of the *Westminster Gazette*, and his wife, Crystal Eastman (an American whose brother, Max, was spending the summer at the Cap d'Antibes). The Fullers were about to go permanently to the United States where Walter had been offered a job, taking with them the young English nanny they had brought to the south to look after their two children. This girl, whom we often met on the beach, took a fancy to – one could almost say, fell in love with – us as a family: not with Peter, not with me nor yet with the baby, but with all three; and, though warned that she would never be able to count on her wages and that the prospects for her future were far from good, she elected, in a rush of pure love, to leave the Fullers and attach herself to us. Her name was Jean Pateman, but Janna called her Jix and so she was known to us for all time, as she came to be part of our lives for many, many years, to remain a friend until her death in 1989.

An attractive, healthy, simple-hearted creature of nineteen or twenty, she was naturally a huge success with all our friends and could have made a dozen more fortunate marriages than the one she eventually contracted, rather late in life, with a scoundrel who robbed her of everything she had and then deserted her. She never married again but became a pillar of the church and of the RSPCA, caring for injured birds and animals in a resort on the south coast of England. Quite recently Anthony West, Rebecca's son in America, told a journalist, who passed it on to me, that he recalled one evening as a boy having his early supper in the dining-room of the Pension Josse when Gerhardi came in to gobble up a solitary high tea; this was in order not to have to offer dinner to 'the Kapp's nanny' whom he had asked out for the evening.

Although Madame Josse had given us rooms in a pleasant annexe in the grounds of the house, it was no place for Peter to work. He found a rather ramshackle studio – probably a former warehouse – on the ancient ramparts overlooking the small harbour at Antibes – a glorious position – where he started to paint again. This was important after the terrible discouragement he had suffered while in Spain, but it was, of course, unprofitable and we depended for our living upon my inexpert journalism: a precarious existence, so that when Nigel Playfair came to the coast on holiday and offered Peter a part – playing his recorder – in his production of *Le Bourgeois Gentilhomme*, to be put on at his Lyric Theatre, Hammersmith, Peter accepted it. He left for London in the late autumn.

This meant that he needed the Orange Street studio which, when I had left in May, was lent to John Collier, one of the penniless writers lodging with Teddy Wolfe's mother in Notting Hill. Peter suggested that John should simply do a swap and take over the studio in Antibes. This he did, arriving with almost no luggage and absolutely no money, to take up his residence in the draughty old building that had been pleasant enough in the summer but was now rather uninviting. John made no complaints, but the question was: how to feed him? I could not possibly afford to offer him meals at the *pension* very often, even though, with the decline of the season and the departure of the guests, we were accorded a reduced rate. But not reduced enough; and John was always hungry. For a time, though it could not deceive anybody, I would ask for a picnic lunch and then, no matter how chilly, wet or blustery the weather, I would walk to the ramparts and hand over the packet to John. It was not a strategy with much of a future for, quite apart from the fact that this meagre fare hardly satisfied John, while leaving me famished, for I dared not show my face in the guest-house until the lunch-hour was over, I was growing alarmed at the deteriorating state of the studio. Also, I did not think that, when winter came, the staff would even pretend to believe I was going on a picnic.

John had built himself a wigwam, or tepee, of blankets in the middle of the studio to try to keep himself warm. It had also become the shelter for a family of mice who feasted upon the crumbs he dropped and added to the filth, since he never dreamt of sweeping or cleaning the place. I began to feel deeply worried about the fate of Peter's pictures and realized that other arrangements would have to be made. It meant I must find somewhere cheaper to live. What I found was a ground-floor flat of two rooms and a kitchen, quite near to the studio, with French windows that were also the front door opening on to the ramparts. This had been newly converted by its owner, an old boat-builder, now a widower, who had moved into the floor above as adequate for all his solitary needs. The significant thing about this ancient man was that he had once built a yacht for Guy de

Maupassant. It is doubtful whether he had ever built anything since, but this cloud of glory, trailed for some forty years, entitled him to wear a greasy mariner's jersey and a rakish yachting cap. The rent he asked – like the flat itself and its sparse furnishings – was modest. It suited us well and, once installed, I was able to keep an eye on and clean the studio, to buy food in the market and to cook for us all in the tiny kitchen.

In those days Antibes was not in the least a fashionable resort. It had its summer season when prosperous French families opened up their villas near the Cap and the Eden Roc, while glamorous and famous characters – for the most part American – came to stay at the big hotel; but the old town of Antibes itself knew nothing of tourists. Its cafés, its shops and its market stalls catered for the native population of fishermen, artisans and their families, with transient sailors and crewmen from visiting naval vessels and yachts who put in to the port.

I will not claim that I ever became a part of or was accepted by that community; but outwardly I was indistinguishable from the other young native housewives and, since the facilities were lacking, my clothes grew shabbier, untidier and more crumpled as time went on. I did not really care. I enjoyed loitering in the market square above which towered the forbidding grey walls of the Chateau Grimaldi, later to be renovated and become a Picasso gallery, but then a neglected, gaunt shell whose sole charm was the stele above its dark entry arch with its Latin inscription, translated for me by John as: 'Here the northern boy danced and pleased.'

All that winter he and I played two-handed poker in the pale sunshine seated on the long jetty wall beside the harbour. We spent our evenings in the vast, dimly lit, ornate and generally deserted café in the main square. Day and night, endlessly, John talked about the things he planned to write, told sardonic stories about his sordid life in Pimlico – the story of *His Monkey Wife* was even then completed in his mind and retailed to me, though not published until 1930 – and spouted reams of Urquart's *Rabelais*, Florio's *Montaigne*, Marlowe's *Faustus*, *Dead Souls* and *Smoke* in Garnett's versions; and *The Waste Land*. Many of those passages have stuck in my mind to this day and I could quote them now, while they led me to read things I should perhaps never have discovered for myself. John was, indeed, a most stimulating and entertaining companion, though of an arrogant and exasperating character.

On Shrove Tuesday we put on fancy dress and went to Nice for the carnival. Dancing in the street that night and inflamed by draughts of Pernod mixed with cognac – a diabolical invention of John's – I fell over and hurt my back. I wanted to sit down in a café but John wouldn't hear of this: we had run out of money, had nothing left but our return railway tickets, and it would be indecent to enter a café. The argument developed into a scorching quarrel which ended by my demanding my train ticket and setting off for Antibes alone, in some pain and a tearing rage. The next morning he turned up ready to depart for good. I cannot say I was sorry. All he wanted was money for his fare back to England and for food to fill the coquettish little basket he was carrying which made me explode with laughter.

That was in February, shortly after which the Molière play came off and Peter returned to us. He greatly approved of the flat, though he himself was always able to escape from its exceedingly narrow confines to the studio. Our fortunes, despite his relatively well-paid job in the theatre – most of which money had gone on living expenses in London – had not greatly improved and we still relied upon my earnings from the silly little articles I contributed to the women's page of the *Manchester Guardian* and one or two other papers at, I seem to remember, two guineas apiece.

It was at this juncture that one of Rebecca West's many kindnesses came to light. Aware of – but tactfully silent about – our insecure finances, she had recommended me to Mrs Edna Chase, the American editor-in-chief of all the *Vogues*, as a suitable literary editor for the Paris edition. This was produced in English for British and American readers. It specialized in authoritative articles on the vagaries of *haute couture* and the cosmopolitan *beau monde*, written by experts on these subjects who, naturally, had only a nodding acquaintance with spelling, punctuation and grammar. Mrs Chase, wishing to do something towards correcting these shortcomings once they had been brought to her notice, planned, while taking a holiday in Europe that summer, to scout for some deserving but literate character to do the job. Following Rebecca's advice, she wrote asking me to come for an interview at the Hotel du Cap in Antibes at noon on a Sunday in August.

The day before, having made an inspection of my sad wardrobe and recognizing that it could not produce anything fit to be seen at the Hotel du Cap, let alone on a person aspiring to work for *Vogue*, Peter and I went to Cannes determined to spend whatever it might cost to rig me out for this momentous interview. After a rather futile round of the shops, by which time both of us were thoroughly discouraged and exhausted, we settled – too hastily – for an elegant silk dress the colour of ripe corn which was several sizes too large for me. It was horribly expensive but, not content with that extravagance, Peter, having spotted a jaunty little black straw hat in the window of a smart milliner's, was set upon putting the finishing touches to the outfit. Bidding me wait out of sight, he went into the shop and, somehow or other, managed to persuade the salesgirl, against her better judgment, to lend him this hat which he swore to return, unharmed, early on Monday morning before her boss – fortunately not there on a Saturday – discovered its disappearance.

That evening he lay on the bed issuing warnings and instructions – 'Don't cut! Don't cut!' – while Jix and I measured and pinned, tried on, pinned and measured again, in an attempt to make the dress a little better fitting all round. At last, when it was long after midnight and we were absolutely worn out, we took up the scissors, slashed into the fabric and utterly ruined the whole dress. When the time came to get ready the next morning I had to put on an old stuff frock bought in London ages before and totally unsuited to a summer's day in the south of France; but at least I had the undeniably chic hat. As I took gloomy stock of my appearance – about as far from that of a likely *Vogue* employee as one could picture –

Peter, conscious that, not even as an armchair, but positively a bad critic, he had been in part to blame for the overnight tragedy, and only too eager to make amends, ran ceaselessly to and from the café on the port, bringing each time a tot of cognac to fortify my nerves for the coming ordeal. By the time he escorted me to the main square, holding me tightly by the arm, and propelled me on to a tram for the Cap I was hopelessly drunk. And speechless. But not helpless: merely rigid.

Thus in the presence of Mrs Edna Chase and throughout the interview I sat stiff and silent, intimating my agreement with all she said by inclining my head in a courtly manner, even when she offered me a gin fizz which I had the prudence not to touch. From my demeanour she could hardly judge whether I had or had not the qualities so generously claimed for me by Rebecca. At least she could discern for herself that I was a person of immense dignity, an impression I sustained until the end of the session when, having been unable to take in pretty well everything she said, with cautious steps and distorted vision, I made my way home.

There was one further meeting with Mrs Chase. She and her husband proposed to come to tea one afternoon. The flat on the ramparts was by no means the ideal interior to entertain such visitors, but we did persuade – indeed, bribe – the local (male) *jeunesse* to forgo for one afternoon the pleasure of standing immediately outside what was in effect our front door to piss into the sea hundreds of feet below. Even with that hazard averted, there was little we could do to give an impression of gracious living, though we did borrow from the boat-builder upstairs his silver teapot, and we did buy a lot of highly decorative fruit – melons, peaches, grapes, nectarines and figs – which we placed upon vine leaves and arranged on a huge platter. We also pleaded with Jix to behave as though she were a parlourmaid: to come in and ask whether we would like tea served now, while Peter would take the baby to the beach.

As bad luck would have it, Mrs Chase and her husband (who was not called Mr Chase but whose name I either never knew or have quite forgotten) telegraphed to say that they could not come on the day arranged and, by the time they did come, the fruit had gone bad, the boat-builder wanted his teapot back – I think he feared we were more likely to pawn it than to use it – and the lads had reverted to their usual sport from which they were not prepared to desist a second time for no matter how many *sous*. What was even worse was that, having given up her free afternoon over and over again, Jix was out and away when the great day came. Thus, at the end of a thoroughly uncomfortable and absurd tea party, as the couple left the flat and turned the corner, they could observe Peter in the street on his knees, trying to feed the baby who sat on the low kitchen windowsill. Whatever Mrs Chase may have thought of me at our first encounter, dignity was not the outstanding feature of our second.

Soon after this we left to take a house in Thorenc in the Maritime Alps, above Grasse. Various people came to stay with us there, for the house, in a valley among pinewoods, was large and comfortable, unlike the tiny Antibes flat. Among our guests was Lilian Mowrer with her little daughter who, six months older than Janna, was now pushing three. Because the Mowrers' circumstances were somewhat different from ours the little girl had the most beautiful clothes, including exquisite underwear, which enchanted Jix who, the dear sweet girl, was confident that when Janna reached her age, she, too, would have such things: you had them when you were nearly three, not when you were only two-and-a-bit.

The great event of our stay was the preparation of a hare. The hunts-man who had bagged it brought it to us and offered, when it should be ready, to cook it. On the appointed day he arrived early in the morning and took over the kitchen. All day long he slaved away there, lightening his task and assuaging the thirst it induced with draughts of the wine he had advised us to lay in for the job. The other ingredients – herbs, vegetables, fruits – which he used in abundance scented the whole house. We were faint with hunger when, at about ten o'clock in the evening he announced, reeling into the living room, that dinner was now served. It was indeed a memorable feast. It can seldom happen that a man will spend twelve hours preparing a dish or know how to do it; while first, as one recalls, one has to catch one's hare.

On our return to Antibes I found awaiting me a letter from Mrs Chase. I had got the job and was to start in three weeks' time at a salary of £1,000 a year, to be paid in dollars, tax free – since I was a British subject living abroad. The proposition appealed more strongly to Peter than to me.

This time it was I who left the family. At the end of September I set off, alone, for Paris to take up my duties.

Part Three

From Literature to Politics

I

I travelled to Paris overnight, to be met at the Gare de Lyon by three or four friends who bore me off to the hotel in the rue Jacob where, in a small room on the top floor, I would live for the next three months: until, in fact, I had set aside enough of my salary to pay for Peter, Jix and Janna to rejoin me. It is true that Peter came for a flying visit on his birthday in the first week of November; but we felt somehow estranged and it was not a particularly happy event.

When I began working for *Vogue* it was housed in the place Edouard VII, familiar to me from the bitter days, seven years earlier, when I had stayed with my parents at the hotel of that name in this cul-de-sac off the boulevard des Capucines. Shortly after my arrival, the offices were moved to the Champs-Elysées where I was assigned a rather dingy little back room.

My status was somewhere between that of the 'technical' staff – typists, filing clerks and the like – who were monstrously underpaid, and that of the expensive and glamorous young men who, having attended the social functions and the seasonal collections of the great fashion houses, wrote the articles and drew the illustrations recording these rites. My work was not arduous, but nor was it entirely congenial, consisting as it did of putting in and taking out commas, introducing such avant-garde concepts as the semi-colon, correcting the spelling and reforming the syntax of those who were above such things.

Occasionally I contributed an article myself and I invented such terms as 'spectator sportswear'. I was also expected to go to some of the fashion shows, to perch upon a small gilt chair and drink abominable sweet champagne in the middle of the day, while – this being before the era of the catwalk – haughty young persons of incredibly long-legged slenderness, in marked contrast to the predominantly dumpy women in the audience, undulated about the salon, bearing down upon one in a most daunting manner, as if about to deliver a deadly insult or demand an immediate apology, only to think better of it at the last moment and, in a swirling movement, glide away to intimidate some other blameless onlooker.

I felt ill at ease in this over-scented atmosphere of lavish spenders. Once I asked the lively little American editor – who later founded a successful *maison de couture* himself – what manner of lives these women led. 'Why, the same as you and everyone else,' he said, rather crossly. 'They marry, have children, go to parties, lunch parties, dinner parties, cocktail parties, house parties: the usual thing. They're just more moneyed than you and everyone else.'

I made the discovery that behind the world of fashion stood the textile trade: that, in places far from Paris, new materials were produced, thanks to technical advances and the skill of fabric designers, and then used in the most imaginative way by the leading dressmakers, who thus determined – as the textile manufacturers had determined for them – what should and would be worn by those who could afford to renew their wardrobes every season. I relished the choreographic possibilities of that scene: the swaggering, stylized *haute école* of the mannequins; the extravagant gestures of mesdames, their managers; and the concordant movements of the potential buyers, who raised their glasses, clapped their hands and turned their heads this way and that in perfect unison. I suggested to Frederick Ashton – then in Paris working with Ida Rubenstein – that this richly comic spectacle should be translated into dance.

For the newcomer, the outsider, this exotic world had its charm and its temptations. I succumbed to Louiseboulanger's persuasion to accept, at cost price (roughly one-twentieth of what a genuine customer would be charged), an evening dress of pale leaf-green chiffon, with uneven hemline, to be worn with a slightly darker leaf-green, short, velvet cloak.

Reality, however, in the rue Jacob was always breaking in. I awoke one morning to find I had ugly spots round my mouth. Horrified, I sped to an American doctor recommended by one of my colleagues. He opened the consultation by enquiring brusquely: 'Husband got spots?' I explained he was not with me in Paris, whereupon the doctor asked: 'Rooming with anyone?', from which it was clear that he had diagnosed the pox. I was only too willing to have a Wassermann test.

At that juncture the Meynells came to Paris for a few days accompanied by Dr Joan Malleson. Dining with them, I naturally refused to touch alcohol. Halfway through the meal Joan asked me whether I was afraid I had a venereal disease. I admitted this was so. 'Well, let me tell you,' she said, 'what you've got is impetigo, probably from a dirty towel. I'll give you a prescription for it. It may take a little time to clear up, but there's no need to worry. And now, do have a drink.' She was, of course, quite right.

By Christmas I had saved enough to send for the family. They left Antibes for good and I took a suite of rooms in the rue de Fleurus, just off the rue Guynemer and opposite the gates of the Luxembourg Gardens where Jix could take Janna every day.

I had made a friend on the editorial staff: a fashion expert who had been brought to Paris originally as one of a team of outstandingly beautiful American girls, selected in New York by Jean Patou himself to become his models. Although no more – and no less – literate than the other writers on fashion, she was an exceedingly modest, kind and practical person: not at all what was expected in someone of her history or her looks. She lived with her mother in an apartment in an expensive quarter on the Right Bank from whose windows she could, and did, closely observe the intimate doings – and the underwear – of her patrician neighbours. With her I went riding in the Bois every morning before breakfast.

That was not my only extravagance: Jix's arrears of wages, long overdue, were at last paid, with interest; I rented a studio for Peter in the Denfert-Rochereau district, off the boulevard St Jacques; and we moved into more spacious and more permanent accommodation, taking the whole first floor of a small family hotel with a good restaurant, a little way further up the rue de Fleurus, my own room, with windows on both sides, looking out upon the rue Madame. I thought of myself as settled here for some time, bought a few pieces of additional furniture and hired a piano to practise the easier of the forty-eight Preludes and Fugues; but gradually, almost imperceptibly, I began to feel that I was a parasite – that all of us working for *Vogue*, and the journal itself, were no better than tiny parasites battening upon a great parasitic system; that our concerns lacked dignity and moral justification.

This disquiet was channelled into furious indignation at the way the young French underlings – the girls doing the menial jobs about the office – were treated. Their poor wages, reflected in unhealthy complexions and shoddy clothing, were a disgrace and a reproach to us all. What were our wealthy American masters thinking of to countenance such sordid parsimony in an enterprise devoted to promoting conspicuous consumption? Though well aware that mine was an invidious position, I sought some way to stand up for those underpaid employees as I sat in my dismal small workroom, well away from the showy offices at the front of the building, where the editor presided at a desk of black glass, and visitors were ushered into reception rooms furnished with deep, soft chairs upholstered in white leather from which only the most acrobatic could rise with grace.

Unversed in the conduct of protest movements and with a lack of finesse guaranteed to ensure failure, I confronted the editor, declaring that if something were not done forthwith to improve the pay and conditions of the cleaners, clerks, typists, stenographers and tea girls, I would resign. The editor took this threat with equanimity. And rightly. For shortly after, while I was on a brief spell of leave with the Meynells in London, they impressed upon me the folly of making any rash move unless and until I had secured some other means to gain a livelihood. I wrote to the editor, withdrawing – though not in so many words – my grandiose ultimatum, upon which he telegraphed: 'Congratulations on taking off your red dress.'

But I had not. Rather, I was learning a little and now pulled back to take a higher jump. I knew that I could not last – indeed, had no intention of staying – much longer doing work that I thought not merely worthless but demeaning. I also knew that such an attitude – censorious and priggish – accorded ill with the mode of casual flippancy much favoured in that milieu. If I expressed my views, rather than being sacked I should simply be mocked; and I had no wish to make a fool of myself.

I decided to play this endgame using tactics my employers understood and might even respect. I would wait for an opportune moment and then declare that I could only stay in the job if I were paid twice my present salary: double or quit. In the meantime, to secure my rear, Peter went to England and took a cottage in the country, which he furnished with second-hand pieces where he with Janna and Jix could spend the summer. I missed the family, but was glad they were out of the city at this season; and I myself, having given up the rue de Fleurus and taken over Peter's studio – for which the rent was paid until the autumn – spent weekends in such places as the Ville d'Avray, Montmorency, Barbizon, Pierrefonds and Fontainebleau.

This time my ultimatum worked. When offered the alternative to my preposterous wage demand, my employers naturally chose to get rid of me. Having demonstrated that I could be as greedy as anybody else, I left with honour, after giving a tremendous lunch party for the entire lower-paid staff in the gardens of a restaurant on one of the little islands in the Seine. It was a huge success. Rumours of it must have reached the editorial staff, none of whom had been invited. Those who had, drifted back to the office very late that afternoon, in no condition to exert themselves.

A few days later, I packed my bags, handed the key of the studio back to the landlord, was driven in style to Dieppe and set sail for England.

2

The cottage was in Great Abington, a village some nine miles south of Cambridge. It had been found for Peter by the Bernals who lived close by in a pleasant, solid old house, with a little tributary of the Cam purling alongside its garden, at Hildersham, said to have been the birthplace of the thirteenth-century chronicler, Matthew Paris. Their little son, Michael, some fifteen months younger than Janna, became – and remained for many years – her best friend. Indeed, once we had settled into the cottage, our two families were inseparable, sharing children, husbands, wives, guests, domestic help, seaside holidays and cars.

It was, in fact, now that Peter, who must have sold some pictures to be able to do so, bought me my first car: a maroon-coloured, bull-nosed Morris Oxford cabriolet, that is, a smart two-seater with an extra, folding seat at the back, known as a dickey. It had a stout leather hood to put up and let down on hinged arms, as on a pram. All that bitter cold winter, stabled in the yard of the village pub, it had to be started with a cranking handle that had a recoil liable to dislocate the wrist, if not the shoulder.

Although I had never before owned a car, I had learned to drive as long ago as 1919 when on tour in Scotland with my parents. The chauffeur had given me a lesson every morning before breakfast but, though I quickly got the hang of it, I could not then hold a licence. As soon as I could – when I reached eighteen – I drove my father's heavy Turcat-Méry open tourer if he gave permission. It was perhaps the most unsuitable car for a young woman to handle, but at least it taught me caution at the wheel.

It is tempting, but would be ineffably boring, to describe all the cars I have had – most of them bought for between £5 and £10 – but I shall say only that, late in life, I formed an emotional attachment to a Simca the colour of butterscotch; and that I finally gave up having a car to celebrate my eightieth birthday, recognizing that, however superbly I imagined I was driving, at such an age, with weakening eyesight and slacking reflexes, one cannot but be an absolute menace on the road. Instead, let me relate that in the 1920s I learnt to sail a dinghy with a centreboard on the Blackwater estuary, and in the mid-thirties to fly an Avro Cadet at Heston; but, since I was incapable of landing – again and again, coming in to hover some ten feet off the ground – I was never awarded a pilot's licence.

The Meynells had bought a house in Toppesfield in Essex, a few miles from the Cambridgeshire border, formerly a farmhouse known as Bradfields, on whose land, in 1800, many Roman antiquities had been found. It was an attractive place with a barn they had turned into a room for indoor games and a reedy pool where, all summer long, visitors could swim. We often went there, en masse, for Sunday lunch and once Sage spent an entire weekend trying to demonstrate how fire could be made by twirling a pointed stick in a block of wood. He failed to elicit a spark, but produced some evidence of charring.

Vera claimed that Sage never looked clean. We were driving to Hildersham on that occasion and I advanced the charitable view that this was owed to his sallow complexion. Upon our arrival at the house, Vera stalked up to him and peered closely at his face. Then she turned to me and said: 'Dirt, pure dirt.'

Sage himself had the best stories about his inability to conform to the

customs of the tribe. One of these concerned a visit to his friend Frank
Pakenham in Ireland. A valet unpacked his minimal luggage and, when he
went to his room, he found laid out on the bed, his spare tie – his single
concession to his host's practice of changing for dinner – and, on the
dressing-table, his slide-rule slightly drawn out of its case, conveniently
ready for use.

Daily we drove the children into Cambridge where they went to
Geoffrey Pyke's Malting House nursery school. They liked best to climb
into the dickey of my car and pull the roof down over their heads. Passers-
by would be surprised to see the small children lift the lid and hop out when
we arrived.

Geoffrey Pyke became an intimate if entirely unpredictable friend. We
also saw a good deal of Maurice Dobb and his then wife, Phyllis, in whose
cottage, immediately behind the Malting House, Wittgenstein was lodging.
As he did not appear to be a member of the university in any capacity – he
was, in fact, there at the invitation of Bertrand Russell – I asked Phyllis
Dobb one day: 'What does Wittgenstein actually *do* here?' 'What he
actually *does*,' said his landlady bitterly, 'is to bang the lavatory door at
night.'

It was now that I began writing my first novel. I showed the opening
chapter to Rebecca West on one of my visits to London. (It was on the
same occasion that, disapproving of my friends, she referred to them as
having 'taken vows of unchastity'.) She was unexpectedly encouraging
about my work and, had I not been diverted by compelling personal problems, nothing would have stopped me from going on with the novel.

The painful thing that had to be faced was that my marriage was falling
apart. Peter, who had rented a studio off Haverstock Hill in Hampstead,
came less and less often to the cottage and, although we spent a summer
holiday together with the Bernals on the Norfolk coast – the grown-ups,
like all English families at the seaside, cowering in the lee of upturned
fishing-boats to shelter from the biting wind, while the children, more

warm-blooded, danced at the edge of the icy sea – our lives were no longer closely knit.

It is usual for outsiders to know better than the two people concerned the rights and wrongs of a failed marriage. For years and years I was to run into Peter's friends who shunned me as the vicious woman who had treated that sweet man so cruelly; while I was doing my best to assuage the fevered imagination of those who commiserated with me as the victim of a lecherous bounder. At this late stage I could not attempt to justify my conduct in ending my life with Peter. There are scenes forever burnt into my memory that cause me, even now, a sense of shame, notwithstanding the complex reasons that made me absolutely certain I must make the break.

Of course Peter had had no interest in my working life on *Vogue*. How could he have had? Unimportant though that may have been, it contributed to the alienation that began to creep into our relationship at that time. At bottom was the sensitive and, in the last analysis, cardinal factor of loyalty: I had ceased to feel in harmony with his values and philosophy of life; I could not stand up for them as one's partner should. That we were less than faithful to one another must also, of course, have played a part in loosening the ties that bound us; yet, in the end, I knew it was not sexual fidelity but mutual trusting and honouring that mattered and had perished.

It was sad that the settled home I had never known during our happy years should now, at last and too late, have been found. For Peter eventually bought outright the Haverstock Hill studio and it became his permanent centre – where, indeed, nearly fifty years later he was to die – yet I stayed in it only as an occasional visitor for a few days at a time; while, over the years, I went there for parties, including Janna's twentieth birthday celebration – on the eve of D-Day in 1944 – and Peter's own eightieth in 1970, it was never my dwelling-place.

The worst aspect of our parting was Peter insisting that, if he could not, then neither should I have the care of Janna. Conveyed to me by Vera Meynell, this edict – a severe blow – did not have the force of law and I could have ignored it; but, conscious of my fault in rejecting him and having, as he put it accusingly, 'deprived him of wife and child', I submitted to the punishment. In any event, the decree was of relatively short duration, lasting only until Peter wished to remarry, when he was anxious that I should divorce him, after which I took full responsibility for Janna in all respects.

My parents, in keeping with their declared – though unflattering – belief that Peter had married me only for my father's money, had taken good care that we should never touch a penny of it in all our years together. When the marriage broke up, they welcomed, indeed celebrated, the divorce, according it the blessing so signally withheld from my wedding. My father even paid the expensive legal fees, accompanied me to the court and took me for lunch with the lawyer afterwards.

While this long-drawn-out and hateful process in its early stages was being worked through, I left Great Abington, said a temporary farewell to Jix, sent Janna to friends with a pack of children of their own in Buckinghamshire and, a solitary person, moved to London. The postscript to this far-off period of misery is that, though the tearing apart was neither swift nor easy, Peter and I did in time attain to a kindly, even affectionate rapprochement, concerned for each other's wellbeing and progress.

I look back upon our years together as among the happiest and certainly the most formative of my life.

3

It was now 1930 and I was pushing twenty-seven. I had really done nothing with my life. Casting off parents, husband, lovers and now – albeit involuntarily – my child hardly amounted to a career.

This was not lost upon my close friends. Sage pronounced me 'a pity', saying I was 'like a lot of good pictures with their faces turned to the wall'.

He also declared that he would never think his life a success unless mine were too. Francis made the provocative statement in a roomful of people that I would never dare to write a book because I was 'afraid it wouldn't be as amusing as my talk'. These opinions stung me; so sorely, indeed, that I have never been able to forget their verbatim expression. Now, alone and without any conceivable *raison d'être*, I felt hopelessly lost and out of kilter. I needed help, and on the advice of Alix Strachey, I went to Adrian Stephen, a strict Freudian, for psychoanalysis.

In common with many at that time and in that situation, I became fascinated by the subject of psychoanalysis. I read the textbooks, subscribed to the international journal, mastered the jargon and, in the approved manner, grew neurotically attached – and then hostile – to my analyst. Many years later he became a good friend.

Given this preoccupation, it is not surprising that, once Janna was restored to me, I should think that she, too, would benefit from analysis. To this end I made an appointment with Mrs Melanie Klein. She enquired into my circumstances. When she found that I was quite open and without the slightest guilt about my love affairs with women, she turned me away with voluble discourtesy, saying, in atrocious English, that it was I rather than my child who should be treated, and leaving me no time – nor, I have to say, the least desire – to inform her that I had been analysed for over a year. This taught me that some psychoanalysts stand more in need of therapy than others.

While it would be rash to claim that Janna did not suffer damage by our final breaking up – as distinct from the many separations throughout her few years – it is a well-attested fact that parents are human too and go in for all kinds of failings and irregularities which, so long as these do not include lovelessness, neglect or ill-treatment, the child has to live with, and live down, as best it can. In the event, Peter forged a close and tender relationship with Janna, seeing as much of her as, I believe, he would have chosen to do had we remained together. He earned her unalloyed and undying admiration; and, since he did not have to take her to the dentist nor, indeed, do anything that could be disagreeable or boring for her, it was always a treat to be with him.

After living for a short time in a horrible little room in Heathcote Street, I leased a flat on the Foundling Estate: the ground floor and basement, leading into a garden, in Brunswick Square. Apart from the fifty-five minutes of my analysis each day and my study of psychoanalytic literature, I did little with my time. In a desultory way I planted the sooty little garden, believing that nothing could thrive there, in which I turned out to be surprisingly mistaken. For the rest I sought as much outside distraction as possible.

For a few months I was caught in the searchlight of Nancy Cunard's dazzling and alarming personality. She was then about to launch her full-scale public attack upon her mother in a pamphlet entitled *White Lady, Black Man*, bearing on its cover a photograph of Lady Cunard with the Aga Khan. I had set eyes on Nancy once before. That was in Antibes in the summer of 1926 when, trailing gossamer wisps, this alluring creature, in the company of Louis Aragon – a no less decorative figure in matelot rig – dropped out of the skies (more probably had landed off a yacht in the nearby harbour) to dine at dusk by the sea wall in the garden of the Pension Josse where we were then living. While oblivious to all around them, absorbed in one another, this glamorous pair could not fail to excite attention. They stayed on until the skies darkened and Madame Josse came out to place a little lamp on their table. When next I looked, they had vanished, leaving behind an impression of magical beauty.

Once drawn into Nancy's magnetic field, some five years later, I found myself shuttling between London and Paris as part of her entourage: dining with Harold Acton's friends in Lancaster Gate one evening, lunching in Lapérousse with a frightfully peevish Norman Douglas two days later; writing, at Nancy's bidding, the programme notes for her private showing of Luis Buñuel's *L'Age d'Or*, and spending night after night until dawn in some *boîte* or other, of which the most reputable was Le Boeuf sur le Toit.

Nancy Cunard

Having no fixed abode – apart from her house in the French countryside – living, whether in London or in Paris, in some small, decayed hotel room, Nancy transacted all her business in these dimly-lit, smoke-filled night clubs to the sound of loud jazz and when, as a rule, she was pretty drunk. Here, at least, she had a table to write on. Fitfully generous, she would make out a cheque for some needy artist who had suddenly crossed her mind. It would be written on a scrap of toilet paper (perfectly legal and negotiable tender, it seems). She frequently asserted that no one could live on less than £1,000 a year, demonstrating to me, even then, her tenuous hold on reality.

Buñuel's film was not, in her company, my only encounter with surrealism. Apart from being taken to the studios of its practitioners, such as André Breton – where I saw for the first time African sculptures – Nancy in London would put up at Rudolf Stulik's Eiffel Tower restaurant in Percy Street and there one night I found an enormous high-heeled purple satin slipper wedged in the lavatory pan.

This *saison en enfer* had its milder interludes. At her wish we went in my

Austin Seven – a dowdy little black box on wheels which had no style but could conveniently be driven all the way home on the pavement after parties – to a country hotel near Oxford in mid-winter where we were the only guests. An ancient waiter served us in the empty dining-room and we walked to the frozen river, crunching the frosted ground underfoot while she recalled a different season: one of fair lawns running down to the water's edge when she was young. The place was full of nostalgia for her, with associations stretching back to the days of the First World War when, together with Sybil Hart-Davis, she had enjoyed recklessly happy adventures.

It was, on the whole, a bizarre episode for me: my world was turned upside-down, shaken and thrown into disarray. All my previous assumptions appeared open to question; everything I had taken for granted appeared in a new light, the parallax making my values look third-rate and contemptible. It was totally destabilizing; but I was not and never have been fitted for total destabilization. My basically petit bourgeois standards reasserted themselves by slow degrees and, long before Nancy, once she had lost interest in me, was to resort to physical violence, I came to hate and dread the surge of her unpredictable aggression.

Her verbal cruelty when drunk knew no limits. Then her shafts flew like daggers of broken glass, cutting and wounding pitilessly. I have sat by, appalled but too craven to protest, while she humiliated some harmless old queen or insulted the waiter with whom she had been to bed the night before. As her *nostalgie de la boue* dictated that she should surround herself with hangers-on whom she considered her inferiors, she never lacked targets for the exercise of this deadly and repulsive skill.

Some of her worst excesses, of a terrifying brutality, were reserved for her good-natured, patient lover, the black jazz pianist, Henry Crowder. One of her slighter, but utterly shocking stabs at his self-respect sticks in my memory. It was late one night, or early morning, when we had gone back with Bryan Guinness and his wife to their house in Westminster, all of us drooping with fatigue. All, that is, except Nancy who commanded

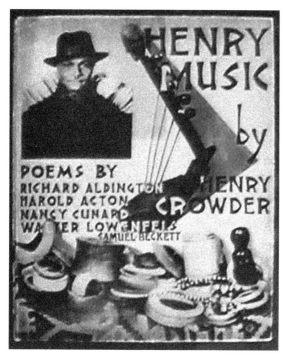

The front cover of Henry Crowder's Henry Music *(published by Hours Press, 1930), and (below) the inscription to Yvonne from Henry in her copy of* Henry Music *which reads as follows: 'How can I frame a sentence or sentences that tell what I feel about Bimbe [Yvonne's nickname]. She is lovely, charming, sweet, beautiful. Of us, and with us.'*

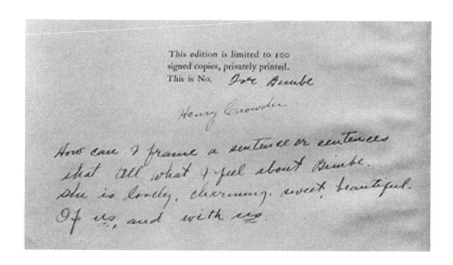

Henry to play the piano and would not let him stop. He rose at last to his feet and, in tones of despair, said to Bryan Guinness: 'I appeal to the master of the house.' 'Everything finds its level in the end,' commented Nancy. And this she could do despite the boldness and sincerity of her campaign for the Scottsboro boys, her fine book *Negro* and her genuine need and affection for Henry.

This bruising experience brought forth in time a short story, called *A Day in a Night-Club* – it was published in *Life and Letters Today* – which did catch a whiff of that unnatural climate, and induced a lasting aversion to the half-cut. It is reproduced in the following chapter.

4

*A Day in a Night-Club**

There is not much light here, but we are growing accustomed to the basement dusk. We look at each other across the unsteady little table – over the top, by stretching our necks, round the side, by ducking, of a flickering lamp which had once a smart red shade, now water pink. It is cold and musty. Your arms are still bare. I go to the cloak-room and find that a tired corner-girl, taken ill, has left her underclothes behind and a pair of fur gloves. I bring these to you and you wrap the cheap silk round your neck, put the gloves on your hands. Far off in the angle of the darkness the waiter is taking off his boots. The trumpeter plays a deep note more than once, then shakes the spittle from his mouth-piece and goes home, on tiptoe, for his children are of school age and below.

You tell me that you are uncertain about your life; that all things change

---

* First published in *Life and Letters Today*, December 1938.

for you, according to where you find yourself. I say: 'We must stay here until everything is decided.'

You agree with me and I fill your glass, which has marks of lipstick not your own and of washing cloth on its surface. You drink a little of the stone-cold red chianti and it runs like iron wires in your guts. I tell you that you are too agreeable; that we should invite others to share you; that nothing seems to matter enough as long as we are alone together and that, in these circumstances, your decisions will be invalid. You agree again. I am pleased and touched by your patience. I invite a group of very small dirty men to sit at our table. They join us and eye us with considerable appetite. I say: 'Do you want any of these?' You shake your head and smile at me with great kindness. I am filled with remorse: you are so flexible and forbearing. The little men say how enjoyable these joints are. They say they have come from a great distance to spend a few hours here. They are unwanted. They have always been unwanted. Their mothers did not want them. They are all mistakes. They prefer, therefore, to travel underground, to work in cellars, to dance in basements. They want to know, in their turn, what brings us here. I reply that we are indecisive: we cannot make up our mind about things. They nod wisely and one of them asks whether we would like to hear a song. I look at you and you say: 'Yes.'

Four of the small men get up and take their positions on the platform. They have heavy, powerful voices, too trained and too resonant for this place and they sing with evident distaste for the words they pronounce. It is a song, written in 1870, exhorting Romans to be a little nicer to Christians, for four male parts.

It has grown dusty in the basement and, the song over, the singers ask us to pay their expenses and let them go. We each drop a half-crown into the coffee pot they hold out and wave them good-bye as, one and all, they go up the stairs, whispering in conspiracy.

'How is it now?' I ask.

'Sadder, much sadder,' you say.

I shake my head in sympathy and you put your hand on mine, stroking me with the cat-fur. I take a book from my pocket and read you a small piece about the Rollright Stones of Chipping Norton. This soothes you and you say you wish to sleep. We move our chairs round the table closer together, you put your head back on my shoulder and close your eyes. When you wake it is mid-day and the waiter brings us each an uncooked trout and a quantity of horse-chestnuts. We divide these eagerly and you say that you think now everything will be decided. I am amazed and watch your fingers, which move so nimbly; but now your gestures falter and you let the conkers fall from your hands. You say it is no use. You prefer indecision. I am keeping you here against your will. That was no part of our bargain. You must be allowed to go. You want to fly, to have your hair cut, to buy a new rug, to see Orleans, to read the *Daily Telegraph*, to roller-skate, to wear an ensemble in yellow, to attend mass meetings, to demonstrate. I say that there will be time for these things tomorrow, even tonight. Let us only have one day here. You say 'Very well', and I am embarrassed by your pliable good temper. I suggest that we talk about the Dolomites, but though you do not refuse, we find that neither of us has seen them and, for an hour, we sit silently.

'It is so hard?' I ask at last. You say it is harder than it has ever been.

'If only there were a telephone here,' you say.

'Let's write down all the people you could call up if there were,' I suggest.

You like this and I get out paper and pencil. You take off the gloves and grow warm and interested as you write. Your face glows, you smile. You make a splendid list and then read it aloud to me. At each name you look at me triumphantly and I lower my head, for every name is that of an enemy. I am utterly defeated and call loudly to the waiter for drinks. He says it is not yet time. I say I will eat as many sandwiches as he pleases, that I am a resident here, that I am a member of the Trades Council, that I will call the police. He says he is an old man now, he has had a lot to put up with in his time and I must wait the same as other people. I protest that there are no other people, that we came here to isolate ourselves from the world and its licensing laws. He must obey me, or I will exercise an unfavourable influence on his entire future. He says he cares nothing for all this: he is a Union man. He says he thinks he can find some dregs left on other tables. Would I like to try them? I say eagerly that I would and then notice that you are frowning disapprobation at me. Nevertheless, though I hold out a hand to stop him, he goes and collects the glasses from other tables. You reprove me for bullying the waiter and say it was an unnecessary display of stupidity and ill-will.

'If you want to blame me, why not do so?' you say. I am very much abashed.

The day wears on. You unwrap the underclothes from your throat and let down your dress. I notice a tiny trickle of blood at the base of your shoulder. You say you are suffering terribly. You bury your head in me and cry. I take out a handkerchief and hold it to your wound. You say it is always the same: patience and suffering. You are happy, you tell me, when you are impatient, goaded, driven by other people, over concerns not your own.

'It is cruel,' you cry. 'You have made me sit here and contemplate my life in sharp wine, ungainly voices, inedible food, your head bowed in persecution-mania; you have made me look at it in silence, in quiet reading, and it is too much. I must stay here forever now. That is the decision for I am quite unfit to face the life I want.'

'How do you know you want it?' I ask.

You tell me again that your life is really full of desire. You recite the things you long for. You speak of rich, loamy soil in gardens which you could cultivate; you speak of running through fields of wet mushrooms to the sea. You say you want things more than anyone else. I laugh a little and say that everything can be got second-hand.

'Outside in the street,' I say, 'there are people telling each other that they want a little grocery place.'

This is quite true and we listen to the voices – one thick and the other sharp – drifting down to us.

'She has everything you can think of,' the sharp voice declares, 'camphorated oil, chocolates, drinks – you know the sort – everything you can think of. Wonderful!'

'Apt,' I comment.

'She can't do nothing in front of me,' is the next remark we hear.

We laugh and turn to each other. I catch your hands and you lean away from me and look clearly into my eyes.

'Of course, I ought never to have asked you to come,' I say, for the tension is released and I am prepared to admit everything and be forgiven. 'It was weakness, not guile. Look, the place is filling up. The day is over. Let's go.'

We reach the street. The lamps are lit, there is a strong evening smell in the air, full of people and petrol and dust. To us it seems fresh. You breathe deeply and look at me.

'It's over,' you say.

'Yes. Our long vigil,' I answer, and add: 'Perhaps now I shall sleep.'

'Yes,' you say very gently, 'go to sleep.'

5

Originally I had met Nancy through that jolly *maquerelle* Wyn Henderson, whose tremendous bulk and bright red hair caused Nancy – for whose Hours Press in Paris she worked – to refer to her as 'the double goldfish'. Wyn was, in fact, very knowledgeable about hand presses and was engaged in setting up some of Ezra Pound's *Cantos* on a fine, antique machine – called the Aquila – in a small workshop off Langham Place. At this point in 1931 she was associated with Desmond Harmsworth and together they planned to start a small publishing business for which the initial capital was provided by Desmond's father, Cecil Harmsworth, the more distinguished younger brother of Lords Northcliffe and Rothermere.

Wyn had read the first chapter of my novel and, with great kindness and greater courage, she and Desmond, backing their fancy, now staked me to the tune of £50 to go away and finish writing the book. That was more than enough to live on in France for, say, six months. Accordingly, I let the Brunswick Square flat and rented a house, known as Les Anciennes Ecoles, in Cassis, filling it with friends and one paying lodger: a young painter of my acquaintance.

Although Janna was now pushing seven, I had no compunction in taking her away from school where, since it was of the progressive persuasion, she had not yet learnt to read or write. I intended to teach her both these skills myself while we were abroad and succeeded beyond my wildest dreams when she could spare the time from pursuing her own carefree life on the beach and in various pâtisseries. On these excursions – wearing on her head as protection from the sun a large and most becoming cabbage-leaf – she was accompanied by Sigrid, a simple, loving girl from Jutland (she would now be called an au pair, I think) who had come with us from England and was enjoying her first taste of life in the south.

It was at this juncture that I learnt that the divorce proceedings were to be heard and I made a dash to London for a few days to give the preposterous evidence required in those days. Apart from this interruption, each morning throughout that spring and summer in Cassis I retired to a tiny back room in the house where, using a packing-case – that housed a family of mice – as a table, I finished writing the novel.

In the autumn, with the collapse of the pound – which marked the end of the British habit of living cheaply on the backs of the French – we went back to London and I delivered my completed manuscript. Wyn and Desmond were under an obligation to submit the books they proposed to publish for the approval of their financial backer, Cecil Harmsworth. He did not approve of my book. In fact, he thought it obscene.

Certainly it was outspoken, judged by the conventions of the day but, although a story of people living in a quite disgusting society, it was couched in such astringent terms of distaste that only an exceptionally prurient imagination could have detected indecency. It had gone to Harmsworth in galley proof and there were passages which had so upset him that he had torn the paper with his savage marginalia. In a bold hand he had written across the top of the first galley, 'I cannot sanction the publication of this book', to which he appended his signature in full. Immediately below, of course, there appeared, in heavy type, the title of this novel. It was called *Nobody Asked You*. So the first thing I did was to have a facsimile made of this delightful juxtaposition of words, had it printed as a Christmas card and sent it to all my friends, wishing them good clean fun.

More seriously I thought about what could be done to save something from the waste of effort and to justify the £50 – and the faith – Wyn and Desmond had invested in me. They had paid for the type to be set up and had bought the paper on which this book was to have been printed. They were almost as put out as I was by their paymaster's veto and conscious that they owed me some compensation for their failure – albeit not their fault – to fulfil their part of the bargain as I had fulfilled mine. They were only too willing to let me have the rights to the type and the paper allocated to my work. Then I bought a very ancient little Citroën deux-chevaux for £5, a large quantity of stamps, some packing paper, string and sticky-backed labels and registered my publishing firm at Companies House as the Willy-Nilly Press. I also took on the publication of *Sanguines* by Pierre Louÿs, translated by James Cleugh, which had been similarly banned, though I did little to promote its sale, I must confess.

My good friend Quentin Bell designed a dust cover for that book and also for *Nobody Asked You*. The latter was made up of two faceless dummies, male and female, wearing eighteenth-century court dress and wigs from the London Museum, placed against a background of the front page of *L'Action française*. Photographed by Barbara Ker-Seymer, a brilliant amateur in those days, it was reproduced for the printer.

As soon as the bound copies came off the press I sent out an advertisement to a few dozen London acquaintances and several names picked at random from the telephone book. As a result a score or so of orders came in. Quentin and I drove about in the Citroën delivering these books, neatly packed and labelled.

Then I had an unmerited stroke of luck: Gerald Gould, at that time the chief literary critic on the *Observer*, suffered a moral crisis over *Nobody Asked You*. On the first Sunday after it came out – 20 March 1932 – he devoted more than a column to it. It raised, he said, 'an aesthetic-ethical problem'. 'Indeed,' the poor man continued, 'I am embarrassed as to what I ought to say . . . If I ignore this book, I do a grave injustice to a very promising and remarkable author; if I recommend it, I do, perhaps, an injustice no less great to many readers who will be shocked and pained by its contents.' On and on he went, in the most titillating way, ending with the words: 'In short, Miss Cloud should have a future as a novelist, but she will not get it – in England – unless she will choose subjects more nearly within the accepted proprieties.'

That did the trick. The next morning droves of rather depressed little men with sacks, sent by every wholesale and retail bookshop and every subscription library in London, arrived on my doorstep. Michael Bernal, who often stayed with us, and Janna, half-naked, as was their wont, but sporting exotic head-dresses, beating drums and blowing trumpets, rushed each time to answer the doorbell. They would then come to me to fetch a pile of books and stagger out to hand them to the startled bagmen.

This went on all day long, day after day, each buyer taking anything up to a dozen copies and sometimes coming back for more on the same day.

After some two weeks of it, the children's enthusiasm having flagged, it struck me that there must be more efficient methods of trading as well as people instructed in their use.

Having had to pay only for the binding and the printing of the dust-jacket, each volume had cost me but a few pence while I was selling it to private customers at the full price of 7/6d and to the book trade at a fraction less, so I was making a huge profit. I had taken note of the fact that the wholesaler, Simpkin Marshall, was among those who sent twice a day for at least ten copies, so I rang them up and had a talk with one of the directors, a Mr Pugh, who was most interested in the Willy-Nilly Press, asked whether we had a traveller in the provinces – a thing of which I had never so much as heard – and was, above all, intensely curious about the author of *Nobody Asked You*. Did we know her? Could we introduce him to her? Yes, we did, we could, and would he like to come for tea? It was a jovial tea-party at which it was agreed that Simpkin Marshall should take over the distribution of the book throughout the country, allowing the Willy-Nilly Press 4/3d on every copy: a fair arrangement which relieved me finally of what had become a most tedious chore.

(At this period Mr Pugh was naturally quite often on the telephone to me and I to him, so it came about that whenever my inquisitive little daughter wanted to know to whom I was speaking, I invariably said: 'My old friend Simpkin Marshall.' It became a family joke, my daughter in later life adopting it as the stock response to parry unwelcome questions about her lengthy telephone calls.)

In a matter of a couple of months the book was sold out and I had made more money on that first novel than on anything I have written since. But then, I did not publish any other of my books myself. However, my riches were largely dissipated in reprinting *Nobody Asked You*, as Mr Pugh had persuaded me to do. This time round I had to pay, of course, for both paper and printing. I have no idea how many copies of that second edition were sold for I had stopped keeping records. However, I never heard that it was remaindered. It has been unobtainable from that day to this.

The episode had various consequences, quite the best of which was that, in the winter of 1932, at a dinner party given by Dorothy Warren Trotter at her house in Maida Vale, I was seated next to a man who told me he was in publishing. 'How interesting,' I said, 'so am I,' and then went on to tell him the story of the Willy-Nilly Press. He found it extremely funny and that was the start of my long friendship with Lindsay Drummond and his wife Bunny. He was, it turned out, one of the senior directors of John Lane The Bodley Head and, shortly after our first meeting, he arranged for his firm to pay me £150 a year – on which one could perfectly well live – in return for the first refusal of any future novels I might write. In the event, though I never managed to earn the advances I had received and was always in debt to them, John Lane did, indeed, publish two further novels of mine.

Moreover, when I fell in love in the late summer of 1933 and wished to join the beloved, who had gone ahead with Janna, in the south of France, Lindsay gave me my air ticket in exchange for the promise of a book to be called *Creditors and how to Escape Them*, the outline and chapter headings of which I roughly mapped out on a tablecloth at the Café Royal – they let me take it away – while dining there with the Drummonds. That book, based upon the accumulated experience, not of poverty, which is something quite different, but of a somewhat reckless hand-to-mouth existence born of false optimism in financial matters, was written as I sat by an open window overlooking the little harbour in the then unfashionable resort of St Tropez. Unfortunately one of those treacherous winds that sweep about those parts lifted the loose sheets of my manuscript while I was out and blew them into the sea. This was on almost my last day and even those pages which I was able to retrieve were illegible. However, on my return to London, by working through day and night, and thanks to a friendly typist who called each morning to pick up the work, I was able to meet the deadline and deliver the work in time for the Christmas market. (It was then September, but in those technologically backward days that was quite the usual thing.) The book was published anonymously and nothing gave me greater pleasure than a review which referred to the author as: 'This prince of debtors in the evening of his life.'

A less welcome consequence of the little flurry of success enjoyed by *Nobody Asked You* was that of being taken up by various distinguished people, only to be dropped rather swiftly, since I proved a dreadful disappointment to them. It is true that I was living in what some people might have thought of as squalor; I was badly dressed and entirely careless of my appearance and, of course, I have always been rather ugly; but those are not reasons enough to account for the cold-douche effect I had upon these admirers of my work.

Sidney Schiff, slapping the volume down on his table, declared: 'Proust would have liked this!' L. H. Myers took me for lunch at the Perroquet restaurant in Leicester Square (I later learned that he owned it) and plied me with delicious food and awkward questions, obviously identifying me with the pitiable heroine of my novel. I had been deeply impressed by Myers's own novel, *The Orissers*, and, as for Schiff, I naturally revered anyone who had not only known Proust but was worthy of adding to his *œuvre*; yet, when I found myself in their company, I was acutely aware that I simply wouldn't do; that I failed to come up to their expectations. It was, so to speak, a case of mistaken identity: they had thought to meet someone different.

6

With the return of spring the children's tortoise awoke. They fed and played with it in the garden, where now I grew lettuces and beans as well as narcissi and other plants just coming into flower. The tortoise, however, was in danger from jets of scalding water cascading from the flat above. I was in something of a dilemma, for that flat belonged to E. M. Forster whose work I so deeply admired that I did not feel I could tell him what to do with his bath water. After some thought I decided to write him a polite letter and posted it. Thereupon he called on me, full of apologies and said he had pinned a notice above his bath saying: 'Do not let water overflow: it upsets the children's tortoise.' He then gave me some sound advice on where I should build a bookcase in my front room and was altogether so gracious and agreeable that I forgave him completely for making some of his female characters of solid wood from the waist down.

One of the people I saw frequently at this time was C. K. Ogden, the inventor of Basic English, at one time the friend of I. A. Richards with whom he collaborated in the writing of *The Foundations of Aesthetics* and *The Meaning of Meaning*. A year older than Peter, Ogden had been up at Cambridge with him where, though not intimate, they had known and liked each other well enough to keep up a desultory friendship. Thus, when he turned up in the south of France, where I first came to know him, he was made welcome in our circle, though he never seemed quite to fit in. I do not think he liked anybody in that circle very much, nor was he accustomed to fitting in; but I found his pale, round face and clever eyes behind large spectacles extraordinarily sympathetic and was pleased and flattered when he took to visiting me in Brunswick Square a few years later.

Nobody ever used his first names (which were Charles Kay). I always thought of him as 'Basic' Ogden, though Janna called him, appropriately enough, Oddikin. He was immensely popular with her. As she sat on his knee, he would say such things as: 'Consider the mountain top, it hums not neither does it spin.' He told her that GHOTI spelt 'fish' (GH as in enough; O as in women; and TI as in nation); he explained to her that he wore three woollen cardigans under his jacket because he felt the cold; and that he had been to India for the day, sailing to Bombay, to which he took an instant dislike, and the next ship back to England. He also taught us a game he called Gaga – derived from Agag walking delicately, backwards – and another where one player had to think of two words that could not, without punctuation, follow each other in any English sentence. The other players had to try to construct such a sentence.

When I could find someone to keep watch over Janna, Ogden took me out to dine at the Escargot in Greek Street where, once this became a fairly regular thing, we always had the same corner table. Afterwards we would go to his house in Montague Street where the staircase was lined with busts of Roman emperors and British statesmen of the nineteenth century, sporting such incongruous hats as bowler, pith helmet, jockey's cap, straw boater and so on. Ogden would whizz about his large, book-lined room in an invalid's wheel-chair and, coming to rest, would hold up a mask and read poetry to me through it. More than once it was 'The Wreck of the *Deutschland*', for he was devoted to Hopkins. He read very well in a slightly rasping voice, with a deep understanding of the verse and none of the declamatory or other mannerisms that can make the recital of poetry so excruciating.

Later, when Rudolf Olden came to England as a refugee and was keen to meet Ogden, he would sometimes join us at the Escargot. It rather spoilt the evening for me, because Olden had a Teutonic way of underestimating other people's intelligence: rather a dangerous thing to do with Ogden. I vividly recall one occasion when Olden was discussing Mach and went to great lengths to explain painstakingly that he did not mean Marx, until Ogden, a very model of patience and courtesy, lost his temper.

When, in 1935, I made my one and only visit to the Soviet Union, Ivy Litvinov told me she was in correspondence with Ogden because she was teaching Basic English to young Red Army servicemen. She had written asking him if he could not provide more suitable material than that put out by his Orthological Institute in Cambridge: in particular, she suggested, exercises that dealt with machines. He had readily responded to this request. 'And guess,' said Ivy, 'what machine he chose: a lawn-mower.'

He offered me the complete thirty-five-volume ninth edition of the *Encyclopaedia Britannica* for £1 if only I would remove it from his house. I gladly did so and it has been my treasured standby ever since. (Once, when Sage spotted it on the shelves of my workroom, he greeted it as an old friend: that was the edition with which he had grown up, he said. He read every word of it up to volume 16 when, coming upon the item 'Metallurgy', he decided this was the subject he wished to study for the rest of his life. He was then about sixteen.)

Ogden was without question the most unaffectedly eccentric person I have ever known and, next to Sage, the cleverest; but the reason I remember him with such affection is that he proved to be also the gentlest and kindest of friends at a time when my world seemed to be falling apart. Precisely because one would not have dreamt of talking to Ogden about one's private affairs or feelings, he was the perfect antidote to preoccupation with self: bracing, immensely knowledgeable, always interesting, even-tempered and aloof, apparently unconcerned with muddled human emotions, impersonal as a tree.

I also saw a good deal of John Rodker – whom we all called Jimmy – at this time. He would go with parties of us to dance-halls and such places. There was also Oliver Strachey with whom one certainly did not go dancing, either to the Mecca rooms or to the Blue Lantern in Ham Yard but, rather, to grand gourmet restaurants, in evening dress.

At the other end of the age scale was John Woodyatt, a friend from Cassis days, still up at Oxford, who often came to Brunswick Square and used to go away with us bringing his gramophone and whole piles of records. He taught me to listen to Brahms (and to distinguish between the good and the bad Brahms); while Sophie Fedorovitch, whom I had first got to know in Paris, came to stay in Great Abington and to join us on many of our holidays.

Those holidays were at Easter and in the summer when, in carloads, we went to a farmhouse or rented a cottage in Cornwall and, occasionally, to

the Isle of Mersea, both East and West – reached by crossing the Strode Causeway over the Pyefleet Creek where Jimmy Rodker had a house. We always took Janna's companions along, including, of course, Michael Bernal, other people's children and also a small niece of mine who, at a very young age, had brilliantly enquired: 'How does the aspirin know which tooth hurts?'

Often on the long drives to the west country, the children, out of bore-dom, would quarrel endlessly over whose bucket was the larger once they had made the discovery that one fitted into the other; or else they did an awful lot of grizzling. As Quentin once put it: 'The children wear their woolly hats, as they are not required to do, in order that they may complain that their woolly hats tickle them.'

We still went for summer weekends to the Meynells in Toppesfield, to swim in the reedy pool and play indoor and outdoor games; we also spent one Christmas there when Sage, incommoded by the blazing log fire, stripped off his clothes and sat stark naked, oblivious to the festivities, reading. In the autumn, staying at Charleston in Sussex, I used to hang about damp woods in the afternoon, trying – and failing – to shoot pigeons with a double-barrelled shotgun that had the kick of a mule.

For one unique adult holiday, I went to Andalucia: to Algeciras, Cadiz, Seville, Cordoba, Granada and Ronda. That was in term-time while Janna was at Bertie Russell's school near Petersfield: a fairly brief interlude for though, like most people, I had been captivated by Bertie himself and his ideas on education and whereas many children – and I think I myself as a child – would have revelled in acres of paper and gallons of paint to play with and unlimited freedom to mess about, it did not really suit Janna's life-style.

At one of my Brunswick Square parties we played a game called Junc-tions. The players had to spot the identity of people who had slept with one another as shown on a chart with lines linking the points: red for heterosex-ual, blue for homosexual connections. No key was provided. Sage won, of course, by recognizing himself as one of the main junctions – a veritable Clapham – with red lines radiating in every direction, so that he was able to solve the puzzle in no time at all.

I was now writing a second and a third novel. On neither of them was the accolade of impropriety bestowed so that, although they received more notice than they deserved, I cannot say that they made a stir nor, for that matter, any money. They did, however, teach me something about writing – which I had thought I knew all about until I got down to it – and a great deal about the necessity to keep disciplined working hours.

It was at this period that I became addicted to the music hall, tracking down and persuading everyone to see my favourite acts. One of these was Nellie Wallace: a scraggy person with buck teeth, a moth-eaten tippet at her neck, a porkpie hat with a single, quivering feather stuck upright in it, bedraggled skirts and huge, dusty boots with upturned toes. This antic figure wandered on to the stage, addressed the audience in a lugubrious way, then sang, executed a grotesque little dance and cut a few incongruous capers, all with an air of unassailable dignity. It was an exquisitely droll performance.

My other favourite was an androgynous trapeze artist who went by the name Barbette. I had first seen his turn in Paris and had followed it ever since wherever it was billed. He would appear to romantic music, cloaked in a shimmering garment, at the top of a grand staircase, a headdress of nodding plumes on a head of golden curls. He descended the stairs with slow steps and, arrived on the stage, discarded the cloak and crown of feathers with graceful gestures, to reveal long, shapely legs and a torso of indeterminate gender clad in an exiguous spangled tunic. With a surprisingly vigorous leap, in strange contrast with his previous delicate, languid movements, he grasped the trapeze and, while swinging wildly to and fro, performed the most spectacular and daring gymnastics. The climax came when, lengthening the ropes of the trapeze, he swung out into the darkened auditorium a few feet above our upturned heads and, as his oscillations grew ever more wild, he plunged headlong forward, abandoning his hold altogether, with arms outstretched as though in terror at this fall into space. At this point someone invariably screamed. At the very last moment, when his death dive seemed unstoppable, he anchored one foot round the rope. It was a brilliant and breath-taking finale which always earned him at least three curtain calls. At the third he would whip off the blond wig, disclosing

a neat head of short, dark hair, with which single gesture he was transformed, on the spot, into an unequivocal male.

Both these acts had a finished, a flawless artistry of a most curious kind.

I gave up the Brunswick Square flat when John Strachey, who planned to be
in America for six months, offered me his flat for that period in Regent
Square. After that I moved into a small house on the corner of Lloyd Street
and Great Percy Street, on the Lloyd-Baker Estate in Finsbury. By then –
for we are now in 1934 – political events in the world – in particular the situation in Germany since Hitler had come to power – began to impinge on
my awareness.

It is true that, when in Mersea, we had listened time and time again to
discredited Weimar politicians making speeches on the radio and knew
what was afoot; but, although I reacted with the ordinary instincts of any
decent, liberal-minded person – as, later, being Jewish and a writer, I was
to be outraged by the anti-Semitic evils and the burning of the books
(events well known to even such ignorant non-political persons as myself)
– the full enormity of the situation was not brought home to me until I
began to meet refugees from Germany, of whom the earliest, in 1933, left
no doubt about the fate that would have awaited them had they not left
their native land.

Little by little my political consciousness was aroused. I became fully
awake to the social scene around me: the misery of widespread unemploy-
ment, the hideous state of malnutrition from which children were suffering; the poverty and degradation in which millions of my compatriots were
forced to live. It was a slow process and, since I was now some thirty years
old, it could be thought a belated one, even overdue.

7

This phase of my development culminated in the summer of 1935 when I
went by sea to the Soviet Union to attend a physiological congress for no
more valid reason than that I had a number of good friends among physiologists and was allowed to tag along with them. The highlights of that experience have never been dimmed. There I saw Pavlov plain, and heard him,
too, speaking in simultaneous translation through earphones. I would
switch about, listening to the speeches in French, in German, in Italian and
marvel at this, to me, novel device.

Late in the light of the long northern evenings in Leningrad I went
bowling down the Nevsky Prospekt in a *droschky* with Norman Bethune or
Frederick Banting, of Banting and Best, whom I knew, of course, by reputation as the discoverers of insulin. I had always heard the names spoken
with veneration and so had visualized Banting as a grave signor, heavy
with years and academic honours, whereas here was a large, jolly, laughing
fellow, still in his early forties, looking like a farmer.

On arrival in Leningrad we had been greeted on the quay with a brass
band, girls with flowers and a red carpet as we stepped off the gangway.
This was all an immense surprise: I had no idea that physiologists could be
regarded as a form of popular entertainment, or as worthy of honorific
treatment; yet as we went about – taken to Peterhof and Detskoe Selo,
driven through the streets in cortege to the Congress Hall – we were
cheered in the streets, people smiled, shouted and waved to us and threw
bunches of flowers into our laps.

As we strolled about the grounds of the former Tsarist palaces, our
hosts, the Russian physiologists, told us the gruesome details of embalming
Lenin's body – not, I gathered, a complete success at the first attempt –
forcibly reminding me that I was not, after all, a member of their profession. The sights in this glorious city included the great paintings – displayed on easels in the Hermitage – from the Morozov and Shchukin

collections. Laboriously I spelt out titles in Cyrillic characters, to come up with the words *paysage*, or *nature morte*, deciphering also the three-letter name of the artist Rouault.

For the second week of our visit we travelled to Moscow. There I swam in the Moskva river and, like everyone else who had come for the congress, waited two or three hours nightly for dinner to be served in the roof restaurant of our hotel which was Edwardian, though the waiters were of an earlier epoch. We were also invited to a tremendous banquet in the white and gold Hall of Columns in the Kremlin. I found myself seated at a table suitably far from the top opposite a number of young Red Army officers who could not speak a word of English. Nevertheless, we held a literary conversation of the greatest interest conducted entirely by gesture. Before each guest there stood a bottle of wine and a bottle of vodka. One of the young men picked up his vodka, placed it in front of me and pronounced the word 'Shakespeare'. He then bowed to me and clapped his hands. I returned the compliment paid to my country by moving my bottle of vodka towards him, bowing, and saying 'Tolstoy'. This went down very well and we continued in this manner, going through Dickens and Turgenev, Byron and Chekhov. I scored a singular triumph by chancing my arm to propose Aksakov which met with great acclaim, after which we got down to wine-bottle reputations: that is, marginally inferior authors, such as the writer they called 'Vells', illustrating their assessment of him by shaking palsied hands. With great daring I advanced Dostoevsky as a mere wine-bottle; to my relief, this was applauded.

It was quite an exhausting game and must soon have come to an end with my severely limited knowledge of Russian writers and total ignorance of the new Soviet literature. On the other hand, my competitors' acquaintance with the English novelists and poets seemed unbounded and – unlike, I could not help reflecting, young subalterns in the British Army – they held opinions on and were prepared to give wine or vodka ratings to Shelley, Charlotte Brontë, Scott, Wilde and Arnold Bennett, though, I have to say, they did not seem to have read anything later and so, like me, were not altogether up-to-date. I was quite thankful when a great voice boomed out on the loudspeaker: a formal speech of great length was being made so, with a note of query I pronounced the word 'Stalin?' to which one of the young men replied by repeating the name and, with forefinger to his temple and furrowed brow, made the motions of writing to indicate that the great man was engaged upon more weighty business.

Then there was my visit to the Litvinov *dacha*. Ivy sent a huge black limousine to fetch me from my hotel and I was speeded in an embarrassingly privileged fashion through the city and out into the countryside, to be met at the great gates of an imposing mansion – not at all what I had supposed a *dacha* to be – opened by an ancient man who took off his cap and bowed low, bending almost to the ground, as we swept in and up the drive.

After lunch with Ivy and her children – her son Misha had that day made his first practice parachute jump – Ivy asked her young adopted daughter to tell the chauffeur to bring the car round at a certain time. The girl went to the internal telephone connected with the remote servants' quarters in this palatial dwelling and gave the message in Russian. Ivy said reprovingly: 'You shouldn't speak to them like that. It's *ancien régime*. You must say, "Would it suit you?" Or, "Is it convenient for you to bring the car round?"' The girl bridled and said: 'Papa doesn't talk like that', to which Ivy retorted: 'What's that got to do with it? Papa *is ancien régime*.' So much for the Foreign Secretary of the Soviet Union.

It was on the journey home, on shipboard, that I reached a crucial turning point in my life. Among the passengers was Harry Pollitt, returning from the Seventh Congress of the Comintern which, in face of the growing menace of Fascism, had overturned its previous – and disastrous – policy of 'class against class' in favour of the Popular Front. I knew Harry slightly, for he had several times come to musical parties at my house to make a short speech at the end of the concert appealing for money from my friends. I had considered that about as much as I could reasonably be expected to do and, though much impressed by what I had seen in the Soviet Union and a committed antifascist, I had not the faintest intention of joining the Communist Party – or any other political party, for that matter – as I knew myself quite unfitted for the responsibilities and duties such membership must entail. Apart from that, I was totally ignorant of Marxism.

During the sunny days at sea I had lengthy discussions with Harry Pollitt. He urged me to join the Party, putting forward arguments that seem to me to have gained rather than lost their force in the half century and more since he advanced them. He did not deny that sympathizers – known then as fellow-travellers – could play a useful part but he insisted that, for such people themselves, it was a thankless role: things could go terribly wrong, there could be the most discouraging setbacks, in any one country at any one time, while in another there might be developments that spelt hope and progress. Isolated, the individual was at a disadvantage in the divided world of our era. It convinced me then; and now, living in the poisoned fog of Thatcherism, knowing whole populations to be suffering inhuman and untold misery in many other parts of the earth, it is heartening to be able to look – against all expectations – to a newly-kindled light in eastern Europe following the advent of Gorbachev.

Though it became modish to deride the thirties' rush into Communism by middle-class men and women as an almost mechanical response to the spirit of the time, my own experience was that of making a difficult and serious decision.

My Communist Party branch – then called a 'cell' – met in the part of a house off the City Road occupied by a building worker and his family. My very first meeting there was more of an aesthetic than a political experience. Either because the electricity bill was unpaid, or the meter not replenished, the room where we sat was lit only by the street lamp outside. It was poorly furnished and uncarpeted, the walls, so far as one could see in the half-light, covered with some dark, scaly material, the whole strangely sad and beautiful scene reminding one of *The Potato Eaters*.

In this setting the treasurer, who was the wife of the building worker, fumbled with the money in a biscuit tin and, after borrowing a pencil, wrote her accounts insofar as she could see to write, while small children, naked from the waist down – who, in my opinion, ought to have been in bed – ran in and out of the room, peeing on the floor. I must say that this turned out to be unique in my later acquaintance with working-class interiors; but at the time I could not know that it was atypical and felt I had entered a whole new world in which I should never feel quite comfortable.

I was also greatly alarmed in those early days by Robin Page Arnot – whom I had met years before playing poker with the Meynells – proposing that I should teach. He even made out a card appointing me as an accredited Party tutor, for which I was utterly unqualified. (I may say, however, that, many years later, I did take some classes for groups of tobacco-workers, railwaymen, engineers and gas-fitters, the last-named lot growing from five men at the start to fifteen, possibly as a result of my having introduced the quite popular idea of everyone reading one or another of the right-wing newspapers for a week and coming to the class with an analysis – and rebuttal – of the political assumptions contained in some report or editorial. This not only enlivened our sessions but it equipped these people to argue with their workmates where before they had felt, so they said, tongue-tied.)

When I first became a Communist I believed that every other Party member understood not only *Empirico-Criticism*, but also thermodynamics and the differential calculus: a conviction not entirely dispelled by a short-lived association with Communist writers' and other 'cultural' groups in which, as the author of a few light-hearted novels, I felt, and was treated as, a complete outsider. It did not take long for me to withdraw from such circles when I realized that my real deficiency was not so much intellectual, as complete ignorance of working-class people and working-class life.

This, I thought, might be remedied. To that end, in a move that proved not at all acceptable in official quarters, I formed a little band of local Party women who, since they were not in full-time work, were willing to give their services to the Care Committee – always crying out for volunteers – at the local school in Risinghill Street. It was a terrible and wonderful experience. For two years or more we sat through the medical examinations of the children, watching as some of them stripped off layer upon layer of the poor, worn, grey cotton shifts that were to be bought in Chapel Street Market for twopence apiece, exposing their rickety little bellies, while even the new intake of five-year-olds disclosed small black milk teeth, already rotten with decay.

These were for the most part the children of unemployed railwaymen. We were expected to visit the homes of those who stayed away from school to find out why. The reasons were always the same: either nits in the hair, the parents prudently refusing to allow their children to mix with others until the parasites had been eliminated, or else a new-born baby in the family when those of school age were needed – and expected – to look after the younger ones during the birth and for a week or so after.

We came to know those families pretty well, dozens of them, living in frightful surroundings: cramped, damp, dilapidated, bug-ridden dwellings whose landlords did nothing whatsoever to keep them in repair; miserable rooms where the out-of-work fathers sat about dejectedly and the mothers – most of whom over the age of thirty appeared to be toothless – fought a losing battle to keep the place clean and the children decent and deloused. Cooking was done on a range in the main living-room so that a hot meal in summer meant stifling the family.

Once a week our small group would lunch together in my house to talk about these families and pool our notes, from which complete and detailed case histories were compiled and entered in a card index. This was material we intended to write up to reinforce the many, more scholarly, studies of poverty being produced at that time. We believed it could awaken, as it had aroused in us, an awareness of how millions of our fellow citizens were living and provide a moving account of a sample of London working-class family life in the years 1936 to 1938.

However, since the district Party leaders frowned upon what they considered a bourgeois enterprise of the slumming kind – an imputation we particularly resented, since what we felt for these families was affection – we abandoned it. The records were destroyed as, in due course, were practically all the houses in and about Risinghill Street when – after, fortunately, the occupants had been evacuated – the entire area was demolished by a landmine in the first great wave of air raids during the war, obliterating the last traces of that scene.

I wandered about what had once been those familiar streets, now so much rubble, and could not but agree with the men cleaning the mess that it was 'a bloody good thing' such wretched homes were no more: 'Not fit for pigs to live in, they weren't,' said the men.

8

This was the period of the Spanish Civil War. We had been on our way, by sea, to Majorca where I had rented a friend's house for the summer holidays, when the war broke out. Plans had to be changed – of necessity, since we had two children with us – and we disembarked at Lisbon to land up in the small seaside resort of San Martinho, never before, I think, visited by English tourists. There we occupied an exceedingly primitive fisherman's cottage – more of a shack, one could say – facing the bay and on the water's edge, which was very pleasant, while we took our meals at a little restaurant nearby where the children adopted the young waiter as their dearest friend.

On my return to England I found antifascist fervour heightened by the tremendous impetus from the open conflict between the Republican government in Spain and Franco's military rebels. Demonstrations, rallies and meetings, indoor and outdoor, took place day after day. Once Britain had declared its policy of non-intervention, turning a blind eye to the troops and armaments being provided by both Italy and Germany to the rebel forces in a hypocritical claim to neutrality, I seemed to spend a lot of my time tramping the streets of London, from Hyde Park to Bethnal Green, or the other way, shouting together with a few thousand others: 'Arms for Spain!'

That autumn was memorable also for the victory of preventing the march of Mosley's Blackshirts from Tower Bridge through the predominantly Jewish quarter of Whitechapel. While the mounted police, whose entire metropolitan strength had been mobilized, repeatedly charged the vast crowd massed at Gardiner's Corner at the junction of the Commercial Road, more to terrorize than to disperse, the neighbouring streets were rendered impassable to horses with mothballs and marbles, others being littered with broken glass, because the inhabitants of the houses lining the street had thrown from their windows every bottle they could lay their hands on. Among the most overwhelming and lingering impressions of that day is the pungent smell of mingled camphor, vinegar, vanilla essence, eucalyptus, kerosene, ammonia, cough syrup, brilliantine, cheap scent and methylated spirit.

For reasons which I do not recall, but which strike me now as slightly demented, I took on the task of organizing a meeting under the title 'Spain and Culture' at the Albert Hall on 27 June 1937 to raise funds for the Basque refugee children in Britain. It was sponsored by the National Joint Committee for Spanish Relief: a body which brought together Labour Party members and Liberals, some rogue Tories and people of no political affiliation, all of whom were so committed to the loyalist cause in Spain that they were even prepared to work together with Communists. This meeting was intended to underline the broad character of that support by bringing to London a platform of internationally distinguished artists and writers from many countries. It was a heavy responsibility and, since I had never undertaken anything of the kind, I did not expect to do it very well: there were so many things that could go wrong. Nevertheless, there was wide and heartening encouragement wherever I turned; I set to work with a will.

In recent years there have been several accounts of this event, but since they were not written by anyone who took part in its organization, I take some pleasure in setting the record straight. The facts are that some people who had promised – and were advertised – to speak, failed to come. The most prominent of these were Picasso and Heinrich Mann. The latter quite simply backed out at the last minute – the telegram announcing his withdrawal was sent twenty-four hours before the meeting – because he believed that the audience would be hostile, even profascist. Why and how he had arrived at that conclusion was inexplicable, for he had not only been reassured by his most trusted advisers that it was not so, but he could have taken heart from the knowledge that his prepared speech had been translated into English and that E. M. Forster had agreed to read it out at the meeting. Mann had asked our committee to pay his travelling expenses from Nice, where he then lived, although it was known that he was obliged to be in Paris at about the same time. While there is no record of our having refused, it is most unlikely that we could have met such a charge upon our meagre finances, which may perhaps have decided him to stay away.

With Picasso the matter was entirely different. When we went to Paris – which was quite often, for many of our painter friends were then busily engaged in decorating the walls of the British section of the Peace Pavilion for the International Exhibition to be held there that summer – Quentin called on Picasso at his studio and found him totally engrossed in making the preliminary drawings for his *Guernica*: the great and famous picture that became the sole exhibit in the Spanish pavilion.* Picasso had accepted our invitation to address the meeting and, up until the last moment fully

---

* By that time we knew the word Guernica. We had yet to learn how to pronounce Lidice and Oradour, Treblinka and Auschwitz, Hiroshima and Nagasaki.

intended to come. His plane was booked, all was arranged, with Quentin standing by to accompany him but, when the time came, he could not be induced to leave his work.

To compensate us for his staying away, Picasso not only signed the letter – more in the nature of a manifesto – that we sent out in advance to invite support, but he gave Quentin one of that day's drawings, dated 7 May 1937 and numbered twenty-five, which he dedicated to the mothers and children of Spain. He said we could use it in any way we wished and, in the event, we reproduced it on the cover of the programme for the meeting, while the original was framed and auctioned by Wilfrid Roberts, the Liberal MP, who held it aloft and moved among the audience, inviting bids. It fetched a very large sum.

Against these two disappointments – for both names had been given publicity and would obviously have attracted people not otherwise involved in the campaign – was the unheralded presence of Paul Robeson. He was in Moscow then and had promised to record a song recital there if we could arrange for it to be transmitted to the Albert Hall on the night.

Now this presented a great difficulty: the secretary to the management of the Hall, Reginald Askew, refused to allow the installation of sound equipment without the consent of his Council which would not be convened until a date long after the meeting. Unable to accept this ruling, we asked the Duchess of Atholl, who had agreed to take the chair on 24 June, to sign a letter to C. B. Cochran, the Manager of the Albert Hall and final arbiter in such matters, then in New York, begging for permission to let Robeson be broadcast, to which he replied by telegram: 'Have instructed secretary.' A public address system was then laid on. The work was barely completed in time; and was no sooner in place than we learnt, with mixed feelings, that Robeson had arrived in London and intended to be present on the platform. We need not have had the smallest regret at this turn of events, for the splendid man, as good as his word, had indeed recorded a programme of songs for us before leaving Russia, but the reception was so bad, the crackle and thunder that emerged through the Tannoy system drowned his voice. After a few moments of this howling failure, we switched off, Robeson rose and, to extravagant applause, began to sing. Nor would the audience allow him to stop: to ever greater encouragement, he went on and on, making a glorious finale to the proceedings and, it could be said, saving the day.

I had hardly foreseen that the evening would turn out so well. Before the meeting began, hovering behind the scenes, I had been wringing my hands and wailing, so that Isabel Brown, who was to make the fundraising appeal during the interval, said to me: 'You're no good; you've got no fortitude.' This was unkind but only too true. The whole organization of this great meeting was pitifully amateurish. It could scarcely be otherwise since I was the inexperienced and unsuitable chairman of a small ad hoc committee of willing and enthusiastic volunteers, similarly unqualified, with little or no resistance to setbacks and reverses such as we should inevitably meet. However, the cause we were championing made an appeal to a most varied and distinguished public.

More than half a century later it is interesting to recall the names, still resonant today, of a few of those out of the many who explicitly agreed to appear on the platform, to lend their names, to sign the letter of appeal, to attend the meeting in person or otherwise associate themselves publicly with the occasion. Here are some two dozen of them. Lascelles Abercrombie, W. H. Auden, Philip Noel Baker, Arnold Bax, Vanessa Bell, J. D. Bernal, Patrick Blackett, John Boyd Orr, Havelock Ellis, Gwen Ffrangcon-Davies, Barbara Hepworth, Lancelot Hogben, Julian Huxley, Rose Macaulay, Desmond McCarthy, Naomi Mitchison, Henry Moore, Paul Nash, Ben Nicholson, Harold Nicolson, Stephen Spender, Sybil Thorndike, Sylvia Townsend Warner, Rebecca West, H. G. Wells, Ralph Vaughan Williams, Virginia Woolf.

For me the Basque children were by no means the faceless recipients of charity: I had spent some days, together with my schoolgirl daughter and a gifted young Indian photographer, in the camp at Stoneham, near Southampton, where the 4,000 children, mostly from Bilbao, were temporarily living in tents upon their arrival here. It had been an intensely moving experience, coinciding as it did with the news of the bombing of their home town and, immediately upon my return to London, I wrote a short book – *The Basque Children in England* – illustrated with photographs by Edith Tudor-Hart and my Indian friend, the proceeds of the sale to go to the refugee fund. (It is a matter for laughter now, but at the time I was incensed because, while both the photographer and I were glad to give our professional services in aid of the children, our rather wealthy publisher sent me a bill when the little book – not, as might have been foreseen, a bestseller – had failed to meet the costs of its production.)

Only a few weeks ago, and because I had just had the pleasure of meeting one of the 'Basque children' – now a grandmother – here on a visit from Madrid, I managed to get hold of a copy of the book for her. She had the most vivid memories of the camp; what was more, she herself, then at the age of twelve, figured prominently in one of the photographs in the book. Before I gave it to her I had the curiosity, after fifty-four years, to flip through it. To my surprise I found it quite readable though of only marginal historical interest today.

For a short time I acted as the secretary to the committee of the English section of writers in an organization called 'For Intellectual Liberty' which met at the William Ellises' beautiful rambling old Romney's House on Hollybush Hill in Hampstead. Among the active members of that committee I recall only the names of Cecil Day-Lewis, Goronwy Rees and Rose Macaulay. The last, invited to represent the section at an international conference in Paris, declined to go and, offering to pay all the expenses, proposed that I should attend in her stead to report back to the committee, which I did.

At this time we had holidays in Merioneth – where we camped, together with a family of Penroses, and cooked delicious meals in a great cauldron on an open-air fire – and in Northumberland. There we lived in a cottage in the tiny one-street village of Sharperton on the swift-flowing Coquet river. In the summer we would swim under a waterfall and in the still pool below it; in harvest time I helped to sickle the little cornfield belonging to an old woman no longer able to do it by herself; and there we sometimes lived off the land, eating mushrooms, bilberries, blackberries and the occasional rabbit caught by our little dog Hinny. I have indelible memories of Alnwick and Craster; Housesteads, Bamburgh and Thropton; of the Salmon Pub at Holystone, the ruined Vanburgh mansion at Seaton Delaval; the Hexham cattle market as well as the leaping and wrestling at the Autumn Feast in Bellingham.

In the summer of 1938 members of the Artists' International Association went as a party to the Ile de Ré off La Rochelle. Everyone contributed to a great wall-painting – which one of our number persisted in calling a 'muriel' – in the restaurant where all met to eat while lodged in houses dotted about the island. On our journey home it was thought that the diesel train to Paris, with its small number of carriages, had been reserved for us, only to find that, through some form of mismanagement, it had been double booked and, at the first stop, an equal number of French passengers got in. There was great indignation on all sides but, as the train sped on and there was plainly going to be no relief, we rather ungraciously took our enormous children on our laps, while some of the men gave up their seats to the Frenchwomen until a degree of civil if not cordial relations was established and everyone made the best of it.

9

The little house in Great Percy Street was large enough to put up a succession of refugees, more particularly when Janna went to the Dragon School in Oxford (where Peter knew the old headmaster, Lynham). I was able to meet the fees at the Dragon and, later, to send her to Frensham Heights because by this time – in 1934, in fact – my father had entered into one of those seven-year covenants undertaking to provide for his granddaughter's education.

During term-time refugees would stay in my house as a touchdown point on their arrival here, leaving when they had found more permanent quarters. One of these short-lived migrants left me – unwittingly – a permanent legacy. He was a strange fellow whose behaviour during his brief stay disquieted me. In the first place, he would go away for two or three days at a time telling me on his return that he had made a raid into Germany to contact the anti-Nazi resistance fighters. I thought it odd, not to say unwise, that this particular man, with the most pronounced Jewish features of anyone I had ever seen, should have been chosen as a courier. Surely he must endanger not only himself but everyone he met on such expeditions.

Another thing was that, before leaving on these trips, he always asked me to keep in a safe place and lock up a packet which, he said, contained passports. How and why he should be in possession of a collection of passports bothered me; and, although I should not have dreamt of opening the parcel, I could not suppress my curiosity, nor my uneasiness. When, without consulting me or asking my permission, he arranged for certain letters to be sent to my address and in my name, but bearing a special mark – a code – on the envelope indicating that they were meant for him, I felt things were getting out of hand.

By this time he had found other accommodation, and I was glad to be rid of him; but he called every few days to pick up these mysterious letters; and on one such visit he said he must have a serious talk with me and then, to my alarm, broke down and wept. In a terrible state of distress he told me that he faced expulsion from the German Communist Party which would deprive him of every reason to go on living. He insisted that he must get to Paris to plead with the leadership in exile, which had decreed this awful fate, but he had not the means to travel. Would I give him the money? If he had not the chance to put up a defence, if he did nothing to reverse this frightful sentence, he would kill himself.

Fortunately, by this stage, I at last recognized my total ignorance and incompetence to deal with such matters as secret journeys into what amounted to enemy territory, fishy passports, false addresses and the like. I had begun to feel such mistrust, and even horror, of this man and his activities that I made up my mind to go to Party headquarters to seek advice from someone with the political experience I lacked.

I was told to see comrade Bob Stewart and directed to his room. As I opened the door, he looked up and said: 'Come in, lassie. I've been waiting for you.' This greeting struck terror in me, yet so began a friendship that was to last, unbroken, until he died at the age of ninety-six. At that first encounter, Bob heard me out in silence, though, as he nodded his great head every now and again, it became clear that he already knew most of what I was telling him. At the end of my recital I put to him the heart of my dilemma: should I or should I not furnish this man with the means of going to France to plead his case? If I refused, his death could well be on my hands. Bob would not advise me, beyond saying that the man knew perfectly well that his presence in Paris could not influence the decision one way or another. Yes, Bob conceded, he might or he might not commit suicide though, he hinted plainly, I had given the man ample proof of my gullibility; but, however that might be, it was entirely up to me to decide what to do.

Never before had I wrestled with a moral predicament of such gravity. All that night I lay awake trying to resolve it. By the morning I had come to a decision and when the man kept his appointment with me later that day I refused him the money. He became extremely abusive, accusing me of being, like all politically illiterate bourgeois individualists, subservient to the orders of the Party hacks: an ignorant, slavish, contemptible ninny, useless in the Party. Then I knew I had reached the right decision. It was a crucial and momentous one, that bridged the gap between accepting a theoretical analysis of society and a total commitment to striving for social change. (In parenthesis, I should relate that my erstwhile lodger very soon emigrated to South America where, far from killing himself, he lived an active political existence.) However this episode strikes the reader – and it even strikes me – as one of outstanding sectarianism in the light of today's developments, at the time it marked a most important stage in my personal and political development; and I would not have it otherwise, for hindsight is all very well, but in political life there is no living backwards.

Bob, who had been a joiner and cabinetmaker in Dundee, was a foundation member of the British Communist Party in 1920. He and his wife, Meg, became honoured guests in my house shortly after that first meeting and we spent many Sundays visiting them. With Meg's death in the early 1950s and his advancing age – for he was over sixty when I first put my head round his door – his life took a melancholy turn, not made happier by retirement and the gradual onset of blindness, so that I visited him as often as I could and he would come to us on Christmas Day. At one point I took him to see an ophthalmologist who told him that his eyes had done their work and there was no cure for his failing sight.

He was always resolutely cheerful and uncomplaining, put on so brave an air of being in good spirits, took so lively an interest in what was happening in the world and, though unable to read the newspapers, held so clear-headed a view of events as they unfolded (including, in 1968, when he was over ninety, telling young people – in their sixties – that the invasion of Czechoslovakia by Russian tanks, was a terrible mistake), that it was an education to be in his company and a privilege to be his friend. As his strong body lost some of its resilience, and to his blindness were added other infirmities, the Party arranged at considerable expense for him to live in a kindly if rather slapdash home for old people. There I went to see him every week during his last years and did so almost to the end though, as ill luck would have it, when he died at the age of ninety-six in 1973, I was away on holiday.

Bob, the wisest of old men and also the most generous and great-hearted, was the first person I had ever known who was entirely good, all through. I could not have had a better teacher. His was the permanent legacy my shifty lodger left me.

My last refugee was John Heartfield who, when I met him some years later at a party, rushed towards me across a crowded room with arms outstretched and, never having entirely mastered the nuances of the English language, screamed: 'She was my first woman in England!' During his short stay with me – and this was the reason why it was short and also why he was the last refugee I housed – I made preparations for leaving Great Percy Street. Johnny helped me sort the books for packing. My father had offered to stand as guarantor to enable his sister Florentine and her entire family to leave Germany and come to England and I was moving out so that these ten people could be accommodated there.

I took a flat on the first floor of a house in Chalcot Square – formerly St George's Square – near Primrose Hill. (I seem often to have lived in a corner house, which is nice as it faces two ways. This one fronted both the Square and Berkley Street.) The flat was shaped like the prow of a ship and was too small to offer hospitality to refugees. The rent, I remember, was 35 shillings a week until the outbreak of the war when, because I kept it on despite being evacuated with my job, it was reduced to 27/6d.

My aunt Florentine, her husband Sigmund, their two daughters whose own husbands had been interned in Dachau for short periods, and the four grandchildren managed somehow to squeeze into the little Finsbury house, one room being turned into a dormitory for the three boys, while the one girl shared her parents' bedroom. The place was completely, if cheaply, refurnished for them by my parents whom I had never before liked and respected so much as for this move of pure benevolence.

The missing member of that family was my cousin Hermann. The plump little boy of my childhood memories had grown up to become a gifted singer and was engaged by the Paris Opéra when the war broke out.

Arrested as a German Jew and, after the Occupation, transported first to North Africa to work with other prisoners on building a railway and then, with health and strength destroyed, sent to Auschwitz, he perished there, as was ascertained only many years later.

When she arrived here, my aunt Florentine was totally blind and deaf. In her old age she had grown very stout, though she presented not a gross but a truly majestic figure. She had a measure of noble beauty and great dignity, with that air of complete serenity owed, I am sure, to the unwavering devotion of her husband and her children who adored her and had made her modest, undemanding life one of perfect happiness. Her mind was still so alert that, despite her handicaps, one had only to start spelling out a word on her hand for her to nod, smile brightly and reply, having fully understood.

The children were aged between nine and fourteen. The two young sons of my cousin Eva had suffered cruelly before leaving Germany. Forbidden to swim in the river with other boys and told they would pollute it, stoned in the street and insulted by schoolfellows and masters alike, the younger child, then six or seven, would rush home to his mother to collapse in a storm of tears, while his older brother – a large, handsome, fair-haired, blue-eyed boy whose looks, inherited from his grandfather, caused him to be singled out in error by a visiting Nazi before the whole school as a model 'Aryan' type – retreated into himself, becoming silent and withdrawn. I was particularly moved by this clever, morose, difficult youngster, who wrung my heart. I loved him dearly.

Though not of a religious disposition at that time, the parents, unable to endure their children's persecution, removed them from the local school and sent them as boarders to a Jewish seminary in a neighbouring town. There they suffered the terrible experience of witnessing their teacher seized by storm troopers who invaded the classroom and, under the eyes of the horrified children, beat and kicked the man into unconsciousness.

The only real trouble in this otherwise harmonious household of three generations was that my eldest cousin's husband was an Orthodox Jew who insisted upon the strictest observances, including a kosher diet with separate utensils for meat and milk dishes: no easy regimen when the needs of six others have to be catered for and their meals prepared in a very small kitchen. However, in due course, the old people moved to the Midlands where the Orthodox couple cared for them until they died, whereupon they and their children emigrated to America.

As for my cousin Eva's family, who remained in England, I was able to find work for her husband and, when the war came, to ensure his exemption from internment, and that of her elder son, now fifteen, by getting them drafted into the reserved occupation of forestry, while she herself became housekeeper to a large group of refugee foresters – mostly Czechs – in the Cumbrian village of Caldbeck. Meanwhile the younger boy, evacuated with his Finsbury school, joined his family there for the holidays. At the end of the war I housed them for a while in London, until they found their feet, homes of their own, good jobs, their way back to the faith of their practising forefathers, material prosperity and no further need of me.

It was Margaret Mynatt, the member of a small team of voluntary relief workers, who had asked me if I could give hospitality to a 'very special refugee'. This was John Heartfield. His advent was memorable for a number of reasons. In the first place I was told he would show up at my house on the day in October 1938 and at the very hour when some 100 International Brigaders were arriving back from Spain. They included those friends of mine who had not been killed there and I had dearly looked forward to meeting them at Victoria Station where a tremendous reception awaited them. As it was, I had to stay at home in expectation of this special refugee. In vain: he did not appear, so that I took rather a dislike to him before we ever met. I was told he would certainly arrive on the next evening; but he did not. So it went on from day to day for the best part of a week. Exactly how he had managed to miss one flight after another I never found out; but, when I got to know him – and to like him enormously – I was not in the least surprised, neither by his missing planes nor yet being unable to explain how or why.

When, at last, Margaret Mynatt brought him to the house – a very small man with bright blue eyes and a shock of pale yellow hair standing on end, which gave him a startled look – he was obviously exhausted. He refused all offers of food and, upon being shown to his room, said he wished to go to bed. It was barely eight o'clock, but we left him at once and I heard him turn the key in the lock, though no one would have dreamt of disturbing him.

The next morning I went upstairs with a breakfast tray at about nine. I knocked gently, but there was no response, so I went away to repeat the performance an hour or so later. Still I could get no reply. This went on at intervals until, by noon, when I rapped very loudly indeed on the door and also shouted his name, I became seriously alarmed. I knew he had but recently come out of a concentration camp and it struck me that perhaps he had been through experiences so ghastly as to have driven him to take his own life.

In something of a panic I rang up Margaret Mynatt and begged her to enlist the aid of a strong man and come at once to break down the door of the room where her special refugee was lying, possibly dead. She came speedily with a stalwart German friend, Heinz Schmidt, who did, indeed, force open the door and there we discovered Johnny sleeping like a baby, impervious to the frightful noise made by our breaking in. It was, of course, his first peaceful sleep, without fear, for many a long and dreadful night.

We stole quietly out of the room, Heinz Schmidt departed and until, at last, Johnny awoke, Margaret and I sat talking. This was not the first time I had met her, for she worked in the office of the Antifascist Relief Committee in Litchfield Street which had been my headquarters in the early days of organizing the Albert Hall meeting. I had not taken to her. She showed not

Margaret Mynatt, 1938

the slightest interest in what I was doing and seemed obsessed by some evil German Communists of whom I had never heard – and did not specially want to hear now – who had evidently driven her into a state of persecution mania. Now, however, quietly talking, she seemed eminently sane, very interesting and pleasant. So began my friendship with the one who, some eighteen months later and in the most unexpected circumstances, was to become my partner and companion until the end of her days.

I O

Margaret's life had never been easy. Born in Vienna in 1907 and christened Bianca, she was the second daughter of an Austrian Jewess of Czech

descent and an English father, the sixth of the thirteen children of a Blackpool cobbler by his two marriages.

The grandfather, John Mynatt, born out of wedlock in 1825, did not do
much cobbling because he was addicted to music. What he liked to do was
to play the fiddle and how he supported his vast family is not at all clear,
though it is known – and understandable – that they lived in considerable
poverty. One day a violinist in the local theatre orchestra fell ill and John
Mynatt was invited to fill the gap. His fate was sealed: he set himself to
master every instrument, in case some player or other should need replac-
ing at short notice. He had also, of course, to learn the orchestra's entire
repertory, so that he should never be found at a loss. What was more, he
'put the children to music', as his descendants expressed it, as soon as they
could cradle a small violin under the chin or reach a keyboard.

With the sole exception of Margaret's father, none of them achieved
professional status; but one and all, through the generations, shared this
passion, so that no one's occupation was described without reference to his
or her musical accomplishment. Thus: 'tram-driver, cellist', 'carpenter,
French horn', 'waitress, mezzo soprano', and so forth; while those without
any marked executant skill had season tickets to the Hallé concerts, made
occasional forays to London from their provincial centres in order to go to
the opera in Covent Garden, and spent their holidays, alternately, in
Bayreuth and Salzburg, for their tastes were catholic. This propensity was
passed on – perhaps symbiotically or by contagion – to their spouses, so
that the widow of one who, like his father before him, had been a shoe-
maker and violinist, augmented her pension by taking in lodgers, advertising for them at the university but specifying that, whatever might be the
nature of their academic studies and according to her current requirements,
they must be viola players or flautists.

Margaret had no contact at all with her father's family until, one day
some time in the 1950s, she found herself in Manchester with time on her
hands and had the curiosity to look up Mynatt in the local directory. There

she came upon the entry of a hardware shop kept by someone of that name. She decided to find out if this could be her cousin Leonard whom she had last seen when she was four years old and he of much the same age.

The shop was a modest one in Moss Side. It had an old-fashioned tin-kling doorbell which, as it announced Margaret's entrance, brought from the rear of the shop an assistant of – despite her spectacles – distinctly Wagnerian looks with blond plaits wound about her head. Margaret asked to see Mr Leonard Mynatt, whereupon the assistant said he was out but that she was fully able to deal with any business that concerned him.

'Oh, it doesn't matter,' said Margaret and was about to leave when, at the door, she turned and said: 'Could you perhaps tell me whether Mr Mynatt's father was a watchmaker who played the clarinet?'

With one hand the assistant clutched the counter for support and with the other at her throat in a highly dramatic gesture, she asked in a strangu-lated whisper: *'Who are you?'*

When all was revealed, it turned out that this was Leonard's little sister, Amy, of whose very existence Margaret had not known. Amy now ran to the back of the shop, which evidently led to private living quarters, shriek-ing as she disappeared: 'Mother, mother, Bianca has come back', quite as though this long-lost cousin had gone missing for a few hours.

A little, elderly woman now emerged and, with tears running down her cheeks, embraced Margaret, crying: 'My dear child, I'm so happy we've found you at last!', which was absurd, since they had done nothing of the kind; she had found them. Naturally they could not know that she had not used the name Bianca for the past twenty years or more.

Margaret's little aunt Emily, beside herself with excitement at this dénouement, shortly afterwards invited the entire Mynatt clan, scattered about Lancashire and North Wales, to meet the newly recovered niece and cousin. It was an enormous, slightly eccentric, proletarian family that went in for self-respect and doing a fair day's work for a fair day's pay. As all these people sat placidly about the high-tea table, Margaret felt she could not impose upon their solid good nature in accepting her as one of themselves without letting them know that she was a Communist. Her announcement met with a momentary silence while the information was digested and then her aunt Emily said: 'Well, dear, if you're a Communist, I'm sure you're a good, hard-working one.' Everyone nodded and murmured agreement. After the tea there was, by general consent and in deference to Margaret's Viennese associations, a lengthy Mahler recital on records.

Margaret's father, John Charles Mynatt, known as Uncle Jack to his innumerable nieces and nephews who venerated him for having succeeded in making music his career, had been picked up as a young boy busking in Blackpool and adopted by a middle-aged man of somewhat mysterious antecedents and a decidedly louche appearance – as the one contemporary photograph testifies – who took him abroad, taught him manners and placed him with some of the finest teachers of music in Europe, including the great Leschetizky in Vienna, so that, at a fairly early age, the young man began to enjoy some success as a concert pianist, becoming sufficiently popular to be invited to perform at the court of Franz Joseph, where he was a general favourite. He then changed his name to Giovanni Carlo Minotti and married his landlady's daughter, because she was pregnant. He did not, however, renounce his British nationality and Margaret's birth – as that of her elder sister – was registered at the British Embassy and she was baptised in the Anglican Church.

As Bianca Minotti she was known to everyone until, at the age of twenty-seven, she came to England – a British subject who could not speak the language – when she sensibly used her real name, Mynatt, and called herself Margaret as less unusual. Her earliest memory was of sitting under a grand piano while her father practised the Schumann A minor concerto. Her next, while still a tiny child, was of rushing out into the street to find someone, anyone, who would stop that father beating his wife. Before she was five years old, after many such incidents, terrifying to the children, he deserted the family for good; which explains why Margaret had not shown the least desire to get in touch with his family when she came to England.

She looked upon her father as a parasite who, since leaving her mother, had lived with and on rich women, one of whom he eventually married. Such was her reluctance to credit him with the smallest virtue or distinction that she flatly denied her cousin Amy's claim that he was the author of serious if incomprehensible books on music. On one of her opera jaunts to London, when she stayed with us, Amy insisted that Margaret should go with her to the British Museum Reading Room and there, sure enough, were the entries: *Die Geheimdokumente der Davidsbündler: Grosse Endeckungen über Bach, Mozart, Beethoven, Schumann, Liszt und Brahms* by Giovanni Minotti, published in Leipzig in 1934, and preceded in 1927 by a lengthy article in *Zeitschrift für Musik* entitled 'Die Enträtselung des Schumannschen Abegg-Geheimnisses'. To satisfy her curiosity Margaret obtained copies of these works and, as she could not understand them, she asked Hanns Eisler to read them and tell her whether they amounted to anything more than the outpourings of a pretentious crank. Eisler, however, reported that they were not without interest or genuine scholarship, albeit of an esoteric nature.

With Minotti's departure the household, an entirely female one, was ruled by a doting Jewish grandmother of great spirit who came from Bohemia, and an equally devoted, if slightly dispirited mother who, during the difficult years of the First World War, when food was hard to come by, displayed a good deal of courage and enterprise, not to mention a certain unexpected cunning, to feed her small daughters. These children were not only jeered at and insulted in the street – their peers, ludicrously, yelled 'Booldog' at them – but, as enemies, they were not allowed to attend school. They suffered severely from the food shortages, despite their mother's efforts, Margaret, in particular, being so underweight when the war ended that, at the age of eleven, she was among those selected for rehabilitation in Denmark and Holland by a British relief organization of

Quaker doctors on a mission to Austria. Nevertheless, the damage done by malnutrition in those critical years of growth had so undermined her constitution that all her adult life, though she disdained fussing about bodily ills, she was liable to go down with one ailment or another, generally written off by the omniscient medical profession as hysteria, or some other psychological disorder.

She grew up with marked musical gifts. Indeed, at the age of fifteen she went in for and won a scholarship to the Vienna Conservatoire where she hoped to be trained as a pianist, an ambition frustrated when her mother decided that she could not afford to let her take up the scholarship, since it would have meant years of a fairly high standard of subvention. What was more and final: in order to eat, the piano had to be sold. Thus, at sixteen, Margaret went into an office to do the most boring job and, from that time on, in a few good but mostly bad times, she supported not only herself but also her mother until Mrs Mynatt's death in London in 1948.

In her late adolescence, her one great solace was singing in the choir under Bruno Walter. This was still the period of light-hearted café life in Vienna, about which Margaret had such tales as that of the regulars who were so familiar with each other and each other's jokes that they gave those jokes numbers and had only to shout out 'twenty-four' or 'fifty-eight' for the whole company to be convulsed with laughter. Shortly, however, like all the other Viennese who had not succumbed to the local infection of levity and lethargy, Margaret was lured by the *Drang nach Westen* to Berlin. That was in 1929 when she was twenty-two.

As a cub reporter on the *Rote Fahne*, for by now she had joined the Communist Party, she fell almost at once into the stimulating environment of Bertolt Brecht's circle. This was the moment when, flushed with the success of the *Dreigroschenoper*, he and his companions were enjoying their first taste of affluence. It went to their heads. They bought motor cars they did not know how to drive, cabin-trunks and other items of expensive luggage with no prospect or intention of travelling and, in general, indulged

*The Brecht circle at a
1931–32 New Year's Eve
party in Berlin (back row
left to right: Margot von
Brentano, Gustav Glück,
Valentina and Alfred
Kurella; front row:
Walter Benjamin, Carola
Neher, Margaret
Mynatt, Elisabeth
Hauptmann)*

*Yvonne (centre)
at Buckow with
Elisabeth
Hauptmann
(left) and
Helene Weigel*

Elisabeth Hauptmann

At Buckow with
Helene Weigel

*With John Heartfield and his wife (top) and with Helene
Weigel at Buckow*

every fantasy of the opulent life conceived by those accustomed to being hard up. Their living conditions improved beyond measure; though, according to Margaret, the newly acquired luxuries did nothing to overcome Brecht's reluctance to wash. He would sit, reading, in the well-appointed bathroom, agitating the water with one hand to make the sounds of vigorous ablutions and, after a suitable interval, would come out, unwashed. It was a close-knit circle of young people who not only collaborated but ate, slept, went about and away on holiday together, identifying so nearly with one another that even the interior decoration of their living quarters was indistinguishable: you could hardly tell in whose apartment you were save that it was unmistakably that of some member of the Brecht entourage.

In common with almost everyone she knew, Margaret took part in the crowd scenes of her friend Slatan Dudow's *Kuhle Wampe*. She also went as a suppliant to the Salvation Army which resulted in a series of articles on its methods and finances and provided the research for *Die heilige Johanna der Schlachthöfe*, that Brecht was then writing.

Her most intimate friend among that lively crew was Elisabeth Hauptmann, Brecht's earliest and most enduring collaborator, a woman of singular charm and great erudition, who remained close to Margaret all the days of her life, throughout the vicissitudes of the Nazi era, when the two were exiled in different parts of the globe, and the separation that followed Elisabeth's return to Berlin after the war and Margaret's permanent domicile in London. That circumstance, however, led to our spending some Christmas and summer holidays in the German Democratic Republic and thus to my meeting many of Margaret's old friends who had returned from emigration. One of these was a woman who had telephoned on the day after the Reichstag fire to ask Margaret, then packing up to flee the country, whether she had a recipe for making orange marmalade as she had a lot of oranges. For years and years this request had nagged at Margaret's conscience: what had been meant by 'oranges'? Were they documents that had to be destroyed? People who must be hidden? In what kind of dire trouble was this friend? Coming face to face with her in Berlin more than fifteen years later the puzzle was solved: she had just been sent a crate of oranges from Israel.

We stayed for weeks on end with Helene Weigel in her Buckow house on the lake; best of all, over the years, we had the chance to see most of Brecht's great plays, as well as many of his shorter works and those by other writers staged by the Berliner Ensemble's Theater am Schiffbauerdamm. We also went to some of Walter Felsenstein's magical Komische Oper productions.

Upon Brecht's death in August 1956, when we happened to be near Dieppe, we dashed across Europe in response to urgent telegrams to attend the memorial meeting in his theatre, where the first two rows of the stalls were occupied by ladies in deepest mourning. (Like Jonathan Wild, according to Defoe, Brecht had 'left several widows behind at his exit; whether they go by his name or not'.) Twelve years later, in 1968, when Brecht would have reached his seventieth birthday, an impressive *Fest* to celebrate his life and work was held in Berlin. It drew people from every country and all five continents, the great and fascinating variety of performances reflecting the tremendous extent of Brecht's influence upon world theatre. It is rather melancholy to reflect that the British contingent – consisting of Jocelyn Herbert, John Willett, Margaret and me – was the smallest present.

When Elisabeth Hauptmann died in 1973 Margaret inherited some of her Brecht royalties so that, for the first time since the age of sixteen, she was not wholly dependent upon her own efforts. It was in her nature to squander this unexpected wealth in reckless generosity, though, sadly, for little more than three years before she herself died; and those the years that covered the onset and development of her terminal illness.

Of late I have been able to read some of the letters Margaret wrote between 1933 and 1937 to Walter Benjamin, one of her dearest friends in the Berlin days. They provide a vivid picture of her life in those early years of emigration. It was a starveling existence, made no easier by her having taken on the task of acting as a liaison with her fellow political exiles while, at the same time, under the practical necessity of earning a living in a country whose language she could not speak.

Neither, for that matter, did she know French, which led to frightful confusion. Her political duties entailed keeping in touch with people in Paris where she went every few weeks. When told on the telephone '*Ne quittez pas*', she inferred that, since '*ne . . . pas*' has to be a negative, the person she was asking for was not there and, while he was being fetched to the telephone, she rang off. As this happened several times a day and on several days running, the poor fellow became unhinged with paranoia.

Reading menus from right to left as in Hebrew – to select by cost – Margaret earned the open contempt of the ABC waitress for ordering unaccompanied Yorkshire pudding, price twopence. Nothing if not indomitable, she made her way, teaching German to her Battersea landlady at six in the morning in lieu of rent and picking up English – though, alas, not English pronunciation – by reading the newspapers with a dictionary.

Early in 1935 she moved to a small room in Doughty Street where she installed a bed she had been lent, a laundry basket that served as a filing cabinet, a gas ring her kitchen and a packing-case her desk. Upon her first arrival with a small suitcase, the landlady had asked when the furniture van might be expected. Margaret affected to think it had been delayed en route but would certainly turn up next day. She counted upon the fact that the landlady did not herself live on the premises and would therefore be unable to see whether any such van arrived or not. As time passed, Margaret borrowed so many unwanted objects from friends that the room became positively overcrowded, though never comfortable.

In her letters to Benjamin she describes her difficulties in adapting to the bewildering size of London and embarking upon a completely new start in life. She writes enthusiastically about the Reading Room in the British Museum where she is doing some research in German for English writers introduced to her by Professor Tawney, to whom she had come with a letter. (One of the things that had unnerved her when she first arrived here was that, desperate for help and guidance, not to mention a square meal, all the English people to whom she had been given introductions, though friendly and polite, always suggested that she should come for tea 'on Tuesday week', or at an even more distantly future date.)

At one stage she is reading sixteenth- and seventeenth-century Dutch manuscripts at the Museum for an historian, from which – extremely difficult – task she is incidentally learning much interesting English history of the period. For the rest, she gives lessons in German shorthand and picks up any odd jobs where German is needed; but it remains a precarious livelihood and, when an accident lays her up for some weeks, she writes to Benjamin that it's clear one can't easily earn money in bed, at least not in her type of profession ('*Denn vom Bett aus kann man natürlich nicht leicht Geld verdienen, jedenfalls nicht mit dieser Art von Berufen*').

In August 1935, after her first eighteen difficult months in England, she is taking a holiday in Le Lavandou where she makes many friends among the local Communists. Again and again she refers, in the course of the correspondence, to trying, unsuccessfully, to place Benjamin's work which he sends her to read; but, of course, nobody in England had ever heard of him then. He was apparently writing short stories at the time and also an article on Kafka and an essay entitled 'The Author as Producer'. She explains that she would need to find a translator for his work as her own English is not good enough. She regrets that he has quarrelled with Klaus Mann and is glad that he has been to see Brecht in Denmark.

For her part, she reports on Brecht's several visits to London and that there is talk of the Gate Theatre putting on *The Threepenny Opera*. (Nothing came of this: a version was broadcast by the BBC in February 1935, but it was not seen on the English stage for more than another twenty years.) A translation of *Die Rundköpfe und die Spitzköpfe*, she writes, is nearing completion and Hanns Eisler, the last of the close friends still in London at that juncture, tries but fails to arrange for its production. Eisler then leaves for

America in the late spring of 1935. There he goes to see Elisabeth Hauptmann in St Louis and sends Margaret news of her, which she passes on to Benjamin.

In those years, though she did not write – nor, indeed, talk – to Benjamin or anyone else about it, she acted, at the British Party's behest, as a courier for the international Communist movement, for which her possession of a British passport and her lack of regular employment made her ideally suited. She would fly to the Soviet Union, pick up a money belt prepared for her and hand its contents over to a fellow courier somewhere in Europe for the use of Communist parties that had been declared illegal in their own countries and gone underground.

One such – and it was to be her last – trip landed her in great danger. The means for her departure on the first leg of the return journey to Helsinki turned out to be a tiny aircraft accommodating no one on board but the pilot, his navigator and herself. It crashed on a wooded mountain in Finland. Briefly she lost consciousness; on regaining it, she was aware of a searing pain in her head and, simultaneously, on testing out that she could stand and was not disabled, that she must continue her journey and reach her destination without fail to keep her appointment. The pilot had sustained more serious injuries and his companion had a broken leg.

The plane had not immediately caught fire but now, as they dragged themselves as far away from it as they could, the wreck burst into flames which, fortunately, signalled their plight and their whereabouts. After only a few hours' delay a rescue team arrived with stretchers. Margaret refused this aid, afraid that it would mean delivering her to a hospital and, asserting that she was quite unharmed, made her way on foot down the mountainside to the waiting ambulances, which bore her companions away while she insisted that the rescuers telephone the airport authorities and demand that, in view of the accident, a plane should be kept waiting for her. This was done and she was whisked off to Helsinki air terminal where, indeed, a plane had been held up for her arrival. The impatient passengers were intensely inquisitive about this very important person for whom they were kept waiting and who arrived by ambulance, but she took her seat and spoke to no one, leaving their curiosity unsatisfied.

On arrival in Brussels she went straight to the small hotel near the main railway station where she was to meet her contact. He did not turn up at the appointed time on that day, nor on the next. She lay on the bed, fully dressed, sending out for food and fearful of falling asleep until, on the third day, he announced his arrival in the hotel. Before leaving her room, she took off the money belt and put the German currency in a bag. At the bottom of one of the pockets in the belt she found a Russian kopeck and understood at once that, had she been killed, or been taken, perhaps unconscious, to a hospital and there undressed by someone, the precise nature of her mission would have been disclosed.

Now that it had been fulfilled she flew back, thankfully, to London where she called in her good and friendly doctor (in those days doctors were often good and friendly), who diagnosed her as having a fractured skull and said that on no account must she be moved. She forbore to mention that she had been on the go for some six days. She was in bed for close on two months. On the Party's advice, she sued the Soviet air company for damages. She kept the kopeck as a memento of a most horrible adventure but made no further expeditions of this nature.

At the request of Wieland Herzfelde – the brother of John Heartfield who had anglicized his name in an anti-chauvinist gesture during the First World War in protest at the *Gott strafe England* hysteria of the time – Margaret registered under her own name his publishing firm, Malik Verlag. Although John Lane put up on their premises a brass plate with the name of the *Verlag*, and some of its publications bore a London imprint as though issued from that address, none was in fact printed in this country.

As a British subject Margaret did not need, nor have, a guarantor. She received, in fact, no form of financial support from any source. (It does not come as a surprise that Bob Stewart was the only person who, upon first meeting her, asked how she was living and if she was in need of money.) In other ways her life did not much differ from that of thousands of other anti-Nazi refugees and, of course, she was not threatened with internment when that regrettable policy was adopted by the British government.

She had left Berlin on the day after the Reichstag fire of 27 February 1933: none too soon, for on the 28th the Communist press, which employed her, was banned and, three days later, Ernst Thaelmann, the Party leader, was arrested. The events that swiftly followed – the houndings and the persecution, the concentration camps, the tortures and the gas chambers – are known to everyone. Margaret, half-Jewish and a Communist, would have stood no chance.

She had first fled over the border to Prague where with others, including John Heartfield, she lived a vagrant existence, sleeping on the bare boards of an unfurnished apartment and 'borrowing' utensils from cheap restaurants to eat what food could be got out of automatic machines with telephone tokens, until picked up by the police to spend a week or so in gaol. Upon their release, some were sent back to Germany, others, such as Margaret with her British passport, were deported but could go wherever they wished. She went first to Paris and then, at last, to London for the rest of her life.

As the tide of refugees rose, she was enlisted by and became a valued member of an unofficial but effective little voluntary Aid Committee which received contributions with one hand, as it were, and doled out with the other the price of a night's lodging or a meal to the lost and needy émigrés. It was at this point, in the autumn of 1938, that I got to know Margaret over Johnny Heartfield's sleeping body.

Part Four

New Horizons

I

While waiting for my fourth – and last – novel to come out, I took a full-time job with the main Jewish refugee organization, then housed in Woburn Square. Though I was to do plenty of writing in that time, I was not to publish another book for nearly thirty-five years.

The people who engaged me made me feel welcome and I was assigned to deal with doctors and dentists, in what was known misleadingly as the Medical Department. This consisted of one quite small, rather dark room whose walls, when I took over, were lined, neck-high, with piles of documents. Cursory examination revealed that these were letters from and correspondence about individual doctors and dentists desperate to come to Britain. There was no indication that they had ever been answered.

However terrible their plight, all those seeking refuge here had to have a guarantor in this country: a British subject who undertook financial responsibility for them to ensure that they did not become a charge upon the state. Doctors and dentists were not allowed to practise as such in this country. That was the problem and, as I looked more closely into these heartrending letters, I realized that, in some cases and however urgent their appeal, they were many months old. For all one could tell, the men and women concerned could have managed by now to have reached asylum here, to have emigrated elsewhere, to be in concentration camps, or dead.

Confronted by this alarming state of affairs, the first thing I did was to get permission to employ small gangs of the young male refugees working on the premises – four by day and four by night – to go through every single sheet of these stacks of paper and classify them. Once that was done I was able to take stock and start to deal with the individual cases needing immediate attention, having eliminated those, for one reason or another, no longer needing – perhaps beyond – help.

The day-to-day running of this charitable organization had, until then, relied largely upon the services of voluntary workers: for the most part benevolent Jewish ladies of a certain age who had generously abandoned their tea parties and bridge tables to devote themselves to this cause, but who had no more idea than day-old kittens on the management of the administrative problems presented by an ever-increasing flood of German Jews, now swollen by their Austrian and Czech co-religionists, who had escaped from Nazi persecution.

I have described elsewhere* how the gloomy pool of the great vestibule of the building was daily thronged with unhappy men and women who had nothing better to do and nowhere else to go, sitting on benches and hope-lessly waiting for something or other, like out-patients in a hospital for incurables. The organization was clearly breaking down under the huge and manifold demands upon it so that, shortly after my arrival, its gover-nors bowed to the necessity of taking on a skilled and experienced adminis-trator. This was Sir Henry Bunbury, a retired civil servant who had begun his career as a clerk in the War Office at the turn of the century and had risen to be Comptroller and Accountant-General of the Post Office since

---

* In Yvonne Kapp and Margaret Mynatt, *British Policy and the Refugees, 1933–1941*, London/Portland, Oregon: Frank Cass, 1997 (but written in 1940).

1920. He was now sixty-two, a man of undiminished energy and ability who entered with enthusiasm upon the task of bringing order and method into a worthy but chaotic enterprise. As a non-Jew he was looked upon with some disfavour by many of the good-hearted ladies who swarmed about the place and whom he started gently easing out.

I, for one, hailed his advent with enormous relief. I admired his professionalism, respected his advice and appreciated his genial temperament. Since he, on his side, seemed to approve of what I was trying to do, we hit it off from the start. Indeed, when a year or so later a Director was sought for the newly created Czech Refugee Trust Fund – a body, unlike other relief organizations, financed with government money (in this instance, blood-money in reparation for the sell-out to Hitler which had created the Czech refugee problem) – I and everyone I could canvass did our best to make sure that Bunbury, rather than some costive business manager or hide-bound bureaucrat, be appointed. He was, and in due course I was seconded to become Assistant to the Director of the Czech Trust.

In the meantime my prime duty was to concentrate upon preparing with the utmost care, week by week, at least six cases of doctors and dentists in dire need. At the end of every Friday afternoon I would make my way to the Home Office department dealing with these matters and submit my applications. Since I had made absolutely sure that they fulfilled all the conditions laid down for the immigration of such individuals, they were never refused. It took time to build up the cast-iron cases on which I worked with the help of an efficient secretary so that, unlike my predecessors – the kindest of scatterbrained ladies – I refused to receive visits from those who had safely reached England, beyond a formal meeting of welcome. It was far more important to work on trying to rescue those still in danger.

However, I did not wish to give offence and, now that the organization had moved to larger premises – a former hotel in Bloomsbury Street (and therefore known as Bloomsbury House) where the Medical Department occupied several rooms and a corridor – I arranged for one or two of the older and more mature refugees who worked in the place to intercept the callers, explain how the land lay and give them friendly and helpful advice. I knew from unhappy experience that all the new arrivals wanted to do if they saw me was to contend that they were exceptions to the rule and should be allowed to practise here, backing up their plea with unacceptable gifts and copious tears, all of which was terribly embarrassing, painful for both parties and utterly useless.

Then one day it was neither a doctor nor a dentist who had to be thus prevented from interrupting my work but a most persistent lady who had the fixed idea that she must work in my department. Advised that there was no vacancy, she nevertheless called day after day until the poor fellows who had done their utmost to keep her off my back gave up and arranged an appointment for her. She turned out to be a large, athletic blonde of forceful personality who simply would not accept that we neither needed nor had any authority to take on extra staff, however voluntary or well qualified. She brushed aside my reasonable suggestion that she should try some other department since she was so keen to work for refugees. This struck me as rather peculiar, but I did not give it, nor her, another thought until, many months later, in altogether different circumstances, she was forcibly recalled to my attention and her real purpose – a most distasteful one – became clear.

In the early days refugee doctors arriving here had been allowed to requalify in Edinburgh; that facility had long been closed to them and there was no way they could be admitted against the wishes of the medical establishment until, in the early summer of 1939, the pundits felt obliged to look into the matter again and decreed that a committee of such eminent men as the Presidents of the Royal Colleges – Physicians, Surgeons and so forth – should, in the name of humanity, and under the strictest terms of reference, admit fifty refugee doctors to practise, five of such places to be held in reserve for members of the profession still attempting to reach Britain and known to be in exceptional danger.

Since there were some 3,000 doctors on our files it was a formidable task to select those who fell into the specified categories, quite apart from the fact that I was not qualified to undertake it. Happily I was able to call upon Professor Samson Wright of the Middlesex Hospital and Dr Philip d'Arcy Hart of the Medical Research Council: two medical men, both Jewish, of outstanding distinction whose judgment and integrity could not be called into question. They spent hours going over all the names and details of possible candidates, winnowing the list to be submitted to the committee.

In the event, two such selections – of fifty doctors each – were made by this august body whose impartiality had been badly shaken at the outset when its members were bombarded by those who, at one time or another, had treated in some foreign spa or in their private sanatoria a minor royalty or other persons of social influence and now expected to be singled out for recognition and reward. It had to be pointed out tactfully that we, too, humble workers in a relief organization, were equally the targets of such special pleading and had firmly to ignore it if justice were to be done to the great majority neither able nor inclined to pull strings.

These proceedings, for all their good intentions, proved pointless, for within a few months war was to break out and all refugee doctors were admitted to practise, a remarkably high number of them eventually gravitating to Harley Street. Also, at the time, the decisions made created much discontent and ill-feeling, the Socialist medical societies objecting that they discriminated against any doctor of left-wing or trade union affiliations, while Tory MPs made the selfsame charge in reverse: in their estimation only Socialists had been among those selected. All I could do was to send to each the furious letter of the other and leave it at that.

Since the declaration of war put an end to all hope of rescuing anyone still in the Nazi-occupied countries, there was nothing for my department to do but close its files and wind up. By then, I myself had been seconded to the Czech Trust and, with the rest of its staff, evacuated from London, first to premises in Hertfordshire and, after a couple of months, to a mansion, formerly a TB clinic, in Berkshire. In neither place did I live in the building that housed the offices. In the former I had rooms in a cottage at some little distance so that each day that autumn I strolled to work across an open common, while in the latter six or seven of us took over a rambling, rather damp and decrepit Victorian rectory standing in its own grounds and this, again, entailed an agreeable morning walk through fields. The house was large enough to set aside two rooms as dormitories – one for girls and one for boys – so that, when the Christmas holidays came, our children, both those of the English staff and of the Czech refugee employees, could join their parents. There were as many as ten of these young things, and very pleasant it was.

There were now entirely new problems to be faced. It was clear that in wartime foreign refugees, however well-disposed to them the British public might be, would not be allowed to remain the only idle members of society, whiling away their time playing at émigré politics or diverting themselves with amateur theatricals and other cultural activities but, like the rest of the population, would be required to join the armed forces or otherwise play their part in the war effort. The bitter alternative, as I saw it, was as prisoners. It was obviously preferable that they should become useful workers, since if they joined the army they were at risk of being captured by the Nazis when they would certainly and swiftly be done to death.

I set about devising a programme for those of active age to be drafted into industry or agriculture, including retraining for such occupations. Most of the men – though we sometimes gave them the collective designation of 'wine-merchants' – had been middlemen or professional people of one sort or another including a high proportion of lawyers; but there were also many skilled artisans: goldsmiths, diamond-cutters, watchmakers, tailors and so forth, whose trades were not much in demand at a time of national crisis.

In the early spring of 1940, by which time hundreds of the Germans, Austrians and Czechs had been drafted into factories, foundries, mines, forestry and farming, the blow fell. The Director, Sir Henry Bunbury, had been on leave; and during his fortnight's absence, I had been working out certain additions to the employment scheme when I was summoned to attend a meeting in London, called, apparently, by someone in the Home Office, to say what I knew about certain refugees who had worked as filing clerks in the Medical Department and whose credentials as bona fide refugees were now being questioned.

While waiting to be called before this tribunal of enquiry I was taken aside by a strikingly handsome young man of impeccable tailoring, a fluting voice and a delightful scent who wanted to know whether I recalled someone whose name he then pronounced, but which I did not think I had ever heard. He then drew upon a blotting pad a fair likeness of the strapping lady who had so insistently offered me her services. Pleased to know what he was talking about and thus able to co-operate, I said of course I remembered her but had no idea who she was. Had he? To that there was no answer, for he then ushered me into the room where some half-dozen people sat behind a long table while every word spoken was taken down on some – to me – unfamiliar kind of silent typewriter. Nobody introduced themselves and, as I faced the table and scanned the panel, I recognized no one but Violet Markham – the only woman – whose presence I found rather reassuring.

I was now questioned about the refugees who had worked for me and I freely told them all I knew about them which, I had to admit, was not much. I had taken their status as victims of Nazi persecution on trust but, when I came to think about it, their antecedents were rather hazy and one would be hard put to vouch for them as individuals. At that point the chairman switched the subject to ask me about the woman whose name I had just learnt. I said I had found her tiresome and importunate. 'You thought her rather a goose?' suggested the chairman. I had done nothing of the kind nor, indeed, given her any thought at all, but it seemed the simplest way to have done with the subject, so I agreed.

It took me an inexcusably long time to recognize that the matter of the slightly suspect refugees was a flimsy pretext for investigating me and that the 'goose' had been the agent sent to keep an eye on me. It was probably supposed that I had frustrated her purpose by sheer cunning. There can be no excuse for my obtuseness; and I make none.

On my way out, escorted by the same exquisite young man who had received me, I, confident at having acquitted myself well, complained to him that we were rather worried about some of our refugees, known to be Communists, who had been detained on York railway station. The Czech Trust, I pedantically explained, was a charitable foundation which did not and could not exercise any form of political discrimination. We should be much obliged, I said, if the Home Office respected this principle and released these people forthwith. He agreed to look into the matter and I sailed out, fatuously pleased with myself at striking this blow for justice.

Upon Sir Henry's return from leave when, to await him, I had laid upon his desk the revised version of the employment scheme, it turned out that he had been interviewed the night before – it sounded more as though he had been grilled – by someone from the Special Branch. This interview, which lasted until the early hours of the morning, had been timed to catch him in his London home immediately he arrived from his holiday and before he came back to work.

I naturally thought he wished to discuss my plans, but his first words were: 'Can this be done in a concentration camp?' Taken aback, I asked: 'Good heavens, are they planning to put the refugees into concentration camps?' 'Not them,' said Sir Henry, 'you.' Later that day he sent me a formal letter to say that he had been instructed to ask me whether I was or had ever been a member of the Communist Party. Of course the matter did not end there: that was only the beginning. As the Assistant to the Director I was also, consequentially, Secretary to the Trustees: three elderly gentlemen appointed by the Government to represent the interests mainly concerned, the Home Office, the Labour movement and the Jewish community. They met every few weeks in a rather grand flat in Cavendish Square to hear reports on the current state of affairs from Sir Henry and me.

At the next meeting following these developments I was asked to wait outside the room where we usually foregathered and spent an uncomfortable half-hour before being invited to enter when I was formally addressed by the Chairman, Sir Malcolm Delevingne. In a doleful voice he announced that with deep regret he had to inform me of the Secretary of State's decree that I should no longer work for the Trust in any capacity. They, the Trustees, who had the fullest confidence in my loyalty and integrity, would be profoundly sorry to lose my services, and he advised me to write to the Home Secretary appealing against the decision.

Sir Malcolm – a very small, twinkling man of seventy-one who had entered the Home Office in 1892 to become Deputy Under-Secretary of State, from which he retired in 1932, and whose distinguished career had included drafting the most far-reaching measures for safety in mines – beneath the carapace of his calling, was of a truly generous and humane disposition. He now volunteered not only to vet the letter I should write but to present it in person to the Home Secretary, Sir John Anderson, whom he had known as a callow newcomer in the service and, so to speak, helped to lick into shape without, he implied, any marked success.

I drafted my letter and submitted it to Sir Malcolm who at one point commented: 'Is that not a rather purple passage, Mrs Kapp?', whereupon I deleted it. Thanks to such editing, it sounded in the end a fairly reasonable and dignified appeal against a despotic ruling. Backed by what I knew would be Sir Malcolm's special pleading, I had high hopes of its success. It did not take long for me to receive a reply announcing that the Secretary of State could not alter his decision.

The reason why I had not been particularly surprised at questions about individual refugees' credentials was because, immediately after the war started, we had been officially informed that tribunals were to be set up to classify refugees into three categories of reliability. The Czech Trust had thereupon inaugurated a Tribunals Department and placed Margaret Mynatt in charge of it to prepare material for the jurists who were to preside over these boards. Margaret, who had an unrivalled knowledge of the background of the political refugees – as distinct from the Jewish victims of persecution – was now, of course, herself under suspicion and summarily removed from office by order of the Home Secretary. In her case there was less fuss than in mine since her work, though far more important, had been of a back-room nature and she was not required to make any statement in her own defence.

Sir Henry posted a notice announcing our dismissal and declaring his personal regret. For a week or more, debarred from work, we held court in the vicarage, to which many members of the staff came with little offerings and friendly words. Then with six months' salary in lieu of notice and a glowing testimonial both from Sir Henry and also the Trustees, I left with Margaret for the Lake District.

There was a comical little sideshow, or footnote, to this episode. In 1932, as soon as our divorce had been made absolute, Peter had married a young sculptress of Russian origin, the sister of a journalist who, under the pseudonym Ernst Henri, had written a daring and prophetic anti-Nazi book entitled *Hitler Over Europe?*, published in an English translation in 1934. This journalist was then living somewhere on the continent without a permit to enter the United Kingdom. Peter, while in Geneva in the years 1934 and 1935 carrying out his commission from the British Museum to do twenty-five lithographic portraits of the heads of delegations to the League of Nations, personally tackled Sir John Simon – recently transferred from the Foreign Office to become Home Secretary – and obtained an undertaking that, on the strength of his guarantee as his brother-in-law, Ernst Henri would be allowed to settle in England.

Now, in 1940, when the Wehrmacht had overrun the Low Countries and was about to occupy France, anyone who was known as a Communist or for other reasons to be sympathetic to the Soviet Union was deemed to be a potential traitor and a danger to the state in the event of the threatened invasion of these shores. It was argued, whether seriously or not one cannot know, that, given the Nazi–Soviet Non-Aggression Pact of 1939, such people would naturally aid and abet the invader. No one was more suspect than I for, in the time-honoured state of confusion that prevails in such circles, MI5 held the firm conviction that Ernst Henri was my brother. One might have thought that the most slipshod spycatcher could have detected that I was not of Russian nationality.

In fact, my poor old brother who, before the war, though ostensibly employed in the family business, spent his time riding to hounds, helping to exercise police horses and those of the Household Cavalry in barracks near his London home and, in general, living a life of equestrian bliss on his second wife's money, was now an aircraftman in the RAF. It would have curdled his blood had he been told that, as my brother, he was being identified with a dangerous Soviet citizen, known to his intimates as Lola.

2

Our dismissal was not without its uses as a straw in the wind for it preceded by only a matter of weeks the wholesale internment of refugees. We heard the news of the fall of France as we sat in the bar of the Agricultural Hotel in Penrith. The next morning the toy steamer from Pooley Bridge put us off at the Howtown landing-stage. Margaret told me to wait there with the suitcases while she explored the hinterland for lodgings.

As I sat on the little wooden jetty, watching the limpid, pale-blue water rippled by the June breeze and listening as it lapped the pebbles at its shelving edge, I knew in an intense moment of incandescent clarity and absolute certainty that, unless I wished, I need never again take full responsibility for everything. I was flooded by an utterly unfamiliar sense of peace. That was when my life with Margaret really began, to end only with her death nearly thirty-eight years later.

We stayed at first in Howtown and, over the months, remaining on the Westmorland shores of Lake Ullswater, moved about the various scattered farmhouses that catered for visitors. It was a pleasurable enough exile. We scrambled over the fells, followed the unmade road leading up to the ancient church in Martindale, or trod the rough, narrow footpath bordering the southern arm of the lake to end up in Patterdale. There were always new walks to be discovered in that spectacular countryside. Once a week a little bus called and, together with the farmers' wives and housekeepers from the few substantial mansions in the area, we were driven into Penrith. Deposited at the door of the principal grocer, to be welcomed with cups of excellent coffee and biscuits, we would leave our orders there to find the goods packed up and awaiting us when the bus arrived to take us back in the afternoon: a day's outing that, although it almost always rained, had a festive air.

We swam in the lake, we read a great deal, we listened to every news broadcast on the radio and also to much good music; and then we started to write our book on official British policy on the refugee question at the very moment when, in ever greater numbers, those refugees were being interned in their thousands, shipped to Canada and Australia, to suffer in incidents too ghastly to dwell upon, being herded together with and tormented by openly declared Nazis, despoiled by their guards, separated from their families and drowned at sea.

By summer's end we had finished our book – but for checking and amplifying facts not ascertainable in the wilds of Cumbria – by which time the first severe bombing of London had begun. Our retreat swarmed with Londoners who could afford to flee from the nightly air-raids and who now took over every available type of accommodation in the locality, from the most expensive hotels to the meanest cottages and guesthouses. Prices soared and we were no longer quite as welcome to our farmer-hosts as before, while we ourselves were anxious to be in the thick of it back in London.

From the start I had taken my victimization badly. I thought it sinister and unjust, in the same way that I deplored the hounding of the refugees as a disgrace. Nobody could genuinely believe that the sad Jewish victims of Nazi persecution were potential collaborators with the enemy and a danger to the state; while the political refugees, now defamed as representing the greatest risk, had been, above all others, Hitler's most doughty opponents. Many of their comrades had already died fighting Fascism in Spain in the hope of preventing the spread of that foul pestilence. I did not taste the full bitterness of my situation until, once back in London, my indemnity nearly exhausted, I found it impossible to get work. Wherever I applied for a job I was followed by an MI5 dossier. This generally lagged a little behind so that, again and again, I would be short-listed or even asked to start work, only to be called to an interview a few days later and told that, alas, I could not be employed for the reasons the interviewers were unable – to their acute embarrassment – to disclose. As there was said to be a serious short-age of civilian manpower for the various types of employment I was seek-ing, these eleventh-hour rejections became, with repetition, almost farcical.

There was, of course, nothing I could do about this and, after spending a few weeks on twenty-four-hour shifts at emergency centres opened for bombed-out families, where I spent more time playing chess than caring for the people who generally managed, after a brief stay, to find a home with relatives or neighbours, leaving us unoccupied, I accepted that fact that I was to be outlawed from paid employment, so I offered my services as a volunteer to the Labour Research Department. I could not have done a wiser thing, for there it was that I learnt the elementary research techniques which were to stand me in good stead in later years. Nevertheless, it was necessary to earn money somehow or other and, while conscious that I must not be so foolish as to try my luck in any sphere that could be remotely seen as 'sensitive', it did not seem unreasonable to suppose that I might possibly be found suitable for the innocuous post of administrative adviser to the Nursery Schools Association which I saw advertised.

That was how I met Joan Allen again, for she – Lady Allen of Hurtwood – was the Chairman of this body. Indeed, she presided over the committee that interviewed me and she gave every sign of being delighted to see me again. I was found suitable for the job: either my dossier had not caught up with me this time or the committee, out of sheer common sense, had decided that it was irrelevant. However that may be, I was engaged. But when the time came for me to start work I was not put in charge of the administration. Instead I was asked, after a lapse of some weeks when I heard nothing from my new employers, if I would supervise a small exhibition of photographs publicizing the work of the Nursery Schools Association displayed in the booking-hall of what was then Charing Cross underground station (now called the Embankment). I was a little puzzled, but agreed to do this rather pointless job and was accordingly installed at a small table that bore a sign with the word INFORMATION. This led to endless good-humoured chaffing by the friendly ticket-collectors and other railway staff who called me 'Miss Information': a joke that never wore thin with repetition.

Very few members of the public visited the exhibition, never more than two or three at a time, no one at all for quite long stretches of the day. People hurried past on their way to catch their trains, for it was a period of heavy air-raids and everyone was anxious to get home or to shelter in the evening, while during the day they went briskly about their business. In any event, the general public could hardly be expected to regard nursery schools as of paramount interest at that stage of the war. Those who did stop to look round earned my undivided attention and were a relief from utter boredom.

Then some odd things began to happen. By this time Sir John Anderson had been succeeded at the Home Office by Herbert Morrison who, to my great surprise, turned up in Charing Cross underground station booking-hall one day and proceeded very slowly and deliberately to examine the pictures of nursery schools. I did not in this instance rush forward with offers of help and further information: I could not for an instant believe that the Home Secretary had so little else to do or entertained so keen an interest in the under-fives as to be here for any purpose other than to inspect me, though there seemed to me to be mighty little he could find out by doing so, and everything about me must have been already known to his department.

A few days later a burly policeman in uniform patrolling the station in a leisurely way stopped by my table and engaged me in badinage. It was light banter of a very odd nature: this war, he opined, was 'all for greed and profit', did I not agree? Anderson shelters, he went on, clicking his teeth in a knowing way, should properly be called Baldwin shelters, shouldn't they? After all, they were made of Baldwin steel and it was Baldwin's profits rather than the deluded public whose safety they ensured, and so on and so forth. I took down his number.

That evening I wrote to Lady Hurtwood and reported him for danger-ous talk: he was spreading what was called alarm and despondency at a time when people were under the strain of nightly air-raids and should not have their confidence undermined, their fears and doubts stoked. At the same time I enquired about the work for which I had applied and been appointed: it was not that of attendant at a photographic exhibition. In reply Joan invited me to lunch; but before the day of our meeting, I received some enlightenment.

A former colleague of mine in the refugee sphere was one of those good and amiable Liberal ladies who loved foreign Communists because they were heroes, and detested English ones because they were traitors. Her innate sense of justice, however, had been outraged by my summary dis-missal: it made me seem almost the equal of a foreign Communist in her eyes. Now it so happened that not only had she been at Bedales with Joan Allen – then Margery Gill – but for many years she and her growing family had lived in the same neck of the Surrey woods and, on the basis of their long-standing friendship, they met quite often. She was privy to the fact that Joan was on intimate terms with Herbert Morrison. Whatever loyalty she may have felt to her old schoolfellow was outweighed by her strict sense of fair play so she had no hesitation in writing to warn me that I must be on the look-out and, in view of this close connection, I should probably not long remain in Joan's employ. Thus I came well primed to my lunch with Joan. In a somewhat awkward and uneasy manner, she explained that, as a Communist, I could not expect to be paid by the Government which funded the Nursery Schools Association. What damage could I do to that body, I asked. Was it thought that I might signal to the Luftwaffe pilots to pinpoint the location of nursery schools for them to bomb? It was a silly conversation leading nowhere and, as soon as I got home, I wrote Joan an acid little note resigning from the job I had never had. Joan had never quite had the courage either to dismiss me nor yet stand up for rational conduct in face of official hysteria. In that connection, I used – before its time – the term 'premature antifascist', claiming that this was the only accusation that could justifiably be brought against me.

That was in the early spring of 1941. I went back to work at the Labour Research Department through whose good offices I was recommended to the Amalgamated Engineering Union, then seeking a Research Officer. I was interviewed by the President of the union, Jack Tanner, and was appointed to the job, where I stayed for the next seven years.

3

It is now almost fifty years ago that, on a sunless morning at the end of May, I first entered the premises of the Amalgamated Engineering Union in Peckham Road as its newly appointed Research Officer. The officials and the entire administrative staff had been evacuated to Pitsford in Northampton since early in the war, while the greater part of the union headquarters in London had been turned over to the local borough council whose functions – distributing ration cards, providing shelter or temporary accommodation for bombed families, grants for the replacement of household goods destroyed in air-raids and advice on a hundred and one wartime regulations – were vastly changed and increased. The only parts of the large red brick building to be retained by the union were the basement – where a crew of six packers worked under their foreman who occupied a gloomy little office in the underground corridor – and two first-floor rooms which, as I shortly learnt, had formerly been the General Secretary's domain.

It was the packers' foreman, Tom Abbot, the only representative of the union's staff, who welcomed me on that first day, showing me into one of these rooms which was to be my office – the other, adjoining room, meant for typists and clerks, was not then open – and, since nobody had used this place since the last Research Officer had left many months before (a young man now in the armed forces), it was shuttered and smelt musty. The large table at its centre was piled high with unopened journals that had been gathering week by week. It was clear that the essential equipment for the job was not so much a sound knowledge of trade unionism or of engineering as the ability to sweep and dust.

Had Tom Abbot not been of such a congenial disposition – a stout man in his late fifties who had started his working life as a packer for the union long years before, rising to his present status which entitled, indeed, obliged him to wear a good blue serge suit, a heavy watch-chain across a comfortable paunch and, almost always, a bowler hat, indoors and out – I should have been totally discouraged that first day. As it was, he stayed chatting to me for some time, exercising a dry cockney wit and taking a most kindly interest in my welfare. He then offered to bring me a cup of tea. Since I was one person, two floors up, and the packers, with Tom, were seven people, I said it would be more reasonable for me to join them in the basement. Without realizing it at the time, with this proposition I won an acceptance which was to be invaluable. Though the Research Department staff expanded, everyone always went downstairs twice a day to drink with the packers. What this signified, and how it had overcome difficulties and prejudices that I had not even suspected, I found out only when, some years later, during one of the mighty drinking bouts with which the packers celebrated any half-holiday at the Walmer Castle, the pub conveniently situated on the doorstep of the AEU premises, Tom Abbot, primed with five pints of beer, dug me sharply in the ribs with his elbow and said: 'You're the only Research Officer we've ever had, and you a female, what doesn't put on side.'

'And you a female': that, of course, was the stumbling block for others than Tom Abbot in that stronghold of male trade unionism. One by one the members of the seven-man Executive Council came up from Pitsford to inspect me in those early days. The very notion of a woman Research Officer was so novel, and so distasteful, to them that these visits generally began on a note of extreme wariness bordering on hostility. I did not go too far out of my way to conciliate or disarm these rather disagreeable callers, but I answered their questions politely and, most of them, whether completely satisfied or not, gradually modified their initial antagonism and became, if not friendly, at least civil.

One of their most offensive members started out so badly that I was convinced I should never be able to neutralize his misogyny and, since he was among the oldest of the Council members with the influence to which his seniority entitled him, I thought it quite probable that he would get me dismissed unless I could persuade him that, despite my regrettable sex, I was doing a good job. His attitude was not encouraging, nor meant to be, and his remarks were so far from well intentioned that I wondered whether I might not as well burn my boats by asking him to leave and let me get on with my work when, to my surprise, he suddenly broke off and asked me,

'Do you drink?' 'Not to excess,' I answered defensively, thinking it was really the last straw that, having failed to trip me up on other grounds, he was now insinuating that I was an alcoholic. But that was not the object of his query: he just wanted to know whether I would join him in the Walmer Castle where he had in mind to treat me to a modest glass.

Another official who came to look me over was quite put out, even outraged, to learn that I fully expected to attend the National Committee, the annual delegate conference and the union's sovereign body, where, I believed, the information I could provide to the executive would be useful. 'Oh, no, no, no,' he said. 'You can't go to National Committee. It's quite out of the question. You're a woman.' 'Why not?' I said. 'Do you mean they tell dirty stories or something of that sort?' 'No, no,' he said, 'you just can't go. You're a woman.'

In the event I did not go to the 1941 National Committee, held but a few weeks after my appointment, though I attended – and was quite useful – in every subsequent year. As to being a female, when women were admitted to the AEU in 1943, the officers were only too thankful that they could call upon me to receive the delegates to the first ever Women's Conference because they were terrified of them whereas, by then, they had grown accustomed to me.

In the very early days, with my recent experiences still freshly in mind, I was exceedingly nervous about not keeping the job. There was, however, only one slightly anxious moment when I was rung up by someone who announced himself as speaking for the Home Office. I told him that all the officials were evacuated from London. 'This,' I said, 'is only the Research Department of the union.' 'And this,' said the caller nastily, 'is only the Research Department of the Home Office.' Nothing came of this scare and, with the invasion of the Soviet Union in June 1941, I and my kind ceased to be considered traitors and saboteurs. I sat back and got on with the work.

As the years wore on I had one particular friend on the Executive Council who could see nothing wrong with me. This was Gilbert Hitchings. He was unlike his fellow councillors in other ways too, for he had none of their arrogance but a rigid puritanical objection to accepting anything – even a drink or a cigar – from the employers' representatives when the two sides met, convivially, in a bar after negotiations. Also, he had a passion for classical music and a knowledgeable appreciation of it which he could not share with his colleagues though he had always, when in manual work, had a group of his mates who pooled their resources to buy records of Bach, of Mozart and of Beethoven, to which they listened during their lunch breaks. He also had a deep respect for engineering skill. I would tease him, saying that once his tongue was loosened, his soul was revealed as nothing less than a Bristol aero engine, tuned to fine limits.

When he was in London we sometimes went to Kew and Hampton Court and he would talk about his background, describing how, as a five-year-old, he had made up bundles of kindling wood to sell for a farthing. There were other tales of a needy childhood that both shocked and awed me. Failing to win re-election to the Executive Council, he lost heart at the prospect of returning to the bench once more at his time of life, suffered a stroke and, shortly after, to my keen sorrow, died.

Everyone is said to remember exactly where they were and what they were doing when they heard the news of Kennedy's assassination. Other momentous events, as indelibly impressed upon the memory, come to mind: Hitler's occupation of Austria on 11 March 1938; the fall of France in June 1940 and the liberation of Paris on 25 August 1944; but though to this day I know where I was and what I was doing on all those occasions, the one that remains most vivid is that following the invasion of the Soviet Union on 22 June 1941.

I had heard of it at five o'clock that Sunday morning. In the evening I went to a concert with Geoffrey Pyke who, not having heard the news at all, was all for leaving at once, as though the fate of nations depended upon his leaping into action. Persuaded that there was pretty well nothing he could do, nor was anything expected of him, he sat down again quietly and listened to the concert. Afterwards we went to a snack bar where, since it was a warm evening, Geoffrey pulled up his trousers above the knee, revealing not only his immensely long, thin legs but odd socks of differing bright colours that drew a good deal of attention. We then strolled to St James's Square where he was temporarily living and as we passed the houses on the north side of the empty square we heard, issuing from a basement occupied most probably by a caretaker, the sound of an unmistakable voice from a radio and there, leaning against the area railings, we listened to Churchill's speech proclaiming the Russians our allies.

In the AEU, unlike many other trade unions, the General Secretary was really the office manager and internal staff administrator while the President, rather than a formal figurehead, was the leader and spokesman of the organization. While the General Secretary in my time – at first Fred Smith, succeeded by Ben Gardner – took little notice of me, since his duties lay in the Northampton offices, the President, Jack Tanner, called in frequently at Peckham for a chat and we became fast friends. He was a man of progressive views and liberal sympathies: the only member of the Executive Council, I believe, who, unlike God, did not hold women in contempt but genuinely liked and respected them, believing them capable of playing a greater and valuable part in trade union affairs. To him was largely owed the revolutionary move to admit them to the AEU. On the basis of our good understanding I came to write all his speeches in those years and he relied upon my knowing his mind and understanding his style to such an extent that he reached the stage when, to my alarm, he would publicly deliver a speech without having bothered to read it through beforehand.

I had studied him as a speaker most carefully: his mannerisms, his love of a resounding peroration, the words he stumbled over and those he most favoured. He had a good, strong, even beautiful voice with a good, strong, cockney accent that lent force and character to his oratory. I was writing lines for a fine actor. The trouble was that he came to believe that I would give him exactly what he wanted for any occasion or part he wished to play. He was always well pleased when his pronouncements caught public attention; as, for example, when he was quoted in headlines in the evening papers calling for the opening of a second front. Such publicity sometimes got him into hot water but, on the whole, ours was a successful collaboration. Indeed, it was because, after the war had ended, he did not like the speeches I wrote for him and I would not write the speeches he wanted to make that we had to part company and I left the AEU.

When I first began as the Research Officer I was not only ignorant of the internal workings of trade unions, of the engineering industry, of workshop practices and industrial finance – a formidable aggregate of disqualifications for the job – but, even worse than not knowing how to read company reports, I could not do arithmetic. This was a major handicap and I sought to overcome it by studying elementary textbooks while travelling to work. Seated on the top deck of a swaying tram I secretly – for I was deeply ashamed of what I was doing – practised converting fractions into decimals and percentages.

Fortunately I had at that time a kindly friend in the civil service who sometimes took me out to dinner during which he would instruct me in the use of the slide rule. This may bring pitying smiles to the lips of today's tiny computer experts; nevertheless, it enabled me in those far-off times to indite perfectly cogent wage claims for some million engineering and shipbuilding workers.

I had ample opportunity for my study of arithmetic, for it was a tediously long journey that I made six days a week. In winter it meant leaving my home in Nassington Road in the dark, or by moonlight, crossing the little railway bridge and waiting on the corner for a bus to Camden Town. From there I went by underground to the Oval but, during air-raids, the tube trains did not cross the river and passengers, decanted at Charing Cross, had to walk to the south side to take another train. From the Oval I caught a tram for Peckham.

There were days when, emerging from the underground, I found familiar landmarks reduced to rubble. After one bad raid the whole area was devastated and unrecognizable. In the era of the flying bombs, the V1s, or 'doodlebugs', it became necessary for us to get out of our rooms which had large windows and glass-fronted bookcases. We would stand outside in the corridor with its solid walls until we heard the explosion. Those unmanned weapons were no doubt aimed at the centre, but generally fell short, so that we, in Peckham, would hear the angry buzz of the engine suddenly cut out and know that the thing was about to land nearby. There were days when our work was interrupted in this way more than a dozen times.

Sometimes in the evening we would go with friends to the heights of Parliament Hill Fields and watch these flying bombs come over the far horizon, to fall, bursting with flame and smoke, on the populous town. Eventually I myself was bombed out in Nassington Road by a V1; and the reason we were not all killed was simply because, in our determination to stake a claim to a share of the small garden that overlooked the railway line, we happened to use for the first (and last) time an Anderson shelter.

Gardens in the war years were precious, not so much as pleasure grounds as for the practical purpose of growing such produce as onions, spinach, raspberries and other vegetables and fruits that were unobtainable luxuries. We occupied the two upper stories of the house and, according to our agreement with the landlady, the garden was divided between us and the tenants of the ground floor: a young man who worked in some ministry and his wife who, inexplicably for those times, did not seem to have any occupation at all.

This couple, in what we thought a distinctly underhand way, had persuaded the landlady to grant them sole use of the garden without so much as consulting us and thereupon threatened my daughter when she, in all innocence, went to gather the fruits of our labour, that if she or any of us ever tried to use the garden again, the gate giving access to it would be kept permanently locked. Since the ground-floor flat contained an indoor shelter – known as a 'Morrison' – we applied to the warden's post to ask whether this did not mean we must have the right to use the existing, if rather derelict, Anderson shelter at the bottom of the garden. That night the bomb fell on the little playground in Parliament Hill Fields, a stone's throw from our house. As we lay on our mattresses, the ground seemed to heave up with the blast which shattered the walls and blew out all the windows of the building. Sheets of broken glass had flown across the rooms, tearing everything to shreds in their trajectory. We could certainly not have survived had we been indoors.

At that National Committee of 1941 Jack Tanner, delivering one of the first speeches I had written for him, strongly criticized the managerial in-efficiency that was hindering war production. One of the ministries concerned got in touch with him to say that, since his words had received some publicity, he had better substantiate his sweeping charges. Disconcerted by this challenge Tanner asked me on the telephone what he had better do. 'Substantiate the charges, of course,' I said. How, he wanted to know. 'Well,' I said, rather too airily, 'we'll have to launch an enquiry throughout the union.'

That was the origin of the three production enquiries carried out by the AEU through its shop stewards and Joint Production Committees in the years 1941 and 1942. Three thousand individuals replied to the fifteen questions put to them in the first enquiry; the total for the three investigations covered almost two million workers in some 900 engineering works, ship-yards and foundries throughout the country, many of the shop stewards attached lengthy screeds to the forms they returned, elaborating on matters either not covered at all by the questions or expanding on their replies.

For the first three months of my time with the union, I was on my own;

but with the launching of the first production enquiry – that is in August 1941 – I asked for and was allowed to take on a secretary. As the work increased over the years I was able to engage first one, then two and, finally, three research assistants, all women: Kari Polanyi, Ann Foster and Susan Meadows, while my secretary, Jill Steele, remained throughout. Such a staff will appear derisory to the members of the present AEU Research Department and even to that of the 1960s, for an entire upper floor to house the department was added to the building. But for us – for me and Jill – the full complement of five was a luxury. For a start, we were able to parcel out the essential reading which had added so many hours to our working day: daily papers, weeklies, trade union journals, engineering and other technical periodicals, foreign news bulletins and government publications, including Hansard. The fact that Kari Polanyi and Ann Foster were trained economists – indeed Kari had been 'directed' to the AEU as her wartime task when her call-up came – was a tremendous advantage.

Though unschooled in survey methods, I knew when I drafted the first questionnaire on production that it must elicit a simple 'Yes', 'No' or 'Don't know' answer. This I had learnt from studying previous enquiries sent out by the General Secretary. An enquiry into outworking had been so loosely worded that to one of the questions it had been possible to reply variously 'on a typewriter', 'by train' and 'sometimes', demonstrating that it was open to almost any interpretation.

The final report on the first enquiry, which I wrote in October 1941, was duplicated and sent, marked 'Confidential', to the relevant government departments.* The two subsequent follow-up enquiries – centred on the newly instituted Joint Production Committees and launched, respectively, in March and July 1942 – were based upon the same questions and formula-

---

* The Ministries of Supply, Production and Aircraft Production, the Air Ministry and the Admiralty. The report also went to two national newspapers, to the Engineering and Allied Employers' Federation and to a selected number of MPs.

tions as the first so that valid comparisons could be made. It was explicitly stated at the time:

> It is a matter of principle in our Enquiries that we do not ask questions covering ground that can only be known abstractly to the workers . . . We have investigated factual matters in which we, as a Union, are interested wholly from the workshop angle.

The third report, issued in December 1942 was printed as a pamphlet entitled *We Who Make the Tools* – a reference to Churchill's famous phrase: 'Give us the tools and we'll finish the job.' Copies went again to the appropriate ministries and the enquiry gained a certain notoriety, questions being asked in the House and Tanner being interviewed by the press.

I did not realize, however, how far-reaching was the news of these enquiries until, in August 1943, the American Embassy got in touch with my office to say that Professor Robert Lynd, the sociologist, was on a visit to Britain with the anthropologist, Dr Margaret Mead, and wished to meet the people responsible for the AEU enquiries. He came to Peckham one sultry summer morning, introducing himself to Jill and me – still, at that juncture, the sole staff of the Research Department – with the unforgettable words: 'My name is Robert Lynd, Professor of Sociology in Columbia University, of left-wing views, not a Communist, how do you do?' It was a wonderful day – for he did, indeed, stay all day, having a horrible lunch with me at one of the little local grub shops – and many of his sayings have remained in my memory. For example, he explained his particular interest in our work because, he said, it was the one piece of research that had come out of the war that was, so far as he knew, 'about something that matters'. He said he was bored with people who 'are just counting grains of sand'. This was so gratifying it is small wonder I have never forgotten his words.

He wanted to look into our methods of analysing our returns which were, of course, of the most elementary. Abashed, but unable to refuse, Jill rather reluctantly produced the huge wads of squared foolscap sheets with their columns of ticks and crosses. 'Oh, what a familiar sight!' exclaimed this adorable man, who then proceeded to give us the most useful tips – without a trace of condescension – on the use of coloured inks and so forth. I had naturally read his book *Middletown* and now I turned to its sequel, *Middletown Revisited* which, though equally interesting, is not quite as impressive.

Professor Lynd was not our only preceptor as time went on. Ian Mikardo, then the Labour MP for Reading, whom I knew slightly, expressed an interest in the production enquiries and came to our office where he discovered, as Lynd had done, the clumsy, laborious and primitive techniques we employed, whereupon he introduced us to and provided the necessary equipment for a punched-hole-and-knitting-needle method of analysis. By that time we had our staff of five and we set about working this new system in twos: one reading from the returns, the other punching the cards. It was found quite soon that the pairs had to switch roles every quarter of an hour to avoid falling into a statistically unvarying number of errors.

However laughable all this must seem to the computer-wise generation, to us it was nothing short of a technological revolution. No doubt the task which took us literally weeks, with all hands at it for seven or eight hours a day, on five and a half days a week, would now take as many minutes.

4*

Shortly before Professor Lynd's memorable visit I had embarked upon the work of assembling a library for the AEU. John Burns had died intestate at

---

* This account was originally published in duplicated typescript under the title 'A Choice of Books', with forewords on John Burns by Eric Hobsbawm and Robin Page Arnot, as Pamphlet 16 of *Our History*, 1959.

the age of eighty-four on 24 January 1943 at his house on North Side
Clapham Common. On the day before, the death occurred of the General
Secretary of the Amalgamated Engineering Union to which Burns had
belonged all his life since early manhood. The two obituary notices
appeared on the same page of the union's February *Journal*.

Union membership had expanded vastly during the war years and it had
recently been decided that its north and south London districts, housed in
one central office, should be split and that new premises should be
acquired. This was known to many estate agents south of the river, including the firm which was handling the John Burns property, also in a temporary capacity, until executors should be appointed; and they now offered
the house on North Side to the AEU as office premises. It was thought that
Burns's association with the union would make the property singularly
appropriate.

In May, on our way to attend the first Women's Conference ever held by
this ancient stronghold of male craftsmen, Jack Tanner asked me what I
thought about the house. I did not think it would be suitable, but what, I
asked, was being done about Burns's famous collection of books on the
trade-union and working-class movement. 'Go and find out,' said the President. 'Here's the agent's address.'

Accordingly I got in touch with the agents and asked what arrangements
had been made for the disposal of the library. Could I call and see the
books? The agents appeared grateful for the enquiry. They were not at all
happy: no will, no executors, no arrangements for disposing of the library
and none in view. But, I was told, it would be physically impossible to
inspect the books. A catalogue was being made; when it was completed,
would I care to come along and glance over it? Yes, I should.

Early in June I was notified that the catalogue was ready and the agent
would meet me at the house on North Side Clapham Common. Thus I first
stumbled into the place, tripping over a pile of mildewed books in the hall,
on a grey summer morning – 17 June 1943 – and was received by a very

harassed individual, who started by showing me over the house. It had fourteen large rooms and the numerous passages, lobbies, landings, corridors, attics and storerooms of its period. Although unlived in, it was fully furnished and the rooms could be easily identified as drawing-room, bedroom and so forth by the indestructible Victorian pieces. But every available space, and much that one would not have thought available, was strewn with books. They littered the floors, the tables, the beds, the chairs; they were piled in untidy heaps and leaning towers under the tables, beds and chairs; they lined the treads of the stairs and the long passages on either side, dangerously narrowing them. They tumbled in massive confusion from cabinets and chests and cupboards; they filled the bathroom and, in an outer conservatory, some ancient leather-bound volumes, covered in dust and half destroyed by mould, cascaded from the broken shelving.

The smell of musty paper pervaded the house. This ghastly profusion made the agent very angry. He pulled open doors and lifted lids saying bitterly, 'Look at them!', and on the top landing where, despite the close day, the chill of a big damp house whose owner had been dead six months struck icily, there were five great half-filled sacks slumped against the banister. I asked what was in them. 'Rubbish!' cried the agent, 'papers, papers, papers.' He invited me to stick my hand in one. Fourteen, he said, had already gone – letters, documents, cuttings, papers of every description – and the job was nowhere near finished. Clear things up indeed! It was beyond human strength and endurance. I put my hand into one sack, stirred about a little, and found a few dog-eared Hansards, a page in handwriting, a sheaf of dingy yellow newspaper cuttings, another letter. I was deeply impressed. I asked if the papers had been examined. The agent snorted: he was there, heaven help him, to get rid of them, to make the house fit again for human habitation; thank goodness the war effort called for salvage.

We stepped our way carefully down the stairs in silence. Neither of us, it seemed, had won a sympathizer; and yet, in me lay his best hope; in him, mine. He led me into the 'library', which earned its name by having books effectively dammed up behind glass-fronted cases from floor to ceiling on three sides of the room, with what might be called space in the middle. In the large bay window stood a desk and on the desk a huge bulk of type-script. This was the catalogue. The agent estimated that it contained 40,000 titles; it would not have surprised him if there had been a million – but there it was and all the books had been listed according to the place where they had been found: dining-room, bathroom cupboard, coffer on landing, study, kitchen passage, and so on. He wished me joy of it and left me.

I had set aside this single day to 'glance through' the catalogue; there was much work to be done in the Research Department and I had only one assistant. The tour of inspection had taken up some time. It was now well after ten o'clock. I settled down, but found myself worrying about the sacks upstairs. Not only had no one time or interest to look into the enor-mous mass of papers which poured from every cranny of the house but, though later many claimants were to present themselves, so far no one but the AEU had taken any steps to find out what was happening to the books or asked to see the catalogue and, not knowing that I was the forerunner of a very large tribe, I felt a great sense of responsibility.

From the very cursory glance at the books lying about as I had picked my way through the house it became clear to me as soon as I had started to read the catalogue that some, at least, were no longer where they were said to be on the list. I began to take a more compassionate view of the agent and would have liked a little further conversation with him. But he had gone. I was alone. The catalogue frightened me very much. No dates were given for any volume and the cataloguer had evidently had more of a job than he could tackle to take down the name of the book and the author.

I knew Burns's interests had been very wide but that until relatively late in life he had mainly concentrated, as a bibliophile, on Sir Thomas More, on London, and on the social, political and historical aspects of the trade-union and working-class movement. The only distinguishing feature of books in the last category was that no one had ever apparently regarded it as such. They cropped up in ones and twos, never in sequence, never together. Dispersed and scattered through the lists, they must, I realised, be spread very thinly throughout the house; needles in a haystack. I went on reading and every now and again put a small tick in the margin of the page.

With the limited time I had I thought that it would be advisable to follow the titles of the books rather than the authors, who would probably signify nothing to me in my ignorance, until I came across *The Dictatorship of the Protestants* [*sic*] which was sufficiently arresting to make me look at the author's name and find that it was Kautsky. Very much alarmed, I reversed this rationalizing process and stuck to the authors' names for a few pages. This proved even more unsatisfactory, since the cataloguer – or the typist – made frequent entries concerning what I took to be a lesser-known but prolific Jewish writer called Levin. As they kept cropping up, I turned back – to first-floor landing, drawing-room, and so forth – and found that this author's works included *Empirico-Criticism* and *Letters from Afar*. There was nothing for it; I must plough through – and decipher – the lot as best I could. By early afternoon the great stack of paper before me had barely decreased at all when an unknown lady brought me a cup of tea. She only stayed a moment, but before I had turned back to my task there was another interruption. A very stately old man with a handsome countenance and a small white beard came into the room wearing a dressing-gown and a tweed cap and introduced himself as 'John's young brother, David'. He was extremely tall and broad and soldierly in bearing. He was also practically stone-deaf. He had come to see me, he explained, because he was a member of the union that I had come from – he referred to it as the ASE, a name it had ceased to bear in 1920 – and he launched into a forthright attack upon the habit of visiting the cinema which was degrading the youth of the country. He then told me some very interesting things about the strike during the building of the Eastbourne railway in which he had taken part in the 1880s.

I felt it my duty to tell him what I was about. I spoke very loudly but not loudly enough to interrupt his tales. At last, standing on tiptoe like the fish messenger I yelled into his ear: 'We want the union to have all your brother's books on the working-class movement, so that they won't be sold to America and scattered about.' He nodded gravely and recalled an incident in the union's early struggles which seemed to set the stamp of approval on my purpose. I bellowed that it was a very long catalogue, and drew him towards the desk to show him that I was marking those books which I thought the AEU should acquire. He seemed rather pleased that I should be occupying myself in this way and returned to the subject of idle youths with no skill and less brains who spent their time at the cinema. I thought it better not to spring to their defence, but there was one point I did want to get clear now that I had an opportunity to put it to a member of the family.

Although I chose my words with care, my question about the sacks of paper on the top landing did not somehow sound very subtle as I split my lungs voicing it. 'Young David' came back from a great distance and, in the muffled voice of the deaf, agreed that, yes, they were for salvage. 'He had a powerful lot of books and papers, did John,' he said. It was hard to know rightly what to do with them all, but they would sell, no doubt, and bring in a tidy bit. He nodded rather sleepily. It was plain that he was accustomed to talking to himself, since he so rarely heard other people's questions, replies or comments; but though it went against the grain to persist, I seized on this clear line of thought and reiterated that the AEU was interested in buying books and, perhaps, even papers. He made a few observations on the decline of trade unionism since his active days – but in no provocative spirit – and then, quite satisfied that he had provided all the information I might require, shuffled out of the room. I stayed on until it was too dark to see the page and then, fearing to inconvenience the old man, who would in all probability have forgotten my presence in the house by now and perhaps be startled if he found a light on in the library – even if the light worked, which I doubted – I let myself out.

That one day's work yielded some 1,200 marked items. Much had been overlooked, many books of particular interest to my purpose, as it later emerged, had never been entered in the catalogue at all. As I travelled home, I pondered on what could be done to claim the documents waiting to be pulped; and that night I rang up a friend of mine, the librarian of a working-class institute, and told him about the sacks. I had no suggestion to offer other than that he should present himself at the house as a person willing to remove them – this being the only thing the agent and Mr David Burns were quite decided upon – and give some time to sorting out the papers. But this was never done. Next day I went back to my office and wrote to the President to tell him that, slapdash as my work had been, I had seen enough to recognize that here was priceless treasure and that the union ought to exercise every means to get the books.

Several months elapsed. At last a list of the items I had marked in the catalogue reached me. It looked rather thin, diluted with old Hansards, White Papers, journals and political writings that could be picked up any-where. It was not impressive. However, I sent it to the President who thought I had rather overreached myself and picked out too many things of too little interest, but suggested I should go to the house again with a view to dropping some and selecting others. He also wanted to know how much the union ought to pay for them. I was willing enough to go back and sug-gested that, when a final selection had been made, which might run to 2,000 volumes, the union might possibly offer £500, as some of the items were of real and even rare value. To my surprise and pleasure, the Executive instructed me that I had a free hand to bid whatever I thought reasonable.

But in the meantime – it was now mid-October – things had not stood still. Many events had occurred in Clapham. It goes without saying that the books had fallen into yet greater decay and that claimants had gathered. The National Liberal Club had put its demands based upon a firm promise from the deceased; the Battersea Council had reminded whom it might concern that it was the heir to the Burns collection; Lord Southwood had offered £3,000 for the complete London section of the library; and the family had put their affairs in order and appointed two executors.

We learnt of these changes by degrees. It was one of the executors, Mrs F., who wrote to the President, saying that as her uncle had retained his membership of the union until he died, she wished us to receive as a free gift and in accordance with what she believed would have been her uncle's wishes, all those books which we had already earmarked, and would someone kindly call at the house to collect them.

So when I next went to North Side Clapham Common on 25 October, this time accompanied by my assistant, it was to pick out from the 40,000 books, 1,200 of them known to be dispersed in utter confusion throughout this large house. Even had they been in the places indicated on the original lists, which I knew they were not, it would have been a formidable task to track them down. But now there had been a complete reshuffling of all the books. Although they still littered the house, almost every book had been moved from its former position and put somewhere else. Thus the last feeble clue to the whereabouts of those I was entitled to pick out and take away had been destroyed. This appalling step had been taken in an effort to bring together in the library the collection of books on London, now sold to Lord Southwood for presentation to the London County Council. To do this, every item on the list with which I came inadequately armed had been successfully displaced; though, as it transpired, the success was limited in other ways, for many London books turned up amongst the miscellaneous assortment which finally poured into the basement of the AEU's head office. A second general post was to take place (in the middle of trying to trace the books we wanted) after the London section – or such of it has had been assembled in the library – had gone, and the shelves were filled with any books that happened to get under the feet in a particularly exasperating way.

But there was also a psychological change. In June, Young David had seemed all benevolence and approval. I had, perhaps on too slight evidence, believed that he favoured the idea of bringing together the working-class library for the union. Certainly I had hoped that everyone concerned would understand that the catalogue had been too long and the hours spent on it too short to make a final choice of books and that when the time came to search them out, a certain latitude would be allowed to include others of equal interest, whether originally marked or not. But that had been when a sale, not a gift, had been in prospect. Now it would have been unseemly to make this request. I could only hope for some unimaginable rush of pure generosity to seize the family; for them to fall in love with me; or regard the union I represented in this case as their only friend. With strong claimants in the field, with bidders competing for the pickings, with auctioneers jostling for place, I thought the chances poor.

In fact, Young David, who met me at the door in dressing-gown and cap, had become almost mad with suspicion. The most frightful incidents had occurred. The worst had been the case of a relative who had quite simply pocketed a Shakespeare folio 'promised me by John', and had had to disgorge it in humiliating circumstances. The agents had been sent packing – 'a lot of scamps' – and Young David had adopted a simple rule-of-thumb attitude to all comers: they could take what was theirs by legal definition and in writing and nothing else. That went for us, too. A further move decided upon in family conclave had been to put safely under lock and key all such books as were thought by some unidentifiable authority to be of unique value – regardless of whether these figured amongst the written donations or not – and to lock up every cupboard, closet, chest and book-case in the house with a formidable bunch of unlabelled keys entrusted to Young David. Apart from his advanced stage of deafness, he was a very hale old man of eighty-three and had all his wits about him; but his tempo was reduced and the act of opening a cupboard or bookcase, which entailed finding the right one out of some five dozen keys, was no hasty work.

The first day remains a nightmare, although on this occasion we met Mrs David, a tiny woman of eighty wearing a goblin's velvet cap and suffering from some respiratory trouble which made her hiss like a little engine as she shunted about the place. She put in an appearance after we had stood for an hour, idle and dismayed, in the stone cold dining-room listening to Young David's tale of crimes and enormities committed by the claimants, and telling us what we must not do. I had few opportunities for getting in my shout, but I tried every now and again to reach his ear, and repeat my formula about the union's purpose and desire. Nothing, he said weightily, must be taken that was not on my list. We were itching to search the place, to get started, but he held us with his mild suspicious eye and his relentless talk, saying at last that we could use this dining-room to stack our books, at which point Mrs David appeared with a cup of tea for each of us and, after courtesies had been exchanged, they went away. But not for long.

To find the books on our list was problem number one. To set aside others of equal interest discovered in this process but not included on our list, and to convey respectfully that we were not trying to steal them but would like permission to buy them, was problem two. The third problem was to prevent Young David from disorganizing both activities by his constant irrelevancies. In and out he wandered, issuing his decree that we were to take nothing not on our list, yet each time offering us some rubbishy work with the kindly statement that we ought to have it because it was just up our street.

We did not venture far from the dining-room that day – a gloomy place, with drawn blinds and a feeble light which cast sad shadows over the heavy furniture and book-filled spaces – and yet managed to start our three piles of books: the wanted and listed, the wanted and unlisted, the unwanted and unlisted (these being Young David's offerings). In the early afternoon I stepped boldly up to Y. D.'s earhole and, pointing to the second pile, said loud and clear that these were over and above the listed books, that we were the AEU and wanted to keep the working-class library together – everything, in fact, that I had said three times before. He seemed quite pleased, nodded a good deal, spoke with warmth of the union under its ancient name and remarked that in his time it had cost a man with eight children something to come out on strike. He then called the agent a rascal and a villain and trotted out. I had not perhaps exactly conveyed my meaning, but I was almost sure that I had captured his attention; so, putting first things first, I profited by his next visit to yell, 'Wouldn't you like a gentleman, and old friend of your brother John, who often came to see him here and knows his books well, to come and advise you about them?' The customary general nod. Yes, he could do with some advice, the agent had been a scoundrel, he had no time for him at all. They should never have taken him on in the first place.

There was no telephone in the house – never had been – but with this to go on I immediately ran to the nearest public telephone and spoke to an old friend who had, indeed, been an associate of John Burns and was himself a well-known historian of the labour movement. I described the situation, referred to the letters and papers that must still be lying about the place and asked him if he would come and look them over and advise the family. He agreed at once and arranged to be in Clapham the following day.

I returned to my work of crawling along a ground-floor corridor on all fours with a candle, since there was no light of any kind, trying to decipher sideways the names on the backs of books – where these faced outwards. My assistant followed behind along the opposite wall and from time to time one or other of us spotted something, halted and tried to prise out the book without causing a major cave-in. Then we took our small haul to the dining-room, to find, as often as not, that it belonged to the wanted but unlisted heap, which was growing out of all proportion.

Young David's visits continued throughout the day. 'I think this'll interest you,' he would say. Most often it did not, but we could never make out whether he intended it to go on the pile to which we were entitled, for he always, at the same time, repeated that we must take nothing not included on our list. The conversations, indeed, now followed a recognized pattern, for at this point I always made my usual rejoinder, but at last managed to get in that John Burns's old friend, the historian, would be glad to come next day and advise on all the books and papers. Young David pondered this for some time. 'Is he a member of the ASE?' he asked at last. I advanced his qualifications and qualities, his integrity and closeness to the trade unions, his tried and true friendship for John Burns, his erudition and his literary fame; but, no, I could not say he was a member of the union. Well, in that case, said Young David, he couldn't come. You could only trust the ASE. Only the ASE could have the books, that was what John would have wanted. It was a great triumph for us, but it did not feel very much like it.

I went out to the telephone again and told our friend not to come. The onus was now firmly – and how heavily! – on us. That first day left us dirty, tired, cold and desperate. We knew that here was not the work of days, but of weeks; and further, that it was not one job but two; that of assembling the 1,200 books freely given and that of persuading someone at some time that the union should be allowed to acquire the complete working-class library in the house. Nor was it really the work of one person or even two; but two only were available and from that day on, throughout the end of October, November and the early days of December, whenever the Research Department's work allowed, I went with my assistant to Clapham, while sometimes one of us went and sometimes the other, until we had developed a very high crawling speed and an unerring eye for identifying books in the dark.

Side by side with the sheer physical labour – for we made sporadic raids to remote corners of the house, prompted by our unreliable list, and lugged about immense piles of bound journals and heavy volumes discovered on the way – our manoeuvres to grain grace and favour went on. It transpired that the only known means of alleviating Mrs David's chest complaint was a nip of whisky, and though this presented almost insuperable difficulties in 1943, we managed to obtain a quarter bottle and please her very much.

It was a hateful autumn. Each morning as we entered the cold, dank house we moved as briskly as possible at our work, to postpone the moment when our hands would be too numb to pull out books. Each night when we emerged, filthy and frozen, into the thick fog, we realised how little headway we had made in either of our twin endeavours, but resolved to pull it off; to round up and somehow or other get possession as nearly as possible of the entire working-class literature this old man had so cleverly hidden amongst his hoard of books.

There were days of progress and days of setback. One late afternoon when we returned to North Side after the 4 o'clock lunch we were then now accustomed to take in a neighbouring café, we found a prosperous gentleman standing in the fog-filled hall. He was some relative, a son or grandson of Young David, and took great interest in our work. He questioned us quite closely. I said off pat what I had said in that house fifty times before. He was not deaf at all. He listened to me with apparent interest and comprehension. I laid particular stress on the union's willingness to pay handsomely for books not included on our list; whereupon the gentleman joined most helpfully in this hunt, shinning up steps in an agile way and bringing down books which we had glimpsed on upper shelves. But then he read through the smudged and tattered list in my assistant's hands and if he could not find the exact title and author on it – of which there was never much hope – he shinned up again as nimbly as before and replaced the book.

We never knew whom we should find in the house and what they would be up to and why. We deployed our forces and one day my assistant went to the attic leaving me in some cupboard where she came running to tell me that it was very nice upstairs as an old gas fire had been lit, but that two ladies were in occupation, engaged in socialist emulation, competing with each other to destroy letters and documents in the shortest possible time – those, that is, which had not gone to salvage in the months before. I went up and made a small lame speech about Great Men and the unforeseeable needs of their biographers. The ladies were well disposed. They paused and one, indeed, showed me a letter in a faded, spidery hand which, she said, had been written all of forty years ago by a bishop. She dropped it into a boot-box at her side which, though almost empty, seemed to have been placed there for items worth preserving. I asked if it was an interesting letter. She repeated that it had been written by a bishop and quite forty years ago. We conversed a little longer and then the ladies returned with a will to their tearing up. I could hardly suggest that they – relatives of the deceased – were unable to judge the value of his correspondence. There was, in fact, nothing further I could say at all and I might well have been sent about my business as it was, but I was glad to note that every now and then a little sheet or two dropped into the boot-box, so I went back to my cupboard.

But if we could teach nobody anything, at least we learnt a lot. We learnt a lot about John Burns – though not as much as we were to learn later when, as we cleaned and sorted the books in the Research Department, we came to read what he had written in the flyleaf of almost every one. We learnt then and there, however, that his books had been his filing system: out of every second or third book that we handled fell press-cuttings, notes and pamphlets relating to the subject. These we put aside each day. We learnt a lot about the movement, and we learnt a lot about books. Naturally the appetite grew by what it fed on and I spent most evenings trying to read up about the journals I had found and what numbers should be extant, which led to one of the greatest time-wasters in the whole process.

I vaguely remembered having seen in a footnote to the Webbs' *History of Trade Unionism*, which I owned in the 1919 Trade Union edition, that the British Museum file on the *Beehive* was incomplete and that Mr John Burns had kindly lent his complete file. I looked up this reference and there it was. The next day I turned the Burns house upside-down, ignoring my assistant's pleas to explore the library, where now – the London books having been removed – an entirely unknown quantity awaited quite comfortable and easy inspection. I could find only three bound volumes of the *Beehive* which we had already brought down from the attic. Now I was really on the warpath. I poked into places I had never suspected before. I raced up and down the stairs. I pulled open closets, I threw out books on the shelves and discovered others behind them, but I never found the *Beehive*.

Some months later when, with an increase of staff in the Research Department, my assistant and I had organized our work to devote two hours at the end of each day to examining and listing the Burns books, I found on the flyleaf of *Red Star over China*, published in 1937, the following words in Burns's bold handwriting: 'Read this on my way to give my volumes of *Beehive* to the British Museum.' By this time, having read the inconsecutive diary which the flyleaves of his books presented and come to know his character quite well, I should not have been surprised to learn that on reaching the British Museum, John Burns had turned about and changed his mind. This fact might have been recorded in the flyleaf of the book he had read on his return journey, but whether that book would ever be found, or was in our possession or even still in existence, nobody could say. So I went to the Reading Room and there, sure enough, below the original printed slip was an amendment showing the entire file.

As the search went on and we had explored pretty well every corner prowling about for this *Beehive* and other elusive items, we discovered that some pretty murky cupboards contained sheaves and stacks of pamphlets. I asked Young David if we had permission to take such things if we wanted them and this was readily granted, for not only did they come under the heading of sheer rubbish, for which no buyers could conceivably be found, but our personal relations had gained warmth. As did our persons in due course. The old couple occupied a bright and cosy room, formerly the housekeeper's sitting-room, at the far end of the house and there a good fire was always going where we were encouraged to sit and thaw out every few hours. We were also offered endless cups of tea and made welcome in the sculleries to do our washing up. In short, we had been accepted.

Permission to extract the pamphlets was one thing, extraction another. We stood in turns on steps in the closets of the house, one held a candle aloft and the other rapidly turned over the piles of paper: Robert Owen,

Cobbett, Kropotkin and Bakunin, Blatchford and Hyndman, Bernstein and Shaw – they poured down on us in yellowing and grimy streams. There were Chartist pamphlets and strike leaflets and the reports of trade unionists on trial; there were anonymous records of early nineteenth-century workmen who had been sent into the first factories as orphans; and there were also, of course, old *Strand* magazines and booksellers' catalogues and all the publications of the Free Trade Movement and the old Local Government Board, the Liberal Party's reports and those of organizations for the promotion of temperance and the suppression of every form of vice in whose activities, at one time or another, Burns had been interested. These had to be sorted and sifted in our own interest. But the haul – of several hundred, collected at the rate of perhaps twenty an hour – was very precious, though there were some cupboards we never had the time to broach at all. And one cupboard gave up its secrets in an unexpected way.

Young David's policy of caution frequently broke down. He was often to be found trying to fit one of his sixty keys into one of the sixty odd locks, and, after some hours, he would call upon us to admire a Kelmscott volume which he averred would fetch many hundred pounds and then he would go away and spend another hour locking it up again. To watch him at this work was more than anyone could bear, but we would sometimes hear the jingle of keys and the deep muted voice bumbling away for a long time in a neighbouring room. But after the incident with the ladies, evidently reported in the housekeeper's room, where perhaps it seemed no more than another amiable aspect of our idiotic interest in old papers, Young David beckoned me one day with nods and winks and all his keys ringing, and let me into a small back room which I had hardly seen before.

It may have been intended for what is called a butler's pantry, or even a more private place from which the plumbing had been removed to accommodate more literature. Against one wall stood a high old-fashioned wardrobe and this Young David approached with many smiles and happy mutterings. This time there was no escaping the full performance. Patiently and cheerfully he tried to fit one after another of the keys – and no doubt often the same one again and again – into the lock, interrupting his brisk conversation with himself to promise me great treasure when the door should be opened. As I waited, and waited, I looked round and saw on the floor a large number of very tempting looking papers which my practised eye now recognised as the folded sheets of Robert Owen's plans for society, but I could not pick them up.

At last, owing no doubt to the simple mechanism of the lock and the similarity of some dozen old-fashioned keys, Young David got his cupboard open. He winked at me again with a look of extreme cunning and, as he put his hand inside and withdrew a large plain envelope he said: 'It's worth a Jew's eye!' and repeated this strange saying many times. He then brought out a letter from Admiral ('Jacky') Fisher written to John Burns in 1915 or thereabouts which consisted of a few conventional lines of thanks, or regret, on a sheet of Admiralty paper. I said how gratified I was to be shown the priceless document and the old man, with chuckles and a further reference to the Jew's eye, put the letter back into its obviously new envelope, and tucked it into some secret pocket under his dressing-gown and shuffled away. That was how we acquired the Robert Owen plans and a great many other things, such as the earliest copies of *Reynolds's Newspaper* which were in the cupboard now left wide open and apparently no longer worth locking, even if, by nightfall, a key could have been found for it.

This system of what might be termed self-help had by now become part and parcel of our lawful occasions. It had been found quite impossible to draw a straight line between what we were supposed to have, what we were allowed to have and what was taboo. All I could do to satisfy my own idea of ethics was to lay in a very special corner every book and pamphlet which appeared to be of genuine value, to note it on a separate list, and one day I hoped to be able to make an honest purchase of these items if ever a rational and approachable being appeared on the scene.

And then, as November passed and arrangements for the auction of the 'costly antique style furniture' and effects of the Rt Hon. John Burns were getting under way, Mrs F. arrived. This lady, who had had a long and interesting working life, was now independent. She had not given up her employment until this point and so we had never met her at the house before, though we understood that she called sometimes in the evenings. It was only in the light of her wonderful everyday sanity that we realised how very eccentric and almost demented we had become in the preceding weeks. For the first time the house emerged from its year-old chill and darkness: electric bulbs were put in all the rooms where we had been working and fires were lit. She not only heard, but perfectly understood what was said to her. She agreed that we should take whatever we wanted to complete that section of the library which she hoped the union would dedicate as a memorial to her uncle; she did not give a fig whether the books were on our original list or not. Her generosity was tremendous. She wished to give us a portrait of John Burns to hang in an honoured place in the Memorial Library. Life in North Side became almost normal.

But with order and sanity new dangers threatened. Mrs. F.'s goodwill and sense of justice were impartial. Unlike Young David, she did not consider the AEU the centre of the universe and did not regard either the National Liberal Club or the Battersea Town Council as a set of scamps. She was determined that everyone should have their rights; and she did this despite a very ambiguous attitude to the property in question for, on the one hand, she had an overflowing admiration for the gifts of her late uncle and his splendid sought-after library, on the other she was almost as exasperated as the estate agent had been by the mere sight and smell and litter of the books. One felt she would have liked to give them a good, hearty, housewifely kick from time to time. They certainly bothered her a great deal. But fair was fair. And so a new nightmare began.

We would arrive in the morning to find that Mrs F. had conscientiously gone through our previous day's finds and taken out what she thought was someone else's due. There were endless borderline cases – books on economics and history and social questions, the daily bread of our Research Department – which had simply been removed as more suited to the needs of others. She really felt that we had performed a valuable service by our faithful sorting and piling of the books, which we were now having removed from the house to the union's premises once a week; and she was at heart rather sceptical of the monetary value of any of her uncle's effects. She had, of course, a quite different idea from Young David's as to what constituted value. Most of the special items I had laid aside, she granted me without hesitation – they included the *North Briton* and the *Red Republican* – and thus a two-way process was instituted: before we left at night, the most notable of the day's finds were stuffed into briefcases, leaving for Mrs F. those things that we, on our side, considered fair game for the National Liberal Club and the Battersea Council. In this way we were more cheerfully able to make the sacrifices she asked. What was smuggled out was, of course, eventually smuggled back again and, on a memorable occasion, I placed all these books on a table in Mrs F.'s sitting-room and told her plainly they were worth a lot of money and never had been on our list, but that if we were not allowed to have them then they would almost certainly find their way on to some dilettante's bookshelf, never to be read, whilst leaving our collection not only the poorer but unrepresentative of the best and most interesting of the old Socialist and trade-union publications.

Before this I had written to the President and asked him what I could do about the books not included in the gift and if the executive would allow me to bid for them as originally intended; I also urged that the union should buy at the auction sale some of the well-made book cases from the library, to house our new acquisition. This had been agreed and now Mrs F. was willing to accept a token sum to include such items as the *Black Dwarf*, the *New Moral World*, *The Reasoner*, *The Chartist Circular*, Louis Philippe on *The Trade Unions of England*, Keir Hardie's *Miner*, Reynolds's *Political Instructor*, and Ernest Jones's *Notes to the People*.

Moreover on the day before the sale – which opened on 8 December – Mrs F. allowed me to precede the auctioneer's man as he chalked up 'lots' on the bookshelves in the library and make a final free choice of any book I wanted. On this day, too, I told her that, as my work in the house must now be regarded as at an end, I could not attend the sale but would dearly like to bid, myself, for one object. This was a hideous small cigar-case set with a formless mosaic of small stones and the word Carlsbad stamped in faded gilt letters on the back. Young David had shown it to me and explained that it had been a present from Karl Marx to Frederick Engels – surely one of the very rare gifts to pass this rather than the other way between these two – and from Engels to Burns. In his usual fashion, Burns had written out the circumstances and history of the gift on a small card which lay inside the discoloured mauve satin lining of the case – with a lock of Stepniak's hair, also labelled. This was an amusing trifle not 'worth a Jew's eye' – and I now asked Mrs F. to buy it for me in the sale, whereupon she asked me to accept it personally as a present.

We got our bookshelves and on 14 December the last of the books, together with a perfectly indiscriminate vanload of unsold 'lots', poured into the basement of the union's offices. (In the end, after a little perfunctory sorting had been done, one antiquarian bookseller consulted and every member of the union's packing staff and now expanded Research Department had had a 'good read', this stack of books was sold to a large second-hand dealer at the rate of, roughly, 2d a volume.)

We finished up with some 3,000 volumes and in January 1944 the union's *Journal* was able to proclaim that it had 'become the custodian of one of the most interesting, valuable and complete working-class libraries in England'. Many people came to see our finds in those first months. A large number of books on trade unionism, economics and industrial conditions was housed in our Research Department for immediate use; others, too precious for daily handling, were stored in a basement, and there my assistant and I retired at the end of each day to dust and sort and list our treasure.

The long-drawn-out process began seriously to interfere with our work and we were at length to engage the services of a librarian, who sat all day at the task, completing the listing of books with their dates of publication and removing the letters, leaflets and notes which had been stored inside the covers. A proper catalogue was never made, but the lists were complete when the first V1 bombs began to fall and our department was urged to leave London and join the Head Office in the country. In reply we asked that not we but the books might be sent into safety. This was at last agreed and the entire London 'staff' – packers and researchers – filled great wooden branch boxes, which eventually left an area where an average of fifteen buzz-bombs was falling each day.

I learnt a few weeks later that the boxes were standing as delivered, in the open, and wrote to our newly elected General Secretary to suggest that we should have them insured. The figure suggested was £5,000 whereupon the boxes were taken indoors at once. But nothing ever came of the AEU John Burns Memorial Library. And after the war, when the Head Office of the union returned to London, less and less interest was shown by the 'custodians' of this treasure. In the early 1950s it was given away – 'on permanent loan' – to the TUC, and now in the Research Department of the union for which I no longer work there can only be faint reminders of that proud possession in the form of the bold signature and a little anecdote or comment written on the flyleaves of some of the books.

One footnote to this record is worth adding: Mrs F. retrieved a great many of the papers and in due course I was invited to her house where, for the last time, I met Young David. It was also the first time I had seen him without a dressing-gown and cap. He looked more splendid and erect than ever in his good serge suit and I was witness to the agreement then verbally made that these papers should be handed over to the British Museum. I approached the Keeper to sound out whether he would accept the papers and, one day shortly afterwards, Mrs F. and I called upon him in the Museum and the transaction was agreed. The papers, diaries and documents that had been saved are where they belong. And somewhere I have a copy of the list of the 3,032 books we chose.

5

A less strenuous but quite interesting activity during my term of office at the AEU came my way as a result of Tanner consulting me on how the union could fête its jubilee in 1945. I suggested that it would be a fine thing to mark the occasion by commissioning a history, a play, a song and pictures, all celebrating the engineers, to constitute a lasting tribute to the organization.

It was, of course, unheard-of for a trade union to set foot in the cultural field. Nevertheless, thanks to Jack Tanner's open mind and genuine interest in the arts, he embraced the idea enthusiastically and, at the memorable first of many meetings, presided over the assembled company of the actor and theatre director André van Gyseghem, the writer and poet Montagu Slater, the historian James Jefferys, the composer Aubrey Bowman and the art historian Francis Klingender. (The only item that came to nothing was the song which, though the lyric was approved, failed in some indefinable way to meet Tanner's musical taste, though he listened to Bowman playing his composition over and over again.)

It cannot be said that the enterprise signalled a breakthrough for the arts in trade-union circles. Outside London, no district marked the jubilee with any but the traditional parades, speeches, sports and serious drinking. Montagu Slater's play, *Pioneers! O Pioneers!* was performed on a few consecutive evenings at the Scala Theatre; Jefferys' admirable history never achieved a large readership outside the union, though it remains an invaluable work of reference; while – perhaps the most successful venture – the exhibition of pictures, entitled 'The Engineer in British Life', under the auspices of the Artists' International Association, was opened at the White-chapel Art Gallery by Ernest Bevin, then still the Minister of Labour. In the long run this also proved the most fruitful of our efforts, for it inspired Francis Klingender, who had organized it, to write his fine book *Art and the Industrial Revolution*, published two years later.

Immediately after these festivities were over I took my two weeks' holiday, going with Margaret to Helzaphron, near Gunwalloe, with its tiny church on the seashore of Mount's Bay in Cornwall. There, on 5 July, we spent the whole day indoors listening to the General Election results as they were announced on the radio until the unlooked-for landslide Labour victory was clear beyond all doubt.

To return, however, to my work at the AEU, it had emerged ever more plainly from the production enquiries of 1941 and 1942 that the members' most outspoken complaints and deepest dissatisfaction concerned the phys-ical conditions of their working environment. They varied with the type of industry – docks, foundries, factories and so forth – but the criticisms reflected a widespread disregard for the comfort, convenience, health and safety of the workforce. Ventilation, lighting, the lack of first aid, canteen and washing facilities, coupled with a failure to comply with even the minimal safety regulations laid down, all came under attack. It struck me that what was needed was a health and safety enquiry on the same lines as the production enquiries, but concentrated on this aspect of our union members' experience.

This enquiry was launched, to receive a most enthusiastic response from shop stewards in every kind of enterprise; but it met with almost none from the Executive Council. Indeed, the officials evinced not the smallest inter-est in the subject. I fought a losing battle for the union to take up the matter of the appalling conditions revealed. The report which I compiled was shelved and no action whatsoever was taken. I could not but regard this as a major defeat.

Far greater attention was paid to the draft we prepared on the post-war restructuring of the engineering industry. As the years went on, we found that our files were devoted more and more to the future. From this material we compiled our report which was treated with some consideration, as was the evidence we wrote for Tanner to present on behalf of the AEU to the Royal Commission on Equal Pay for Women. I have always claimed that this had been my one contribution to feminism, though it was, of course, twenty years too early.

6

After the bombing of the Nassington Road house, when it was declared unsafe for habitation, we were rehoused in what was called 'half-way' accommodation – that is an unconverted building with a bombed-out family on every floor – in Belsize Avenue where we occupied the ground floor and basement. It was a hideous, late-Victorian structure, with rooms too lofty and ill-proportioned, draughts too inescapable and all possibilities of heating too inadequate for comfort.

For a while we had housed my refugee cousin Eva and her family there, but they had now departed and the end of the war found us still living in these unprepossessing conditions to which, however, we now settled down and decided that the time had now come to embark upon the long-postponed study of Marx's *Capital*. This we proposed to do together with two of Margaret's closest friends, Peter and Sheila Wheeler, whose marriage many years before she had witnessed.

It is well known that Marx is not an easy author. One can tell at once which of his most trenchant critics have not been able to read him at all by their custom of attributing to him views he did not profess, pronouncements he never made and theories he explicitly repudiated, just as it is common practice to present him in private life, in defiance of the massive evidence provided by published correspondence, as a domestic tyrant, a despot and a lecher who spurned his wife and bullied his abject daughters.

Having now made up our minds to find out what Marx had really said, we found it exceedingly slow going, for no sooner had one or other of us read aloud a passage than we were obliged to halt and discuss at great length what it could possibly mean. The people living above us in our makeshift residence were a young couple with a little girl. They were now having another baby and the husband, recently demobilized, had left his small daughter with friends, and was redecorating the rooms against his wife's return from giving birth in the local hospital. It was a terribly noisy operation, bad enough at any time, but intolerable on those evenings when we were bent on understanding Marx. We sent him a courteous message asking him to desist from his crashing about on those weekly occasions of study. He responded by expressing much interest in what we were reading and, when told, begged to be allowed to join us.

In the circumstances we could hardly refuse; but it emerged that he found Marx even more difficult that we did which led not only to furious arguments and some loss of temper, but brought our sluggish progress almost to a standstill. He was, however, most persistent in his wish to learn and, even after his wife's return home with the new baby, he would not relinquish his thirst for knowledge. This went on for many months and, when summer came, we had made so little headway that we decided that we and the Wheelers with their two little children would go away on holiday together to carry on with *Capital*. Thus in 1947 we set out in two cars for St Tropez where we had taken for a few weeks at a ridiculously low rent a villa with a private beach a little way out of the town.

While I had not been in those parts since the early thirties, both Sheila and Margaret had stayed in St Tropez just before the war, making many friends among the local Communists whom they naturally hoped to meet again. We knew, of course, that there were severe food shortages in France and, though some items were still rationed in England, by pooling our resources we managed to assemble and pack into the cars bags of flour, sugar and coffee, packets of tea and tins of meat intended for the comrades who had been through, as we had not, the dangers and privations of occupation and resistance.

Our journey brought home to us only too sharply what France had suffered. Everywhere in the north the verges were littered with the remains of rusting tanks, armoured vehicles no better than twisted metal, Wehrmacht helmets, guns and other such war detritus. One could have thought that all the towns and villages through which we passed were *en fête*: everyone out in the streets which were lined with stalls; and then one realized that this was because houses and shops had been demolished. Most painful and pitiable to see were the children: undersized, pallid, with troubled little faces, who were invariably a few inches shorter yet a few years older than the sturdy small Wheelers.

Our villa, we learnt, had been briefly taken over not by Germans but by Italian officers. According to the housekeeper and her husband, who had lived throughout the war in a cottage on the grounds after the owners left and who were now there with orders to look after us, the occupiers had done relatively little damage. The lower ground floor, on a level with and opening onto the beach, was designed for children and equipped like a ship, with portholes for windows, bunk beds as in a cabin and a fine old wheel compass. The name of the ship, painted in bold letters on the wall, was *La Discipline*.

Our most immediate need was to get ration cards without which there were few essential foods we could buy. Thus on the first morning we went, all six of us, to the food office in the town and lined up in the long queue. Pregnant women were sensibly told to come to the front and were quickly served; but when at last our turn came we were told that ration cards for visitors were not available: we must call the next day. We did so but were again turned away empty-handed. This happened one day after another and seemed a wicked waste of time when we might have been out in the sunshine, basking, bathing, teaching the children to swim, exploring the coast. What was more, until we had ration cards we were eating the most horrible bread made of maize flour and drinking acorn coffee. We lived mostly on the vegetables grown in the housekeeper's plot of land. Since it was thought that my French was the most fluent, I was made to conduct the negotiations day after day for the best part of a week. Finally, egged on by the others standing behind me, I banged the counter and shouted at the man behind it: 'But the children must eat!' and 'The children need milk!' The crowd took my part, crying: 'She has reason!' 'It is unworthy!' and so forth, which stoked my genuine anger and lent fire to my protests. Nevertheless, there was nothing to be done and, with five disconsolate people trailing behind me, we left the food office yet again without cards.

That evening we had arranged to visit the comrades, having happily found that many from the pre-war days were still alive, though there had naturally been many changes: some deaths as well as remarriages and births, so that various families had regrouped, as it were, and we were invited to call at a house where a number of them were living together in the centre of the town. We collected up our packets and bags of food and, on arrival, laid everything out upon a table to cries of surprise and joy from the women – their husbands were not yet home from work – and we then went out onto a veranda overlooking the leafy main square to sip an aperitif.

As one of the men arrived, his wife rushed indoors and we heard her say: 'See what our English friends have brought for us: look, white flour, real coffee and tea, lots of beautiful sugar. It's magnificent.' Her husband expressed his pleasure and astonishment and then came out on to the veranda to thank us. He was the young man from the food office with whom I had my daily shouting match. As soon as he caught sight of me, he staggered back, as if struck, put an arm up to shield his face in self-defence and cried: 'Why didn't you bring out your Party card? I would have enrolled you as citizens.' He then asked rhetorically: 'What tourists would have saved food for us that they could have eaten themselves?'

Unfortunately for our study of Marx, the villa was not only beautifully furnished, far beyond our needs and above my station, but it had a fine library where we all found such tempting alternative reading that we made no progress at all with *Capital*. Eventually we came to the conclusion that to master a work of this kind one must concentrate upon it in solitude and, if need be, seek instruction from some not too stuck-up scholar. Our little group, having provided the pretext for a delightful holiday, dissolved itself and we reverted to purely social occasions.

During those years, from 1941, Margaret, after a preliminary canter at Reuters' listening post where she monitored German stations, had been appointed to set up and run the Soviet Monitor: the only non-Russian ever to be in charge of a Soviet institution in this country. At Reuters Soviet broadcasts were heard and taken down by White Russians. One of them rushed around the offices in great excitement one day to announce that he had just picked up extracts from an anti-Soviet book and should he, did his colleagues think, flash it round the world? Margaret asked what the book was called. '*Anti-Dühring*,' she was told. She thereupon encouraged him to put it out world-wide and, although her motives must have been purely mischievous, his true friends in their innocent and fervent hatred of the Soviet Union egged him on.

The Soviet Monitor operated on a twenty-four-hour basis with a staff of some two dozen men and women who listened through earplugs to Russian broadcasts while simultaneously transcribing them in English onto the tape machines connected with the Fleet Street office where runners took the material to all the newspapers then still in that quarter. So efficient was this service that it beat all others in speed and accuracy, issuing bulletins throughout the day and night on the campaigns waged on the Eastern Front from the early days of near-disaster, the great battles that ensued and on to the victory of Stalingrad and the triumphant advance to the west as far as Berlin itself.

The members of the staff had to be bilingual and politically committed, to live in domestic circumstances permitting them to work alternate day and night shifts and to have quick wits and journalistic abilities above the average. People possessed of this rather unusual combination of attributes are not necessarily compatible and Margaret, an accomplished peace-maker – or 'soothsayer', as she called it – would sometimes after a long day at the listening post in Whetstone, be roused from sleep and recalled to deal with ructions and 'say sooth'. There were, nevertheless, some star-crossed love affairs among the staff, a few marriages and several bonny Soviet Monitor babies over the years.

Whenever we went on our brief holidays Margaret would generally find a telegram awaiting her which read: 'Stay where you are.' This meant that she should return at once because a vital piece of news had broken – some major battle being waged – and, after spending her first day closeted in the local public telephone booth to find out exactly what was afoot, she would take the next train back to London.

At the end of the war the Soviet Embassy sent for her. She did not expect to receive a medal nor yet a word of thanks for her services; but neither did she anticipate the thorough dressing-down she was now given for having failed to report and disseminate an item which, she explained, contravened the British libel laws. That was not considered a valid excuse and she was roundly accused of taking altogether too much upon herself in suppressing statements by prominent Soviet leaders. Margaret held her ground and refused to give the speech publicity. In due course in the early 1950s when, though still of interest, the Soviet Monitor had outlived its original function, it was summarily closed down by the government on, precisely, the grounds of violating the laws of libel. It was also true, of course, that its continuation was in conflict with the new times of the Cold War.

During the difficult period of winding up the Monitor, Margaret thought it would be a good thing that I should go away. I went to Rome where I had not been for three decades. I had an introduction to the Italian Communist Party from Harry Pollitt and accordingly called at its head-quarters in the via delle Botteghe Oscura where I learnt the most fascinating things about the Italians including the fact that the Communists in some of the poorest rural districts, unable to meet their dues, paid in kind by sending cartloads of farm produce to feed the Party workers in the towns.

I was asked if there were anything they could do for me and I said I should very much like permission to attend an ordinary branch meeting. It was arranged that I should do so that same evening at eight o'clock in the campo di Fiori. I was advised to take my Party card with me: 'In case,' they said, 'they mistake you for an American.' I arrived punctually at the place where the meeting was to be held but found it almost empty. However, as the evening wore on, the room began to fill up not only with young men and women but also their babies and their dogs, creating a rather jolly atmosphere with a great deal of noise, the loud excited chatter being aug-mented by barking and howls. Everyone was most friendly and I early established that I was not an American while my British Party card was passed from hand to hand and examined to cries of astonishment and plea-sure. Many nods and smiles were cast in my direction, the card was tapped with approval and fingers were pointed. Wherefore, I asked my neighbour, this outstanding display of enthusiasm? He explained that never before had anyone seen a Party card stamped up to date.

The meeting at last got started at about 10.30 by which time the babies and the dogs were sound asleep. It went on until the early hours of the morning, for a tremendous argument raged on whether or not war was necessary to bring about social change, the Russia of 1917 and the recent events in the countries of Eastern Europe being cited in support of this view. The very young Party official who had come to address the branch advanced a quite different opinion but had some difficulty in impressing it upon men and women whose fathers and uncles had been done to death by

Mussolini. Nevertheless, he was able to persuade the majority that the horrors and sufferings of war, though perhaps an effective if terrible forcing ground, were not essential to the cause of social progress and that peace was greatly preferable. When they dispersed, everyone was ready to canvass for signatures to the Stockholm Peace Appeal of those days.

By the time I got back to London the Soviet Monitor was dead, its staff scattered, its premises vacated and Margaret herself starting a new career as managing director of a political bookshop. Later she transferred to the publishing house that, upon her initiative and under her editorship, was to bring out the first complete English edition of the works of Marx and Engels, a task that engaged her fully into the days of her last illness.

It was in 1947 that the local council offered to rehouse us in a flat on premises requisitioned in the decidedly expensive neighbourhood of Heath Drive. We were given little choice: it was this or nothing, now or never, take it or leave it. We took it. The rent was far above anything I had previously paid (£4 a week, I seem to remember), but conditions in Belsize Avenue had become so intolerable – the ground-floor rooms lofty, ill-proportioned and unheatable, the basement dangerously damp and the ancient geyser in the bathroom shared by three families, liable to explode at any moment – that we did not long hesitate.

My father came to see me there just once, for he died in the following year. He approved of my new surroundings, saying that at last I was living in a manner fitting for a gentlewoman. I did not spoil his pleasure by telling him that the gentlefolk who had abandoned the place to escape from the bombing would soon come back to reclaim their property when I would revert to the squalor of what he considered my gypsy lifestyle.

What in fact happened was that the many occupants of requisitioned houses throughout the borough formed a lively pressure group to protect their precarious position. It met irregularly in my flat and exerted some, if marginal, influence upon the local councillors whom we never ceased to harass with demands and petitions. Most vexatious of all was our insistence upon being received by the full council in session when we delivered well-prepared statements of our case. We even took the town hall on one occasion, when excellent speeches were made to an eager and attentive audience. One of these was delivered by a handsome woman with a highly trained and beautiful voice, the mother of two young schoolboys housed by the borough in disgusting conditions. She became a good friend of mine for the rest of her life and, at that time, I went to see her quite often in the terrible place where, in two rooms far apart, in an enormous, derelict building, she and her sons lived, to meet in the communal kitchen in which, at seven cooking stoves, as many families tried at one and the same time to prepare their meals.

The day came when, as foreseen, these houses were 'de-requisitioned' and given back to their former owners so that we were one and all thrown to the wolves: that is, private landlords. A few people, but very few, were eligible for housing by the council: the rest found that things had greatly changed since pre-war days and that rented accommodation was practically unobtainable. It was not only that, in my case, I had not the means to buy a place, but Margaret had quite rooted objections to owning property. That, however, seemed the only prospect if we were not to be rendered homeless: and so it turned out.

We had bought what was then called a 'small dwelling' on the basis of a fifteen-year mortgage from the local council, the ten per cent deposit on it having been given to me by my mother. Since then, it has been found to be of architectural interest, is listed as a Grade II building, and I am simply not numerate enough to compute by how many thousand per cent its value has increased. All I know is that, on first going over it I was convinced that – despite the clutter of furniture, the dingy curtaining that hid the fine windows with their delicate glazing bars and the depressing paintwork decoration in shades of dried blood – if the proportions were indeed as my yardstick told, then the rooms must be decorously beautiful.

Nineteen fifty-six, the year when I moved house for the last time, was of course the traumatic year of the Hungarian uprising, crushed by invading Soviet troops, and of Suez, that last-but-one fling of British imperialism. But before – and above – all else, March 1956 was the occasion for Krushchev's speech to the 20th Congress of the Communist Party of the Soviet Union, disclosing the horrendous character of the Stalin regime behind the Socialist rhetoric.

In our new surroundings we entertained members of the Berliner Ensemble, in London on the first of their two guest seasons, when they performed *Mother Courage, The Caucasian Chalk Circle* and *Trumpets and Drums* at the Palace Theatre. And there it was, at the very weekend when we settled in, that, with everyone else, we were able to read the Kruschev speech, conveyed after three months to the western press.

I was of those who felt the necessity to examine the political orientation and basic principles, to re-assess – literally – the home truths of British capitalism that had initially motivated our adherence to Communism. Whatever delusions about the Soviet Union we may have fostered, they had never determined, though they had certainly confused, our compass readings. We had to take new bearings. Though we were not deflected from our course, it marked a turning point. 'Never glad confident morning again.'

7

As soon as I left the AEU I took the longest holiday I had had in years – some full six weeks – going back to Helzaphron in Cornwall. I knew that, this time, there was not likely to be any blacklisting and that I should probably have not too much difficulty getting a job. Although it had been ignored and never distributed, the health and safety enquiry I had conducted for the AEU was mentioned in the applications I made and I was shortly offered work by the Medical Research Council.

The best thing about it was that I had to spend most of my time in factories: at Vauxhall's in Luton, ICI in the Perry Bar district of Birmingham
and the Morris works in Cowley. Otherwise there was little to be said in
favour of the job. I was attached to a unit working on what was called
industrial psychology – a group of pleasant young men under a mild,
charming, elderly leader – which engaged in the childish pursuit of assess-
ing degrees of what was known as 'job satisfaction'. This entailed inter-
viewing men from the workshop floor who were given time off, with pay,
for the purposes of this unscientific research. They were asked a series of
rather impertinent questions by our group of middle-class people who
were doing this with the management's blessing. The answers, purporting
to establish on a five-point scale the exact degree of satisfaction the men
took in their work, were then subjected to the most rigorous statistical
analysis, quite as though the data had some objective validity and were to
be taken seriously.

I did not find this at all interesting and disliked the rather patronizing
role I played so that, once the unit came in from the cold of provincial life
to be incorporated as a group in the Department of Psychology at University College London, I asked and received permission to undertake a
project on my own. Since my interest in the subject of health and safety in
the workplace was still lively, I planned to look into what provisions of this
nature were made in a particular area: I chose the West Ham district which
included the docks, Silvertown, the railway workshops of Stratford East,
and still bore the scars of war damage. It was many years before it would be
rebuilt with tower blocks, overpasses, underpasses and, finally, the wholesale obliteration of dockland.

I intended to find out what general facilities for health care existed –
where there were factory doctors, nurses, first-aid posts, rest rooms and
suchlike – in this part of the Factory Inspectorate's metropolitan divisions
on the fringe of the city. Apart from the fact that this district was where the
highest number of accidents, both fatal and non-fatal, had occurred,

according to the latest report, it also, for historical reasons, included an exceptionally high proportion of industrial processes that involved handling noxious and dangerous substances, many of them carried on in premises so small – mere sheds – as to fall quite outside any form of supervision. I also wanted to know whether the local general practitioners were concerned with the working environment of their patients and the specific health hazards to which these might be exposed.

It was an absorbing investigation, carried out in an area that, as I came to know it well, I found ever more fascinating. Although it cost me my job with the MRC, for the report I produced was deeply frowned upon by my chiefs, I have never regretted doing it. With great care I composed a Wagnerian letter of resignation to the professor, making it clear that I thought they did not only dislike the character of my work but also the fact that I was a woman and no longer young.

If I have a regret it is that the report never saw the light of day. It may lie buried in the MRC archives, if not destroyed. Naturally, its findings will have been superseded with the passage of time but, on the other hand, that will have lent it a certain historical value.

At one point during this period I had to go into hospital for tests. My GP's letter referring me to the consultant must have mentioned that I worked for the Medical Research Council. I did not know this and was perplexed by the attention and consideration shown me until the registrar, on one of his visits to my bedside addressed me as 'Dr Kapp'. I told him I was not a doctor, whereupon all was changed and I was treated like all the rest, that is to say, like cattle. I was called 'dearie' by some very young men and suffered one indignity after another until the consultant who, having mislaid my notes, had decided that nothing could be done for me, apprised me of the fact by turning back after he had whisked past my bed to say: 'What, you still here?'

Since those days, medical treatment has gradually declined into more of a do-it-yourself service, as people are loath to bother their doctors unless they are in need of heart or brain surgery. We shall soon all be out to gather healing herbs in the hedgerows, where these have not been bulldozed.

I started translating more or less by accident and came to wish that I had never done so. Whereas my work for refugees and in the AEU served the interests of people I cared about, the MRC job – at least until I embarked upon my own project – did not. It was boring, time-consuming and included, among other unwelcome concomitants, living away from home in dingy hotels for frequent short periods. Thus when I was asked as a favour to the publishers to knock into shape a particularly clumsy trans-lation of a short novel by one of the editors of *Humanité*, I was only too happy. Little did I think that this pursuit, which had the teasing appeal of crossword puzzles and was as pointless, would become my full-time occu-pation and means of livelihood. Yet that is what it did. Some of the books that came my way were of so trifling a nature that I felt ashamed of myself and translated them under a variety of different pseudonyms. I also spent more time than I care to remember on editing the English versions of modern Russian fiction: novels for the most part so predictably awful as to constitute anti-Soviet propaganda. In fact, with two exceptions, I got nothing out of this experience but acute financial anxiety, for the work was abominably underpaid.

The two exceptions were, firstly, Brecht's *Tales from the Calendar*, which gave me a fresh and valuable understanding of the possibilities of the German language. This also led to my being given the assignment by Helene Weigel of overseeing all the translations of Brecht's plays then being published here (though, on the debit side, it landed me with a commis-sion from the widow of Johannes R. Becher to produce an English version of her husband's uninspired lyric to Eisler's music for the German Demo-cratic Republic's national anthem: words, I am damn sure, that have never been and never will be sung). The second exception – this an unalloyed bonus – grew from my translating the correspondence between Frederick Engels and Marx's daughter Laura and her husband Paul Lafargue, for this fired my initial interest in Eleanor Marx and led, in the fullness of time, to my writing her biography.

Were it not for those benefits I could not look back upon the years of full-time translating as anything other than an iniquitous waste. Having, as was proper, responded to the demands made by the refugee era and the war years while, it could be hoped, maturing in the process, I ought now to have gone back to writing.

It was at this period that my morale was boosted and I acquired a new friend. I was laid up with flu reading *The Times* in bed, when I came upon an article in the series *Pleasures of Reading* called 'Re-readability' by Jocelyn Brooke and there, of all unexpected things, was a reference to my novel *Mediterranean Blues*. This had been written some thirty years before and, while it had a few moderately good jokes, I had never thought much of it; yet here was this distinguished and discriminating writer recalling it after all this time with relish and re-reading it with pleasure. I was amazed, touched and immensely flattered. Over the years I had read a number of his books, enjoying in particular *The Goose Cathedral* and *The Dog at Clamber-down* with their haunting evocation of magic places. I wrote to thank him for his words and expressed the hope that, unlike me, he would never have to be recalled as one who had fallen silent. Thus began a correspondence that lasted until his sudden death at the age of fifty-seven, four and a half years later.

His letters, some 120 of them, added greatly to the gaiety of my life. At first he and I agreed that we should never meet; but, after a year or two, when I was stopping with friends in Kent, not too far from the village where he lived, it seemed so artificial a resolve that, one late summer after-noon, I went to the wine bar where we had arranged to meet and came face to face with my enchanting correspondent. He was drunk. I was never, in

*Jocelyn Brooke,
photographed in the late
1940s, some ten years
before Yvonne met and
knew him (courtesy of
Jonathan Hunt)*

fact, to see him when he was not, save one early morning when we walked in the woods on an orchid hunt: on orchids he was an expert. There were occasions when I thought it might have been better had we never met.

After his death, when *The Times* printed a singularly grudging and un-generous obituary – on the lines of 'he never quite made the First XI' – I sent one of those afterwords, 'A friend writes', to redress the balance a little in which I said:

> Jocelyn Brooke's field may not have been wide nor his output large,
> but everything to which he set his hand showed a delicacy of feeling

and perception – for language, for landscape, for his own beloved East Kent and for the acute experiences of childhood – which has given extreme pleasure to his readers . . . Behind the work was a gentle, sensitive man, of a nature saved from sweetness by a fine sense of irony.

Throughout our brief friendship, what had preoccupied us both was writing and writers, making me ever more bitterly regret that I was not producing anything. Our discussions made me increasingly conscious that, niggling away at translations, I was committing an unforgivable mistake. As Shaw said in another context: 'It must not be supposed that I did this solely because it was wrong though there was no other apparent reason.'

8

My mother died in May 1961 at the age of eighty-three. In one of his rare interventions, my psychoanalyst had said: 'I think you're fonder of your mother than you know.' At the time I repudiated this, as with every other of his rare comments, but years later – perhaps as many as ten – I woke up at three in the morning, screaming, to the self-knowledge of the truth in his words.

As an adult I had not liked my mother. Her empty life, her petty vanities, her lack of interest in everything other than herself, aroused in me nothing but distaste. Now, at her death, I experienced an emotional turmoil, grieving not for the woman I had not liked but for the one who had borne me: it was as though I wept amniotic tears and I felt not only an irrational sense of loss but aching pity for that poor, futile life.

For my brother who, upon her death, acquired control of the family business from which she had drawn her income, she left a letter of such bitter cruelty that, not surprisingly, he contested the terms of her will by which I inherited everything. It passes all comprehension why, having relieved her feelings by penning this odious missive, she had not destroyed it rather than allow it to be her last word to her son from beyond the grave.

She had appointed me her executor and I now inherited not only her own private investments but also the income from the trust fund my father had set up to provide for her as long as she lived. It looked as though, for the first time in my adult life, I would be financially secure. Apart from paying off the mortgage on my house, I immediately – and, as it turned out most rashly – fulfilled certain long-cherished desires: I joined the London Library and the Wine Society, I bought a Riley and a delicate little Clementi square piano, restored by Morley. But, as one should have foreseen, there ensued years of such sordid wrangles with my brother that, halfway through, utterly sickened by it all, I turned my back upon it, appointing a deputy to deal with the lawyers while I flew to Rome to stay with friends.

The main bone of contention was, of course, the provision by which I came into my mother's share in the family firm. The last thing I wanted was to have any part of it in view of my brother's fury now, quite irrationally, transferred to me. It is true that he had shown little consideration for his mother – or for anyone else, if it comes to that – during her lifetime. Indeed, when first widowed she had looked to him for help and advice in dealing with practical affairs, my father having, in the time-honoured way, kept her in total ignorance of such matters. My brother simply brushed aside her needs and, throughout the twelve years that she outlived her husband, he paid scant attention to her, seldom visiting her in Yorkshire – the birthplace to which she had returned as soon as widowed – and then but briefly. She had often complained to me in those years about his unfilial attitude and certainly the bond between them was – perhaps had always been – weak; yet it was hard to find an excuse for her last vindictive gesture: a letter of such intemperate ill-will that, though I was the one who was made to suffer for it, I could not really condemn my brother for his smarting sense of outrage.

Other unpleasantness of a Balzacian character grew naturally out of this situation. My mother, having quite sensibly wished to see her three grand-daughters enjoy the small legacies she intended to leave them, had given them the money a few years earlier without, however, altering her will in accordance. As her executor I was, of course, legally bound to honour these bequests, though my daughter declined to accept her portion at first, saying she had already had it. Then, destroying the last vestiges of civilized family relations and knowing full well that, until probate was granted, I did not have the means to pay out anything, my brother dictated to his two daughters peremptory letters to me of the greatest insolence demanding their legacies. While I left it to the lawyers to deal with my nieces, I faced the unwelcome fact that, although in no way his aggressor, my brother had decided that I was the enemy and was bent upon declaring a state of war between us. In that he succeeded. We never communicated again.

Hateful though this whole long-drawn-out episode was, it came to an end at last and by 1964, slightly the worse for wear and considerably less well off than had been intended, I could see my freedom ahead, at which point I encountered an even more daunting obstacle. I had fully made up my mind that I would drop translation of Ilya Ehrenburg's memoirs, four lengthy volumes of which I had worked on with Tania Minorsky in Cam-bridge, at which juncture Ehrenburg himself ran into trouble over the pub-lication of his next instalment. The text had always first appeared serially in the journal *Novy Mir* from which we made our translation. Now it sud-denly failed to come out. Throughout the years of our collaboration, and although Ehrenburg was frequently in England during that time, neither Tania nor I had ever met him, so I had no means of knowing the truth of the matter, but we were given to understand, at second or third hand, that official exception had been taken to his references to the mass murder of Jews under Hitler. (When the book was eventually published it struck us both that the objections would more probably have been to passages relat-ing to anti-Semitism in the Soviet Union under Stalin.) However that may be, it was rumoured at the time that the editor of *Novy Mir*, by way of protest, had absented himself from his desk and gone on a three-day bender; and we were advised – by Ivor Montagu, I think – that in this instance we should hold things up until the accepted text came out in book form. The affair was finally resolved, it seems, by Ehrenburg appealing in person to Krushchev and publication followed. But I felt we could not in decency elect that moment to withdraw: it would be interpreted as our having sided with the censoring authorities and sharing their views. Thus I felt under some obligation to continue with this, by now, wholly irksome task, wondering miserably which of us – Ehrenburg or I – would die first. He did; and, although the manuscript of yet a further volume was found among his papers, I felt I could without dishonour refuse to work on it.

At last the decks were cleared: my brother – though not his hostility – had been bought off at a price; probate had been granted; I had paid back the debts incurred in settling estate duty, as it then was, and a small but regular income was being paid into my bank, while by now I was also receiving an old age pension from the state. In 1966, at the age of sixty-three, I started work on the biography of Eleanor Marx.

9

I have said that the idea of writing the life of Eleanor Marx arose from my translating the correspondence between Frederick Engels and Laura and Paul Lafargue. Eleanor flits in and out of the pages of these three volumes in a most tantalizing way. Every reference to her evoked an interesting personality who aroused my curiosity. I wished I knew more about her, but when I enquired I found there existed no biography of her.

At a Christmas party in the early 1960s, I told Maurice Cornforth, then the managing director of a small publishing firm, that I should really like to write such a book. 'And we'd really like to publish it,' he said. There it

Yvonne with her daughter Janna, around 1970

rested for some years and then, when I had been plunged into research on the subject for about twelve months, there appeared, in 1967, the first biography of Eleanor Marx, written by a Japanese scholar. I was not deterred by this as, even at that stage, it was quite clear that I had an entirely different standpoint from this author.

A joke my daughter and I have always enjoyed is the admission that we are not among fortune's favourites. Never was this better illustrated than in the writing of *Eleanor Marx*. Thus in July 1969 I went to East Berlin for the second time to do research at the Marx–Lenin Institute and had not been there more than twenty-four hours, had done just one day's work, when I had an accident in the street and smashed my kneecap. (I fell, as I had occasion to tell the doctors, on the same day as the Bastille.) I was in hospital for the next five months, going home only at Christmas. Thus it was that I never got to Moscow at all, as I had intended to do. However, the Moscow Institute could not have been more helpful or generous, sending me photocopies of all the original material I had hoped to study there.

That, of course, is not the same as being on the spot, as I had discovered when, after my earlier researches in Berlin (where I had gone in the first instance to attend the Brecht festival), I went to the International Institute of Social History in Amsterdam. All the documents I had requested in advance, taken from lists sent to me, were ready and waiting for me but I found a great deal of equally relevant and valuable material about which I should never have known had I not been there in person.

While stuck in the GDR hospital, where I received the most excellent treatment and my patella was skilfully repaired, the Institute laid on a courier who brought and changed over files every week, some of them containing material that is generally only inspected by special permission. Were they not afraid, I asked, that I might spill soup on it? But no, they were perfectly unperturbed and anxious that I should pursue my work, though it must be admitted it was slow going in view of a fact pointed out by Corporal Trim that: 'There is no part of the body . . . where a wound occasions more intolerable anguish than upon the knee . . . there being so many tendons and what-d'you call -'ems about it.'

While still in plaster, I was visited by two people from the Moscow Institute: one the joint author of a little book entitled *The Three Daughters of Marx*, published in both Russian and German, the other justly famed as the expert decipherer of Marx's abominable handwriting. They had long talks with me which, I like to think, resulted in their believing that I was to be treated seriously and quite probably helped towards my being accorded the unstinting co-operation of their Institute.

Because of this dreadful interruption in my life I was forced to reconsider my work plan and, if necessary, entirely re-jig it. The structure of the book had been most carefully worked out at the start; but now, in 1969, I came to the conclusion that it would have to be in two volumes. I doubted whether I should ever write the second volume but felt it would be something to complete the first.

Although it took ten years in all – from beginning the work until its final publication – the actual writing occupied little more than eighteen months for the first and perhaps two years for the second volume. The rest of the time was spent on research, the building up of a chronological table on a week-by-week – sometimes day-by-day – basis as an essential 'scaffold' and, of course, endless reading and note-taking.

One of the most difficult problems that has to be solved when such an amount of material has been amassed is that of selection. It is not so much a matter of *discarding* as of how much weight to give the facts: how far it is legitimate to condense and where it is vital to expand. No doubt many errors of judgment crept into the making of these decisions, but such deliberations themselves take up many unproductive hours while the greatest time-waster of all was that, as the research progressed and the picture began to be filled in with greater clarity, there came the need to go back over the same ground, again and again, rereading things whose full import had escaped me at first, nor could be recognized until one was better informed.

Many weeks were spent reading through files of the contemporary local press, not quite knowing what I was looking for but taking note of items that caught my attention and accumulating, almost unconsciously, a sense of time and place. This was greatly enhanced as I wandered many times about the several neighbourhoods and visited the houses where Eleanor had lived until I was familiar with their very smell. No amateur historian, as distinct from a highly trained academic, can do research entirely in libraries or the study. It could be said that all my research was a voyage of discovery – both the archive kind and the leg-work – and if I could say to myself 'Well, fancy that now', and feel that I had come upon something of astonishing interest, it would quite possibly interest others too.

Just at that time, I was cutting back a climbing rose with a long pruner which, as everyone knows, has a vicious recoil, when the quadriceps of my weakened leg gave way and I fell, breaking the ankle bones on both sides. This meant another six months' incapacity. Only after three weeks in November at a rehabilitation centre was I able to discard my crutches. Again, of course, the work was held up – indeed, the second volume did not go to press until 1976 – and, though I worked during this second bout of disability, I was hampered by the fact that I live in a house built for squirrels and in those many months could never get up the stairs to my work-room.

It was at this stage that the publisher, afraid that I really would not ever produce the second volume, applied to the Arts Council for a grant. The first volume had been widely and, on the whole, favourably reviewed and in the event I received two grants in consecutive years: one for £1,000 and the second for £750. Since I had never had an advance and, naturally, had been unable to earn anything during the six years I had now been engaged on this work, while meeting out of my small inherited income the not inconsiderable expenses of foreign travel – to Berlin, Paris, Amsterdam – and the other costs of research, the grants not only represented encouragement but were of tremendous practical value.

It would be impossible to speak of writing *Eleanor Marx* without reference to the help I had at every stage and in every way. In the early days when I needed to consult the old St Pancras ratebooks I was assisted by an architectural student of my acquaintance: a young man not afraid of the dirt and dust in the basement of what is now Camden Town Hall and who was extremely nimble and good at mounting ladders and pulling out the huge heavy volumes from shelves near the ceiling. These volumes had not been touched for decades and were in a terrible state of dilapidation, while they had no indication on the outward-facing spine of the wards they covered, let alone the dates to which they referred. This was in the winter of 1966–7, so that those cellars were not only filthy but bitterly cold and even damp. There was nothing – no table or bench – on which to rest the ratebooks once they had been taken from the shelves and one day when this agile boy had climbed to the top and extracted a volume on the off-chance that it might prove to be the one we were seeking, the book, the boy and the ladder fell in a heap and both of us narrowly escaped death in that awful place. Yet when I wanted to pay for his services, he declared it had been so interesting that he could not accept any money until, under strong protest, he allowed me to give him the price of a seat at the cinema. There were many incidents of this kind: several youngsters, some of them the children of my friends, helped me handle the heavy volumes at Somerset House – where the registers of births, marriages and wills were still then housed – and they were one and all so fascinated by these records that they refused any other reward.

My greatest good fortune was in having Elizabeth Whitman to work with me copying letters and documents in Paris and Amsterdam in 1968. (Incidentally, we were working in St Cloud during the famous Happenings of that May and in the house of Professor Bottigelli who taught at Nanterre, where the student demonstrations first erupted. He went to work wearing a crash helmet.) A year later Elizabeth, whom I had originally borrowed, as it were, from the Labour Research Department for these excursions abroad, now came to work with me full time. (It was she who had prepared all my papers for Berlin, to which she appended a message wishing me good luck and, in the German style, ironically enough: '*Beinbruch*'.) While I was in hospital she carried on the work in London. A brilliant researcher and a most expert technical worker, ordering the complicated files that were being built up, she also typed out my many drafts. So long as they were practically illegible, with deletions, balloons and amendments, she enjoyed doing this, remarking only, without rancour, 'As soon as you've found the *mot juste* you find the *mot juster*', but when it came to the final draft – a matter of copy-typing – she could not be bothered with anything so boring and passed it over to one of her young daughters.

She suffered from severe respiratory trouble which became progressively worse as time went on. When, in May 1972, my first volume was published, she was in a parlous state of health but was at least able to see the work in print and read some of the reviews, which gave her immense pleasure. To my sorrow she died that winter in her early fifties. Following her death, her youngest daughter told me that she had been ecstatically happy doing the Eleanor Marx work, which was a little solace. Certainly it had stretched her fine intelligence as perhaps her previous activities had hardly done.

She had passed on her admirable working practices to a newcomer when she had felt too ill to carry on, but that young woman, though competent and much interested, shortly became pregnant and gave up the job. After that I had the assistance for a time of a young woman from LSE and, as I neared the end of writing the second volume, Nicholas Jacobs gave me the inestimable help of sorting out my reference notes. As was inevitable at my time of life, deaths hovered about the writing of the book. In 1973 I lost the comradeship and support of that noblest of old men, Bob Stewart, who was then aged ninety-six. But the greatest grief was the terminal illness of my companion Margaret Mynatt. After years of hospital treatment and operations during which she still attempted to carry on her work, she was now dying at home.

The second volume of *Eleanor*, delivered to the publishers in September 1975, took an unconscionable time to appear and it was proposed to publish it in the spring of 1977. It seemed unlikely that Margaret would live to see it and I finally persuaded the publisher to bring the date forward to the end of 1976. In this I prevailed and the second volume was indeed issued in December 1976. Although it was too heavy for Margaret to handle in her weak state, she had the satisfaction of seeing it in print before, in February 1977, she died. Before her end she also watched with interest a television serial about Eleanor Marx and was visited several times by the actress, Jennie Stoller, who had played the name part and who now came to read Chekhov aloud in her lovely warm voice during those sad last days. Jennie became and remained a close friend.

It is impossible to refer to the years of writing these books without referring to the librarians, archivists and other specialists whose help I sought: they were a revelation. Their eagerness and enthusiasm were infectious. I was keen enough, but sometimes wanted only a particular fact. They, however, would not be content with that: they must offer me reams of related material, indicate further sources and generally fire me to go more deeply into matters that I had hardly thought I needed for my purpose. In that way I got stuck in all manner of unlooked-for researches, and even had some difficulty in extricating myself from the mid-nineteenth-century sewers of Kentish Town, a subject of infinite appeal.

Then there were the owners of family papers and reminiscences. For these I travelled about the country and met some delightful people. One old lady in her eighties, living in a coastguard's cottage on a bleak spit of land near Hastings, a niece of Edward Aveling, rushed to an outhouse to find an album of wonderful Victorian family photographs. Those I admired, she tore out to give to me, saying that she was too old to do anything useful herself and only too glad to contribute to the activity of others. I had the photographs copied and they were reproduced in my book, while I returned the originals to that generous old lady.

Although it must have happened to every researcher since the beginning of time, for me it was totally unexpected to come upon the 'smiler with the knife' who had been at work everywhere. I would take out some obscure little local paper of a certain date and find that the page containing the one item I sought was missing, neatly cut out of the file. The most startling instance of this vandalism – with a fortunate sequel – turned up at the Public Record Office, then in Chancery Lane.

It is, or was, a fact, that while the documents in the PRO are kept in an exemplary fashion and the responsible members of staff were of the highest excellence, the auxiliary workers in my day, those who trundled trolleys of documents about and generally fetched and carried, appeared to lack concentration: it took me a week of days to obtain the census returns I had applied for and I was in a frail state of dementia by the time that the right rather than the wrong file reached me, only to find that the relevant page was not there. I stood up and shrieked. All the people examining Elizabethan rent-rolls in the Long Room lifted their heads like startled waterbirds disturbed at feeding. I took the file to the desk where the young lady, though shocked at my behaviour, listened patiently but denied that such a thing was possible. 'Look, look!' I screamed and showed her that, indeed, there was a numbered page missing. 'Was it anyone special you were looking for?' she asked. I told her it was the Karl Marx household. Then she, too, stood up and screamed. On quietening down she informed me that, though grave, the matter was not a final disaster because these were photocopies: the originals were too precious to let researchers loose on them because so many documents were stolen in regular numbers each year.

I reminded her that the *Survey of London* covering that particular parish had been published only a few short months before. The compilers of that volume, which had included the details I was trying to track down to their primary source, were absolutely above suspicion, so I suggested that the PRO should apply to all those who had indented for this file, after the *Survey* people had completed their work. Since everyone fills up a form of which they leave a carbon copy it was possible to trace the twenty odd researchers who had used that file in the last period. Each one of them was sent a letter. None admitted to having mutilated the records, but a fortnight after all had replied the missing page was found, loose, slipped into the back of the box containing those census returns. No doubt the thief had copied and probably sold it.

The PRO authorities were so grateful to have recovered it that they presented me – without a fee – not only with a photostat of this special page but also with that of another most interesting document of whose existence I had not been aware but which they thought, quite rightly, would be of particular value to me. Moreover they gave me permission, against all the rules, to park my car on the forecourt. The porter would come out intoning

'No parking, no parking', then peer into the car and say, 'Oh, I see. It's Mrs Kapp. Go to the end on the left', and he would open wide the great gates. I felt extremely privileged.

That was not all. I had put in for the Home Office file on Marx's application for British citizenship. Day after day I called at the PRO: the file could not be found. Eventually it turned out that somehow, against all the odds and in a totally inexplicable manner, it had vanished from the trolley on its way to the photocopying room. I had to abandon all hope of tracing that item; but a year or so later, working in Amsterdam, I happened to glance through some supplementary catalogue in the International Institute for Social History and spotted this British Home Office file listed there. Though it had naturally not been among my advance requests – since nobody could have supposed that it might be in Holland – I asked to see it whereupon it was promptly produced.

On my return to England I wrote to the PRO to tell them that these documents – clearly their property – were to be found, photocopied, in the Dutch archives. They wanted to know when they had been acquired and from whom, but that I could not tell them, for I had not liked to ask such questions, thinking it best that the PRO itself should do so. How that ended I cannot say, but this unscrupulous pilfering and the disgraceful mutilation of records were a dreadful eye-opener: I had not thought scholars capable of such acts.

Among the more entertaining telephone calls I had were those to Buckingham Palace (the Royal Archives, housed in Windsor, when approached proved to be a model of efficiency and courtesy), the Army Museums and the Cemeteries Department of what was then the Greater London Council. Scotland Yard was another interesting contact. Having studied reports in the contemporary press of the crowd that followed Alfred Linnell's funeral in 1887 and the length of its route, I thought there was something wrong and wondered just how many miles 120,000 people in procession would cover. When I put my question to the sergeant who answered the telephone

*Yvonne on her eightieth
birthday*

he enquired politely: 'Are you planning to organise such a march, Madam?'
Reassured on that point, he turned to ask someone in the background:
'CND was never as large as that, was it?' He then instructed me on the difference between a journalist's and a police estimate of a crowd and that
between an orderly parade and a straggling mob, adding that the largest
turn-out in his experience had been that of the trade unions on May Day in
1973 when police had been stationed on roofs along the route. He enquired
whether I were of a 'mathematical turn of mind' and, giving me the figures
and calculations used by the police, advised me to work it out for myself.

One unlooked-for incident with a most agreeable outcome occurred during the writing of the second volume and as the result of an advertisement
which I had placed in a Kent local paper in the hope of tracing possible

descendants of Eleanor Marx's landlord, or others, who might have reminiscences of her sojourn in the area. There were no replies until I was rung up one evening by a man who opened the conversation by saying: 'My name is Demuth. Does that mean anything to you?' As this was the name of the Marx family's faithful, lifelong servant, Helene Demuth, said to have borne a son by Marx, I was breathless with excitement. I managed, however, to control my voice and to say that, yes, his name meant something to me and how could I help him. 'Are you a journalist?' he enquired. When told I was not he explained that, had I been, he would not have wished to have anything to do with me, but his curiosity had been aroused by my advertisement.

He then proceeded to tell me a horrifying tale of how some journalist, having unearthed the Marx connection, had visited the present speaker's grandfather, who owned a book of family photographs, including those of Frederick Demuth, his father and Marx's putative son. These, which he promised to return, he had simply taken away and was now hawking round Fleet Street. The old man had been deeply upset by this experience but, as his grandson now explained to me, there could be no redress. To lay a charge against the journalist was out of the question since the victim, a man of nearly ninety, could not in any circumstances be expected to give evidence. However, the incident had put the family upon its guard against strangers who showed an interest in the Demuth–Marx association. All I could suggest was that this particular Demuth should read my book – I did not offer to send him a copy but advised him to get it out of his local library – and, if he thought well of it, to get in touch with me again. I waited, not at all sure that I would ever hear from him and wondering whether I should have shown more eagerness and not let him suppose that it was a matter of indifference to me. But I had been right not to press him, for he did, indeed, read the book and then passed it round to his father, aunts and uncles who all agreed that he should get to know me. So began a most congenial acquaintance with David Demuth whose delightful young family I visited on several occasions and who took me to meet his most remarkable old grandfather, Harry Demuth, the only son of Frederick and thus supposedly a grandson of Marx, with whom I spent a most profitable afternoon.

There is, of course, no end to reminiscences of this kind: in the course of some ten years' work, the encounters, discoveries and adventures never failed to enthral me; the grandeurs and miseries of research to throw me into alternate ecstasy and despair. There were matters that forever eluded me, others that dropped like ripe fruit into my hands when I happened to be in the right place at the right moment. Of the scores of people and institutions I was in touch with over those years, here and abroad, I met with only one single person who proved obstructive and unpleasant. Everywhere I met with co-operation and encouragement. What this meant to an amateur historian venturing into an unknown field cannot be overvalued. It left me with an enormous debt of gratitude and, while I learnt a great deal about Eleanor Marx, I also learnt much about and from countless of my fellow creatures. In short, the writing of *Eleanor Marx*, which drew in one way or another upon my whole accumulated experience, left me wonderfully enriched.

THE END

Envoi

Since the second volume of the Eleanor Marx biography was published at the end of 1976, I have written two short books, contributed an essay to the volume marking the centenary of Karl Marx's death in 1983 and produced these memoirs.

In these years, approaching and hoping to attain to my ninetieth year, I have enjoyed, to my own astonishment, not only the satisfactions of work, but the miraculous and surpassing happiness of love; the charm of friendships, old and also new; the tranquillity of a small garden, with the sense of fulfilment that comes of growing things; and the splendour of the seasons.

I have celebrated the birth of step-great-grandchildren, delighting in them as babies and in their sweet and healthy childhood, while sharing my partner's pleasure in four grandsons, the youngest of whom was born as lately as 1984.

I have stayed longer than is thought necessary in Urbino; revisited Venice, Amsterdam and Paris; pottered about Lake Garda, the Dolomites and Verona; explored Split in a golden autumn and Dubrovnik in a grey spring; sailed up the Danube, embarking east of Bucharest to Vienna,

stopping off in Belgrade, Budapest and several left-over Habsburg spas on
the way; walked over the Sussex Downs, the Quantocks, the Yorkshire
moors, the banks and escarpments of the river Wharfe, the cliff tops of
southern Cornwall from the Pendene lighthouse, and made pilgrimages to
almost every one of the glorious churches of Norfolk and Suffolk.

Above all, I have learnt in old age that, despite what appear to be sudden
dramatic spurts, the march of history is unconscionably slow; but that a
love of justice and a belief in the potential for human progress is inextinguishable.

Now, as the short day closes, everyone will be out with a lighted candle
in Wenceslas Square.

November 1989

Afterword

Yvonne Kapp – a reflection

Charmian Brinson

It was in the early 1990s, when Yvonne Kapp was already almost ninety, that I had the good fortune to meet her in connection with some research I was carrying out into German-speaking refugees in Britain during the 1930s and 1940s. In fact, my initial interest was not in Yvonne but rather in her companion of many years, Margaret Mynatt, who, as a refugee from Hitler, had played a significant role in the affairs of the German political emigration. Margaret, younger than Yvonne by four years, had died of cancer in 1977, however – hence my approach to Yvonne in her stead.

Although, when we met, Yvonne was already physically frail, she was – and remained – a formidable intellectual presence, by no means inclined to suffer fools gladly. She demanded exacting standards of herself and expected others to comply with these; if they fell short, she could be un-relenting in her disapproval. The acuity and candidness that were among her most outstanding characteristics are evident throughout these mem-oirs. Yet so too are her humour and innate curiosity, pronounced even in extreme old age, as well as – a quite different aspect to her personality, this – her striking affinity with children. (My, then, six-year-old daughter, while in awe of someone so evidently 'old', grew to adore her and was shattered by her death some years later.)

In the event, my initial conversations with Yvonne soon came to concern not only Margaret Mynatt but also Yvonne's own dealings with members of the anti-Nazi German and Austrian exile communities. For Yvonne, as a British Jew and, from 1935, a committed Communist, had herself been involved in refugee aid work during the 1930s, being employed by the Medical Department of the Jewish Refugees Committee and, like Margaret, by the British Committee for Refugees from Czechoslovakia (later known as the Czech Refugee Trust Fund). Her experiences while in the employ of these bodies are told in these pages, as is the abrupt termination of her employment in 1940 when, during the period of the Nazi–Soviet pact and at a time when a German invasion of Britain was daily anticipated, Communists – both native and refugee – became a particular object of suspicion in Britain.

This ordeal, shared with Margaret Mynatt, was a searing one, leading her to identify still more closely with the refugee community, many of whom, Jews and/or committed antifascists like herself, had by then been interned on the Isle of Man or deported to the Dominions. During 1940 and 1941, Yvonne and Margaret compiled a report on the subject, *British Policy and the Refugees*, a devastating attack on British government policy; this, at the time of my first meeting with Yvonne, still lay in a drawer, unpublished (the publisher for whom the work had been intended having gone back on the original agreement).* It is very much to the credit of the publishing house Frank Cass, who recognised the intrinsic and enduring interest of the manuscript, that *British Policy and the Refugees* was finally published in 1997, nearly sixty years after it was first written.

---

* For the background to this, see Foreword to Yvonne Kapp and Margaret Mynatt, *British Policy and the Refugees, 1933–1941*, London/Portland, Oregon: Frank Cass, 1997, p. xviii.

Just as I was privileged to be asked to write a foreword to that volume, so I feel honoured now to be writing the afterword to *Time Will Tell*, memoirs of a remarkable woman whose life almost spans the century in which she lived. On meeting Yvonne, I learned of course very quickly that her work with refugees, our initial point of contact, had constituted only one episode, though a significant one, in her long and variegated life; and indeed *Time Will Tell* charts the progress of that life, from *enfant terrible* and best-selling novelist in her youth, through refugee aid worker, political activist, union functionary and translator in her middle years, to acclaimed biographer in old age. Moreover, *Time Will Tell* goes beyond the personal: there is much about Yvonne's life that reflects the intellectual, cultural and political climate of the age in which she lived, with Bloomsbury (in the shape of her friend Quentin Bell) juxtaposed with Harry Pollitt or, on an international plane, with Helene Weigel (for some years, Yvonne advised Weigel on English translations of Brecht). Figures as diverse as Rebecca West, Noël Coward, Francis and Vera Meynell, Max Beerbohm, Clifford Allen, John Collier, Melanie Klein, Nancy Cunard, C. K. Ogden, Rudolf Olden, John Strachey, Paul Robeson, John Heartfield, Kate O'Brien, Herbert Morrison, Jack Tanner, Jocelyn Brooke and Ilya Ehrenburg people these pages.

Not a homogeneous life, therefore, by any means, though all the more interesting for that. Born of somewhat restricted and restricting parents, in 1921 Yvonne met the painter Edmond (Peter) Kapp, a man more than twelve years older than herself, who drew her into the artistic, Bohemian circles in which she was to move as a young adult. After her marriage to him the following year, she learned – indeed, had to learn – to make her own way in life. By the time the marriage came to an end, Yvonne was embarking on her career as a novelist. Memorably, she describes here the circumstances surrounding the publication – under the pseudonym Yvonne Cloud – of her first novel, *Nobody Asked You*, in 1932: considered so outspoken by her prospective publisher (who then backed out of the agreement), it necessitated the setting-up of her own short-lived publishing house, the Willy-Nilly Press. She also recalls the ambivalent and embarrassed *Observer* review that turned her work into a bestseller,* all this recounted with the combination of ironic distance and at times disconcerting frankness that characterizes her approach to autobiography. *Nobody Asked You*, published when Yvonne was still only twenty-nine, was soon followed by three further novels: *Short Lease* (1932), *Mediterranean Blues* (1933) and *The Houses in Between* (1938).

All four novels, dealing in brittle and brilliant social comedy, were very much of their time; and with the worsening world situation and, in particular, Yvonne's own growing political awareness, her novel-writing career reached a natural conclusion. Indeed, in old age, Yvonne tended to be rather dismissive of these early works. Nevertheless, it is with pleasure that she recalls stumbling unexpectedly across a tribute in *The Times* to her *Mediterranean Blues*, almost thirty years after the book's appearance, in which the distinguished writer Jocelyn Brooke referred to 'that hilarious novel about English expatriates at Cassis' as still occupying 'a place on my shelves next to [Norman Douglas's] *South Wind* and [Compton Mackenzie's] *Vestal Fire*'.[†]

Yvonne was, so Brooke reflected in this 1962 article, 'among the writers whom one tends to forget because they no longer write'. Yet, despite her change of course, Yvonne herself remained well aware of where her true metier lay, recording ruefully and retrospectively that 'having, as was proper, responded to the demands made by the refugee era and the war years, while, it could be hoped, maturing in the process, I ought now to have gone back to writing'. Instead, after the war, she spent long years translating, 'an iniquitous waste' in her view. On the other hand, as she herself relates here, it was precisely her work as a translator that led

---

* Gerald Gould, 'New Novels', *The Observer*, 20 March 1932, p. 6.
[†] Jocelyn Brooke, 'Re-readability', *The Times*, 8 March 1962, p. 15.

her to the project in which she was really to find herself, her two-volume biography of Eleanor Marx on which she embarked in 1966, at the age of sixty-three, and which she finally brought to fruition ten years later.

Since Yvonne herself is modest about her achievement, something of the exceptional nature of the reviews she received for her *Eleanor Marx* should perhaps be indicated here: from *The Guardian*, for example, which termed her first volume 'immensely scholarly, positively hypnotic . . . a superb book',* or from Michael Foot in the *Evening Standard*, who described it as 'a work of scholarship but also a work of art'.† After the appearance of the second volume, Eric Hobsbawm would write in the *New Statesman*: 'Yvonne Kapp's magnificent and definitive Eleanor Marx [is] one of the major biographies of our generation.'‡

As Foot intimates in his perceptive review, what sets this biography apart is the combination of the scholarly – and Yvonne describes here in these pages the painstaking care with which she set about the biographer's task – and the artistic: for this work, just like her novels before it, displays an exceptionally high degree of stylistic craftsmanship. 'As soon as you've found the *mot juste* you find the *mot juster*,' the typist of *Eleanor Marx*'s many drafts would remark wryly.

It was after completing the biography that Yvonne then applied herself to her autobiography, *Time Will Tell*, concluded in the politically significant year 1989. She lived to experience the belated publication of *British Policy and the Refugees* in 1997, when she was ninety-four years of age; but *Time Will Tell* remained unpublished – a source of some considerable disappointment to her – at her death in 1999. Betty Lewis, the companion of Yvonne's final years, remembers the slow emergence of the typescript over several drafts, as well as Yvonne's stated intention to position her

---

* Gwyn A. Williams, 'Full Marx', *The Guardian*, 15 June 1972, p. 11.
† Michael Foot, 'Meet the Marx Sisters', *Evening Standard*, 1 August 1972, p. 20.
‡ E. J. Hobsbawm, 'La Fille du Régiment', *New Statesman*, 7 January 1977, pp. 21ff.

personal progression through life against the background of some of the major events of the twentieth century that played their part in shaping it.

For, while *Time Will Tell* functions as an autobiography on several different levels, the work is first and foremost a *political* autobiography. The turning point in Yvonne's long life, as she describes here, came about in 1935 when, following a visit to the Soviet Union, she met the British Communist Party leader, Harry Pollitt. Though very much a committed antifascist by that stage, she recalls, she had had not the slightest intention of joining the Communist Party, or indeed any other party, until persuaded of the rightness of that course of action in conversation with Pollitt. The mid-1930s were a time, certainly, when many right-minded intellectuals were choosing to join the Party, yet it was still very much 'a difficult and serious decision' for all that. Moreover, as a newly fledged Communist, Yvonne was to find herself challenged in a number of areas: in her understanding of Marxism, for instance; in her work as a Party tutor; and in what she herself termed her 'complete ignorance of working-class people and working-class life'. It was in an attempt to remedy this last deficiency that she set up, as she recounts here, a little band of Party women to minister to the health needs of the local unemployed, in the process falling foul of the district Party leadership who criticised the work as 'a bourgeois enterprise of the slumming kind'.

If this constituted merely a small-scale brush with the Party, then a much more serious problem was to arise – for Yvonne and a great many other Communists – following the signing of the Nazi–Soviet pact in August 1939. From her intimate knowledge of the German situation, built up during her work with refugees, Yvonne remained convinced that, contrary to what was being decreed by Party doctrine at the time, the war was antifascist rather than imperialist in nature. Interestingly, while this dilemma is not articulated as such in *Time Will Tell*, it is elsewhere: in an interview with fellow Party member Mike Squires, for instance, in which Yvonne describes being 'swung this way and that' on the matter, leading to 'a state of appalling confusion'.* In the same interview, Yvonne also recalls her immense relief in June 1941 when, following Hitler's invasion of the Soviet Union, she was finally able to feel at one with her compatriots where the war was concerned. This emotion, if not the preceding turmoil, *is* reflected in *Time Will Tell* when, of all the momentous events that have impressed themselves on her memory (from the *Anschluss* to the assassination of President Kennedy), it is the German invasion of the USSR and subsequent developments – 'Churchill proclaiming the Russians our allies' – that Yvonne selects as the most memorable.

While this particular dilemma resolved itself satisfactorily, another crisis point was reached, of course, in 1956, with the Hungarian uprising and with Kruschev's speech to the 20th Party Congress, disclosing the true nature of the Stalinist regime. In a short but moving passage, Yvonne reveals something of the fundamental re-examination of her position that these events brought with them when, quoting Browning, she writes: 'We had to take new bearings. Though we were not deflected from our course, it marked a turning point. "Never glad confident morning again."'

Some disenchantment there may well have been. Despite that, however, Yvonne remained within the Party, retaining her essential political beliefs until the end of her life. By that time, she records, she had learned that 'the march of history is unconscionably slow; but that a love of justice and a belief in the potential for human progress is inextinguishable'. Yvonne Kapp's fundamental optimism, as expressed here, is entirely in keeping with the encouragement she derives from the 'newly kindled light in eastern Europe, following the advent of Gorbachev', just as it is in harmony with the historic words, dated November 1989, with which she chooses to conclude her narrative:

---

* Interview carried out on 2 July 1994, held by Mike Squires as part of an oral history collection.

Now, as the short day closes, everyone will be out with a lighted candle in Wenceslas Square.

Charmian Brinson
November 2002